To my parents, Lowell and Miriam Sloat

(not for loan)
(personal copy—)

The Dangers of Growing Up in a Christian Home

Donald E. Sloat, Ph.D.

Thomas Nelson Publishers
Nashville • Camden • New York

For the sake of easier reading, the pronouns, *he*, *him*, and *his* refer to both male and female in the generic sense except where the context dictates otherwise.
Details in the anecdotes used in this book have been changed to protect confidentiality.

Published in Nashville, Tennessee, by Thomas Nelson, Inc. and distributed in Canada by Lawson Falle, Ltd., Cambridge, Ontario.

Printed in the United States of America.

Scripture quotations are from THE NEW KING JAMES VERSION of the Bible unless otherwise noted. Copyright © 1979, 1980, 1982, Thomas Nelson Publishers, Inc.
Scripture quotations from The King James Version are marked KJV in the text.
The Bible verses marked TLB are taken from The Living Bible (Wheaton, Ill.: Tyndale House Publishers, 1971) and are used by permission.

Library of Congress Cataloging-in-Publication Data

Sloat, Donald, 1941–
    The dangers of growing up in a Christian home.

    1. Family—Religious life.   2. Family—Mental
health   3. Christian education of children.
4. Christian education of youth.   5. Pastoral psychology.
I. Title.
BV4526.2.S515   1986   248.4   86–21699
ISBN 0-8407-3064-0 (pbk.)

                3 4 5 6 7 8 9 10 - 97 96 95 94 93 92 91 90 89

Contents

Foreword

One of the most positive and encouraging sentences in the New Testament is found in 2 Corinthians 1:3-4: "Blessed be the God and Father of our Lord Jesus Christ, the Father of mercies and God of all comfort, who comforts us in all our tribulation, that we may be able to comfort those who are in any trouble, with the comfort with which we ourselves are comforted by God."

This truth practiced in our lives ensures that no experience, regardless of how painful or difficult, is destined to be negative. We are able to glean the lessons from these experiences and share them with others either to help them avoid these hurts or to provide alternatives and strength as they go through them.

The Dangers of Growing Up in a Christian Home is about just that. Dr. Sloat has experienced either the reality or the perception of the application of certain legalisms to his early life. As in all our lives, it doesn't really matter that much whether the experiences are real or perceived. If we feel they are real, they affect our lives, often forever unless we confront and resolve them.

It is probably unavoidable that, in our good intentions to raise our children as Christians, we pass on a good deal that is the excess baggage of our misunderstandings of the faith or even the result of the failures, fears, and prejudices of our experience.

This book should help those of us who are parents to see

how certain of our manipulations, though intended to accomplish good purposes, can bring harm or resentment into the lives of our children. Even in the best of circumstances and with greatest forethought, it is inevitable that some of this will take place. The Bible reveals the limitations of numbers of parents, from the priest Eli to the mother of James and John. We are often too close to the forest to see the trees in regard to our children, and we allow our love to become obsessive, indulgent, manipulative, possessive, or frightened and protective. We find herein warnings of this possibility and, in a sense, not just the author's experiences but also our universal experiences. There is no such thing as objectivity in parenting. There are, however, grace, forgiveness, insight, and understanding in Jesus Christ.

Dr. Sloat addresses these truths in a most pointed and practical way.

For those of us who have found the crippling wounds of legalism in our adult lives, we can find help in this book to love and understand our parents while remaining objective about their mistakes. It helps us to love the church and its various attempts at redeeming us and protecting us from worldliness while still seeing through the mistakes of a human institution run by fallen men and women.

This is a freeing and forgiving book, but also a confrontational and sound-minded one. All of us who have been raised in the evangelical Christian subculture will see ourselves in this book, and I hope we will love both Christ and His church more when we are finished. We will also be better able to let Christ make us whole as we are freed from the misapplied truths and human errors of our youth.

We should be better parents and better sons and daughters for having read this book.

Jay Kesler
President, Taylor University

Acknowledgments

Although the ideas in this book have been developing in my mind for many years, an unexpected chain of events brought this project into reality. In 1982 I sent an article to *The Church Herald* for their consideration, and they published it. Two months later an editor from Thomas Nelson Publishers contacted me. He said he liked my article, and he asked if I had ever thought about writing books. "I do happen to have this idea," I replied, and I described the idea for this book. So began my relationship with Larry Weeden, senior editor at Thomas Nelson, and his support has resulted in this book. I believe God made the arrangements; I can take no credit for it. Larry has been my editor for this book and has been very helpful.

John Stapert, Ph.D., editor of *The Church Herald*, not only published my first article several years ago that originally caught Larry's attention, but he has also become a valued colleague and encourager. As both a psychologist and an ordained minister, he has been a sounding board for my ideas and has provided me with insights from the Calvinist viewpoint. He also read early drafts of the manuscript and gave valuable advice.

Youth for Christ has always had a special place in my

heart, and I am proud to have been a part of YFC. I often miss the fellowship I experienced with them. I have appreciated knowing Jay Kesler through the years, and I am grateful he is supporting this book.

My parents have played a major role in my life. I recognize that much of what I am today is the result of their influence; their consistency has laid a stable foundation and has been a support. Their actions that I liked have been very meaningful, and their actions that I did not like have helped me develop the ability to help others reach toward their own maturity. In retrospect, the knowledge I have that is most valuable in my work is not what I learned in school, but what I learned as I worked through my own struggles.

One of my fifth-grade assignments was to memorize a poem and recite it to the class. Not knowing much about poetry, I turned to my dad for help. He looked through his scrapbook of quotes he had collected and gave me a poem to memorize. I have forgotten all of it except for two lines, but these lines often come to mind when I have to deal with a mistake I have made and I wonder if I should keep trying. The lines are, "Mistakes are made we can't deny, / But only made by folks who try." The wisdom my dad gave me has helped me attempt things I would not have done otherwise.

The fact that my experiences with my parents have so easily transferred to others' lives demonstrates that my parents' methods and my early church experiences were not unusual or unique—many others have had similar experiences. My parents, as have many other parents, used their best methods as they raised their children. Since the focus of this book is on hurts and struggles, the examples I use from my family experiences reflect the hurts more than the good times. But I have many happy memories from my days on the farm in addition to the painful ones. My parents' willingness to let me tell you about our experiences together is gratefully acknowledged.

Through their personal therapy, many people have shared their struggles with me and have been a source of personal support for me even though they were unaware of it. As we have struggled together with the issues in their lives, they have helped me clarify and improve my own ideas. They have helped make this book possible.

Three people have had the most profound effect on my adult life and have been instrumental in helping me become my own person. Paul Tournier, through his books, has been a consistent source of insights that have helped me not only in my personal life but in my psychotherapy work as well. Dr. Kenneth U. Gutsch, my major professor at the University of Southern Mississippi, also has provided valuable insight and encouragement, particularly in the area of personal autonomy. My wife, Linda, deserves the most credit for helping me recognize and express my emotions and for sticking by me in love as I struggled for years with agonizing frustration and depression.

My daughters, Amanda and Molly, have been special blessings who have shown me a new concept of love and life itself. They have added so much to my life, and I wouldn't trade them for the world. They also have been patiently tolerant while "Dad is working on his book." The patience Linda has displayed while I have been working on this manuscript would rival Job's.

From a technical standpoint, I am grateful to be living in the personal computer generation. I have written this book on my Macintosh, which has been an absolute marvel in terms of editing, printing, and just plain fun in writing. "Thanks, Steve Jobs!"

PART ONE

Why the Christian Home
Can Be Hazardous
to Your Faith

CHAPTER 1

When Honest Feelings Erupt

The sun was shining brightly through a blue sky as I sped in my yellow '65 Mustang convertible down Detroit's Ford Freeway toward Cobo Hall. It was a Saturday morning, the day before Easter Day in 1967, but my inner feelings did not match the sunshine. The joy of the Lord about which I had always heard was not in my heart—even on this, the weekend of a most special Christian day. My heart was heavy; I felt alone, afraid, and unhappy. A sense of heaviness surrounded me, which I later learned was depression. It seemed no one cared or shared my feelings. The sturdy concrete columns that supported the overpasses were bathed in bright sunlight, but to me they offered a strange appeal—I felt like jerking the wheel of my car and crashing headlong into them. Dying didn't seem so bad compared to what I was feeling.

What's happening to me? I thought. I had always tried to do the right thing, including being "nice" as my mother had taught me to be. I had grown up in a Christian home, attending church services every Sunday morning and evening and every Wednesday night, spring and fall revival meetings, fall camp meetings, Youth for Christ (YFC) meetings, singspirations, and whatever else was offered. I had changed colleges and majors because I felt God had clearly called me into YFC work. In spite of that, my fourth year in full-time Christian work saw me coming apart.

The past year had been a struggle as I began to have twinges of emotions that were foreign to me. I doubted God; even worse, I wasn't sure He loved me. Christ didn't seem the greatest person in my life either.

After reading *The Taste of New Wine* by Keith Miller, I had gone on an honesty kick and was consequently devastated by what I had begun to see in myself. I didn't really care about saving some kid's soul. Actually, I liked the show business part of YFC. No burden for lost kids burned in my heart. My inner conflict and confusion were intense, for YFC had been "my calling," and I had planned a career in YFC. My goal had been to learn all I could about teenagers and to build a program that would train men and women to be effective workers with teens. Having come this far, I found that the very foundations of my career and personal beliefs were falling in ruins.

It all built up on this Easter weekend when Christians celebrate the joy of Christ's resurrection. Ironically, I was en route to help direct a concerted effort to proclaim Christ to the lost teenagers who would be attending the Teen Fair in progress at Cobo Hall.

But I didn't feel like saving anyone. I was afraid—deeply afraid of and even angry with God. Christ wasn't real to me—at least not in a positive way. He seemed to be more of a hindrance than a blessing. I had been told and had even told others that He was the way to abundant living, but I surely didn't feel it. Yet here I was, going to tell lost kids the good news of the risen Savior.

I didn't want to do it. I could hardly believe it myself. "Just let me out of all this!" was the anguished cry inside me. "Why was I born in the first place?" I felt I could die— or wished I would. My inner secrets, my fears, were locked inside, and I felt I had to discuss them with someone—at least to get rid of some of the load. But to whom could I talk? And worse, what would another person say about my feelings?

Our booth at Cobo Hall consisted of a background wall built of alternating red-and-white door panels fastened side by side, with an awning hanging over the forward side. On the wall were the words *Physical, Mental, Social,* and *Spiritual,* with a twenty-by-twenty-four-inch photograph mounted under each word—the photo depicting the concept of the word. I had photographed the pictures and made the enlargements, something of which I was proud. In front of the wall was a platform, about six feet square, enclosed with a railing. On the platform sat two bucket seats. Wire mesh was taped to the seat bottoms and was connected by wire to a battery. Beside each seat was a switch controlled by the person who sat there.

The intent behind this arrangement was to call two people from the crowd who wanted to challenge each other on the electric seats. Each person would take a seat, place a hand on one chair's switch, and watch the signal light. When the controller switched the signal from red to green, the first person to push his switch would give the opponent an electrical shock. If a person tried to beat the system by pressing his switch before the light changed, the person pushing the switch would receive the shock.

It was great fun, and the kids had a screaming good time. While this was going on, other YFC staff members and trained Christian teenagers were taking a religious survey, with several key questions designed to set up an opportunity to share the Four Spiritual Laws—Campus Crusade style. This, of course, was the real purpose for YFC's participation in the Teen Fair, which was a commercial enterprise consisting of teen-oriented displays and appearances by prominent rock bands.

Feeling as I did that day, I stayed away from the survey work, believing that I could at least handle the booth in spite of my inner misery and agonized feelings. As I worked the booth, my inner pressure continued to build, and I knew something had to change. With considerable effort I struggled my way through Saturday, but Easter Day loomed ahead and my inner agony persisted. I knew I had to talk to someone, but who would understand?

Diane was a teacher who had volunteered her time to work with one of my clubs, and I had been training her. Not only did I feel closer to her than to anyone else in my life at the time, but I also had romantic feelings for her and had wanted to date her. She had been reluctant to become involved, however. She was a very spiritual person, having become a Christian in her early twenties after having lived out the wilder side of herself. Knowing her deep spiritual commitment, I knew that if I told her what I was feeling, any hope of developing a romantic relationship with her would be quickly doomed. I was in a bind. I had to talk to someone and I wanted to talk to her, but the risks frightened me. My need to talk finally won out, however, and with great fear I took my first big step toward honest self-disclosure. In the journal I kept at the time, I described the incident in the following manner:

I didn't think my boss could understand me. No one else could be trusted. Diane was the only one. Finally I decided to talk to her. What could I lose? The way I was feeling there was nothing anyway. Yet even though I decided to talk to her, it didn't work out during the morning.

Finally, Sunday afternoon I got a chance out in the hall. "You're miserable, aren't you?" Her remarks told me she knew what I was feeling, and slowly I began to empty my heart—filled with frustration, bitterness, and misery. I didn't like God! I thought He was unfair, and Christ was not real. Why should I love Him? I felt that He owed me all He gave. Why not? He started the whole mess. Nobody really cared about me. Why should I love Him?

I had to admire that woman. She never flinched but stuck solidly to her faith and cried. She said it made her "love Him more." Then she really hit me with "You're looking for the same thing I was—love and happiness!" And she was right. "And you knock God for the very things you want—to be loved." And that really hit me! I'd never thought of it before.

I told her I wanted to take off a few days to find the answer, and if nothing happened I'd quit after the April 8 rally. That generally covers the talk we had. It meant so much. I went home early, wracked.

I talked to her some more Monday night, and she assured me she'd listen no matter what I did. That got to me.

Diane listened and gave support that I desperately needed, but I never felt that she really understood. The part of our conversation that has stuck in my memory was her statement that hearing my feelings made her "love Him more." Somehow I did not take comfort in that, but at least she listened and gave acceptance—something I had felt only once before in my life.

Much has happened since those days in Detroit. As I have cautiously ventured into new relationships through the years and encountered many struggling Christians through my psychotherapy work, I have realized that my feelings were by no means unique. Many Christians have felt as I have, but most, as I was, are afraid to air these feelings for the same reasons I experienced. These feelings do not fit the expectations of the general church community. It is not the type of thing one stands up in Wednesday night prayer meeting and announces. It is a terribly frightening thing to think *I am the only one who feels this way*! This fear in turn creates other fears that add mercilessly to the fears already too heavy to bear.

Through my own experience as a Christian, and as a psychologist observing Christians struggle in my office, I have come to a couple of major conclusions. First, sensitive, struggling Christians who have grown up in Christian homes, hearing the gospel since their earliest years, often are overlooked by the church as they wrestle inwardly to make sense out of the scriptural truths they have been taught. Since personal struggles are very seldom mentioned from the pulpit, sensitive, struggling Christians are left holding the bag with feelings they do not understand and feel are wrong in light of the Scripture they have been taught to believe and follow.

I have also concluded that for certain personalities, growing up in a Christian home can be dangerous because there are many subtle obstacles at work in the home and the church that make it difficult for these people to develop meaningful adult Christian lives. In all my years of church attendance, I have not heard this problem and its dangers discussed. I am convinced that there are many halfhearted, struggling, reluctant Christians whose needs are not being acknowledged or met by the church, but they are afraid to voice their concerns because no one has brought these issues into the open for discussion.

Not all Christians will be able to identify with the theme of this book, and that is expected. But if my observations strike a chord in you and you find yourself agreeing with what I am saying, you are the person to whom I am writing. If you are a sensitive, struggling Christian who has often felt alone with your feelings, wondering why your Christian life is not as great as the examples you hear from the pulpit, I have good news for you. *You are not alone, and it doesn't mean you are a bad Christian because you struggle.*

If you're a sensitive, struggling Christian
and you've often felt alone with your feelings,
wondering why your Christian life is not as great
as the examples you hear from the pulpit,
I have good news for you.
You're not alone.

Some of you who read this may have minor frustrations, and others may have experienced or may be experiencing a definite personal crisis when everything suddenly and un-expectedly seems to come apart and inner confusion mounts. And in spite of your earnest inner searching and praying, nothing seems to make sense, others do not understand, and your despair begins to prevail. To you I want to say that it is okay to hurt, to think, to ask questions, and to struggle. I believe with Paul Tournier that "God is over all of life" and He accepts us in our struggles.

Of course there are no easy answers, and not all answers will be found here. But I invite you to walk with me through my life and the lives of people I have known as together we explore the struggles that many second- and third- generation Christians face as they try to make sense out of their faith. In the pages that follow, you will read about the dangers that exist in the Christian home and the church, how many of us have reacted to these dangers, and some suggestions for dealing with the frustrations they cause us.

This is not a complete guide to personal healing, but by reading about others' struggles you will gain support for your own. Also, I have learned through the years that when we can make sense out of the things that give us trouble and develop clearer directions for our thinking and our lives, we often can make adjustments that help us live with less fear and tension. The ideas in this book should help you see more clearly the path you need to follow to become your own person and know the difference between emotional struggles and spiritual ones. God wants us to be the best people we can be, and my goal is to help you fulfill God's plan for you.

CHAPTER 2

God Has No Grandchildren

"We came to see you, Dr. Sloat, because we are concerned about our daughter. She stayed out all night last Tuesday and said she was going to be at her girlfriend's, but we found out she was walking around town until 3:00 in the morning. She doesn't mind anymore and has been writing these horrible notes that her mother found just lying on the table." Father had been speaking, and he stopped as he turned toward his wife, who was seated at the far end of the couch in my office. Their daughter, Susie, was seated between them. It was my first contact with them, and when they called to make the appointment, they inquired specifically whether I was a Christian, so I knew that Christian values were important to them. Susie, thirteen, was a pretty girl who could have easily passed for seventeen, and she knew it. She chewed her gum with an air of aplomb and tossed her blonde curls with a mischievous smile.

"She wants to date; she thinks she should be able to date fellows who are eighteen," her mother began, "but I told her she had to wait until she was at least sixteen. She thinks she is old enough now."

"Mother-r-r!" Susie interrupted angrily. "I am old enough! Goww! What do you think this is, the Dark Ages or something? I need to learn things for myself!"

As we discussed the family background, the situation became clearer. Father had grown up as a rather wild young man and had eventually become an alcoholic. Now in his late thirties, he had become a Christian during the past year and was very active in an evangelical church. His recent conversion and commitment to sober, honest living had narrowly averted a divorce from his wife, Susie's mother.

Mother, no angel herself during her teen years, had borne a child out of wedlock and had placed the baby with an agency for adoption. During the recent conflict with her husband, she had been seeing another man and was planning to divorce her husband to marry him, but these plans fell apart when the fellow returned to his wife. Mother, too, had recently made a commitment to the Lord.

Mother peered earnestly at me. "I know what it's like to be sixteen, and I don't want Susie to go through all the hurt I experienced. I want her to see that there's so much trouble in the world, and it doesn't have to happen to her. I want her to attend church with us and enjoy the peace that we have." Father echoed her remarks, adding, "I see all the mistakes I made through the years and the wasted time. I don't want Susie to go through that!"

As I observed this family, I could see that each one had a point, but things were not that simple. The parents were obviously first-generation Christians, and I could sympathize with their desire to protect their daughter from the hurts they had experienced. However, I could see more clearly than they that their Christianity was so meaningful to them precisely because their present joy of God's salvation was in such contrast to their earlier, painful, sinful lives. Susie, on the other hand, had apparently inherited her father's strong will and desired to do what she pleased. She was certainly not ready to become a quiet little church girl when she saw so many exciting opportunities ahead of her and was inclined to imitate her parents' past examples.

The problem is that Christian values
cannot be easily or automatically transferred
from one generation to the next.

The parents wanted desperately to instill their Christian values in their daughter, but their values were based on their individual painful experiences—experiences that Susie did not and could never share because she is a separate, different person. Their dilemma is typical of the kind of problem faced by evangelical parents, and if you are a Christian parent, you will certainly understand their concern. The problem is that Christian values cannot be easily or automatically transferred from one generation to the next, and this constitutes a foundational concept as well as a potential danger point that can cause untold difficulty if we do not understand it. Let's look at the difficulties involved.

Each Generation Is Different

Each person enters the world with no prior knowledge or experiences, which means each generation is starting out from scratch in attempting to deal with life. Fortunately, technical knowledge accumulates from one generation to the next. For example, the technology regarding the refining of gasoline and the engineering features of internal combustion engines has been developed and recorded by previous generations. Because new generations can study these principles, they do not have to reinvent everything from the wheel to computers, which saves them years of time.

Christian values and knowledge about living accumulate as well. But unlike technical knowledge, they cannot be passed simply from one generation to the next because they have to become personally meaningful in an individual's life and experience. This requires years of living and learning from successes as well as mistakes. Since we all tend to learn the hard way from our own experiences rather than from our parents' experiences, we often repeat the mistakes of prior generations; hence the expression "History repeats itself."

Danger Points and Implications

Several problems, or danger points, can occur as we attempt to pass our values to our children. First, parents (and the church as well) may instill so much fear and guilt along with values that youngsters are afraid to sort out their beliefs in order to stand on their own. This is what happened to me as I grew up, and I believe it is common in the evangelical church. A second problem exists when youngsters accept what their parents have taught them without questioning or evaluating it. They are then simply following hollow beliefs that can crumble easily under pressure. This is especially true when Christian parents either do not teach children to think for themselves or do not even allow them to do so. It is easy for succeeding generations to go along with their parents' teachings, and as a result they live out traditions that have little or no personal meaning. I frequently see this problem in the lives of Christians who come to consult me regarding problems that have developed in their lives. Let me explain.

Parents (and the church as well) may
instill so much fear and guilt
along with values that youngsters
are afraid to sort out their own beliefs.

There's a story about a young wife who, every time she baked a ham, cut off the end of the ham before she placed it in the oven. Since the end of the ham that she threw away had good meat on it, her husband wondered why she consistently cut it off and threw it away. When he asked his wife about it, she responded with surprise. "Well, I don't know," she said. "I never really thought about it. That's what my mother always did!"

So the next time the couple visited the mother's home, they asked her. The mother, as had the daughter, responded with surprise and said she had learned it from *her* mother. She really didn't know why she cut the end off the ham, either.

The next step was to ask Grandma. As expected, Grandma had an answer. "Oh, that's easy," she exclaimed. "I always had to cut the end off the ham because my oven was too small to hold the whole ham. It just wouldn't fit."

A value, a belief, or a way of doing something can develop out of one person's experience, and there are good reasons to believe or do it that way, but this same belief may not fit the next generation. As in this story, Grandma had a small oven, but her daughter had a larger oven and could have baked the whole ham. Instead, she took Grandma's action and made it her own without realizing that what was necessary for Grandma was not necessary for her. The next two generations following Grandma simply went through the motions copying Grandma's action, but the action had no personal meaning to them. When challenged, their behavior pattern crumbled because it was not based on their own experience. It was based on Grandma's experience, and they did not stop to evaluate what they were doing.

A value, a belief, or a way of doing something
can develop out of one person's experience
for good reason, but this same belief
may not fit the next generation.

This same process happens repeatedly in the church and in Christian families. It is particularly true of what we often call the do's and don'ts. For example, someone decided from personal experience that reading the newspaper on Sunday was wrong. This "don't," then, like cutting off the ham end, was given to the next generation, but the next generation most likely did not have a similar personal experience that brought it to the same conclusion. Temporarily, at least, it accepted what it was told as the way things were done. As a result, some people went through the motions of not reading the Sunday paper, but their motions had little personal meaning.

As a boy growing up on an Indiana farm, I lived in a community in which there were many Amish people. Meeting Amish buggies on the road and seeing the Amish in their distinctive dress were everyday experiences for me, and I am reminded of them as I write this. They have made a very determined effort to maintain the same style of life as their founder, Jacob Amman, who lived three hundred years ago. Their horses and buggies are very tangible representations of following beliefs that came out of their church founder's personal spiritual experience, not their own experiences.

Several years ago my brother, who is an attorney in my hometown and who has many Amish friends, asked several of them why they maintained their practices. To his surprised amusement, they were unable to give thoughtful answers. All they could say was, "This is the way we've always done things."

Of course, we often smile rather knowingly at the Amish with their horse-and-buggy way of life in the twentieth century, but their practices are only more obvious than ours. We evangelicals have our own particular horses and buggies, and we probably could not defend ours any better than my brother's Amish friends.

Old Problems

The problems that second-, third-, and following genera-tion believers face in developing a personally meaningful faith are old ones. Examples of these difficulties may be found in the Old Testament. Shortly before he died, Joshua summoned the children of Israel together and reviewed with them the mighty works God had performed on their behalf when they conquered the Promised Land. Joshua concluded his speech by challenging the people to make a choice: either serve God out of gratitude for what He had done for them, or worship the gods of the local Amorites (see Josh. 24:1–28). Like Susie's parents at the beginning of this chapter, Joshua was a first-generation Christian, a man who had witnessed firsthand God's actions in his life. His faith was real and was based on his personal experience. The older men who had served with Joshua also shared his steady commitment.

In spite of this generation's spiritual wealth, however, its experiences couldn't automatically be passed to the next generation. The Bible tells us:

> Joshua, the man of God, died at the age of 110, and was buried. . . . The people had remained true to the Lord throughout Joshua's lifetime, and as long afterward as the old men of his generation were still living—those who had seen the mighty miracles the Lord had done for Israel. But finally all that generation died; and the next generation did not worship Jehovah as their God, and did not care about the mighty miracles he had done for Israel (Judg. 2:7–10 TLB).

Even in the Old Testament days, growing up in the pres-ence of godly parents did not mean that God automatically became real to the next generation through personal experience. The generation following Joshua had not personally experienced God's miracles and did not appreciate what He had done for them.

God's Remedy for Israel

God was still there following Joshua's death, and we can see that He was prepared to help the next generation develop a meaningful faith. He left several nations in the region to "test the new generation of Israel who had not experienced the wars of Canaan. For God wanted to give opportunity to the youth of Israel to exercise faith and obedience in conquering their enemies" (Judg. 3:1–2 TLB). God realized that each generation is different and that firsthand spiritual experiences cannot be handed from one generation to the next, so He developed a plan that would provide the new generation with firsthand experiences. Those who could not participate in the original wars and see the miracles God had performed in the initial conquest of Canaan would be able to see God work in new wars that were unique to their day.

Doing this, of course, would have been risky because their faith was limited, based primarily on the stories they had heard from their fathers about the great victories of the past. But by honestly confronting their enemies in their generation, the young people could see God demonstrate His continued presence, love, and support for His people. In order for this to happen, however, the young people had to take action. Obedient action would have resulted in the type of success enjoyed by Joshua and unique experience of God's support and faithfulness. Subsequent chapters in the book of Judges reveal that when the people of Israel cried out to God and actually were faithful to Him, He delivered Israel and gave peace.

Put simply, *God understands the problems involved in transferring faith from one generation to the next and is capable of providing solutions if people are open to the particular opportunities that exist in their own time.*

A Critical Point

Failing to realize that each generation is different and that each of us must come to grips with his own personal and Christian values can have devastating results. Let me illustrate this with an everyday situation. Karen, an attractive brunette in her early twenties, sat in my office and told me she was unable to tolerate living with her young husband. Several weeks earlier she had moved into her parents' home to escape his abuse. With tears of pain streaming down her face, she blurted through her sobs that Stan had called her derogatory names and criticized her so much that she had become afraid to express her own opinions. On one occasion he had angrily chased her around the house brandishing a baseball bat, which caused her to fear for her life. In her relationship with him, she felt more like an object than a person. As we discussed their situation, it gradually became clearer why Stan treated her as he did.

Stan had been born to a young couple, and shortly after his birth, his mother divorced her husband and moved away, leaving him to raise a small son. This hurt the father so deeply that he developed a deep mistrust of women.

Stan had grown up watching his father abuse his stepmom and had learned his dad's belief that "you can't trust women. They are no good." In fact, his father often repeated these phrases to Stan, who took his dad's conclusion based on his dad's experience and made it his own. Even though Stan married and wanted to be close to his wife, his dad's words kept ringing in his subconscious, putting him in a double bind. He was trying to be close to a woman; at the same time, he was sure that women could not be trusted. As a result, he attempted to protect himself by treating his wife disrespectfully. This finally caused her to reject him, thus confirming in his experience the truth of his father's advice, and he did not realize the part he played in it. Accepting his father's opinion as truth for himself cost him dearly, not only financially, but also emotionally, because he lost a loving wife. If we follow this same principle with Christian beliefs, we can just as easily live according to someone else's distorted notion of what is right for us.

Becoming One's Own Person

Because each generation is different, we have to take what we have learned from our parents and the church, examine it, struggle with it, understand ourselves, and modify or build what we have learned into our own lives. No matter how good and meaningful our parents' spiritual experiences are, the fact remains that they are *our parents'* experiences and we cannot simply transfer their values into our lives without adapting them to suit our personalities and experiences. Understand that the truths of God are not at risk or issue here. What *is* at issue is how meaningful they are in our individual lives.

Each of us is different and has to
come to grips with his own faith
and makes it real through personal experience.

We as parents need to realize this point and allow our children to have experiences from which they can learn, not overly sheltering them. This is probably one of the hardest things for us to do because we love our children and do not want to see them experience pain or failure. Parents who do not appreciate this concept, however, will unknowingly create a danger point for children by not allowing them to develop their faith in their own ways.

The fact that each of us is different and has to come to grips with his own faith and make it real through personal experience is the premise upon which the remainder of this book rests. Personalizing our faith and value system is necessary for us as Christians to be strong, positive, fruitful people. For this to happen, growing children, and adults as well, need supportive environments that provide freedom for struggle so that their faith suits their unique personalities.

How People Are Alike
Even Though
They're Different

It was almost 10:15 and time for the bell to ring, signaling the start of Sunday school. Several adults had already taken their seats in the classroom and were talking quietly. I had started the group discussion class because I believed that too often people in the church are not given enough opportunity to express their opinions and encourage one another. As it was about time to start, I looked nervously at the clock, wondering where everyone was.

Harvey is here, I noticed silently. He was always on time and not very talkative, but any comments he did make were usually meaningful and said with a sly sense of humor. His general approach to things seemed to be conservative, and I suspected he was not much of a risk taker. A few weeks earlier when we had been discussing the idea of people working out their own faith, he quite honestly stated, "I would rather not think. I would be just as happy if all the rules were spelled out and I didn't have to make any decisions."

Just as I was about to begin, Linsey came bursting through the door, her coffee cup trailing precariously in her left hand. As she slung her purse to the floor beside her chair and slid into a sitting position, she glanced around the room and queried cheerily, "You didn't start yet, did you? Did I miss anything? Did your wife pick out your sport coat, Don?" Suddenly catching herself, she looked startled and glanced sideways, quietly observing, "I'm interrupting. I think I'm late."

Understanding Human Behavior

Linsey and Harvey are two different people, and their personal styles are consistent week after week. Because each views life differently, their struggles and the expression of their values are not the same, and each has a different approach to the Christian life. But beneath the differences that are easily observed, how are they really different? What makes Harvey so quiet and Linsey so verbal? Why would Harvey prefer to have decisions made for him? What effect does this have on the way he lives? How will Linsey's Christian struggles compare with Harvey's?

As we look at the dangers and struggles of growing up in the Christian home, it will help us greatly to have a system of understanding people and the underlying personality characteristics that either contribute to some person's struggles or diminish the struggle for someone else. I have discovered a useful system that explains human behavior in everyday language and makes sense to people. It is called the Personal Profile System.

The Personal Profile System[1]

Even though the Personal Profile System (PPS) was developed by a psychologist, it is not a personality test in the rigorous or technical sense and was not designed to reach into the recesses of a person's mind as many psychological tests do. It also is not marketed as a psychological test and is not based on an extensively researched personality theory. It was designed, rather, as a method of describing people's everyday behavior (their behavioral tendencies) in uncomplicated, ordinary language that someone could understand without studying technical psychological theory. The PPS highlights the individual differences in people, identifies strengths that people have, is easy to use, and is useful in helping people understand one another.

The PPS questionnaire booklet contains twenty-four groups of descriptive words, and a person checks the word in each group that is "most like me" and the word that is "least like me." Once the answers are scored (there are no right or wrong answers), the results are plotted on a graph similar to figure 1. A score above the midline, or halfway point, means the person has a definite tendency to show that particular behavior. A score below the midline means behavior will be opposite or different from the high point on that dimension.

Also, one high score (above the midline) will modify another high score as the two dimensions of a person's behavioral tendencies influence each other, but a detailed discussion of that is beyond the scope of this book. For our purposes I simply want to provide an understanding of people's behavior. Therefore, the following material is a broad view of human behavior. As you read, you will find yourself in the descriptions.

We have all heard the common sayings that divide people into two broad categories, such as "chiefs and Indians," "leaders and followers," and "those who make it happen and those who watch it happen." The Personal Profile System also divides people into two categories along these same lines, and then each of these categories is subdivided into two more categories. The two general categories are "active" and "less active."

The active people act toward life and usually are the ones that "make it happen." They have definite ideas about how they want things to be, and they try to make things go their way. The less-active people usually adapt or adjust to what

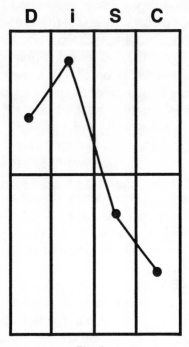

Fig. 1.

An illustration of a typical DiSC graph, this one for a high "i" person.

is happening rather than try to change things. They focus more on the how and why of things and are usually more content with keeping things as they are rather than trying to make changes. The less-active people are the ones who generally "watch it happen."

The active category is subdivided into the "Dominance" and "influencing" factors, while the less-active category consists of "Steadiness" and "Compliance." The four tendencies as a group, "Dominance," "influencing," "Steadiness," and "Compliance," constitute the DiSC system and are usually referred to by their first letters, such as "the 'D' tendency is to take charge," and so on. (The "i" is not capitalized as the result of a printer's mistake when the PPS was first developed. The profile's developers decided it added a certain distinction to the system and so have kept the lower-case "i" through the years as an unusual trademark.)

General Description of DiSC[2]

To gain a general understanding of the DiSC system, let's look at each of the four dimensions briefly before we examine the specific highlights in each category. Since people with the "Dominance," or "D," tendencies like to be in charge, they generally have the results they want firmly pictured in their minds, and they push people to take action that will bring them closer to their goals. They pay close attention to communication that will speed up the action and shrug aside questions others may raise about the "right" way to do things. They also have a natural inner feeling that they can change things, and they are good at overcoming opposition to their plans. Their behavior is characterized by dominance.

People with the "influencing," or "i," tendencies also want to bend things their way, but they do it differently from the "D's." They take charge, not by action, but with words as they work with people and try to persuade them to go along with their ideas. Since the "i's" are interested in people and want others to feel good about themselves, they are especially attentive to others' personal needs and search for ways to meet these needs tactfully as they exert their influence. Because they are more interested in people than things, the method of actually accomplishing a task is considered less important than a person's feelings. Their style is characterized by verbal efforts to influence.

People with the "Steadiness," or "S," characteristics are generally steady, dependable plodders who prefer to keep things the same. Since they are not interested in taking charge of things as the "D's" and "i's" are, they usually adapt to what is going on around them. Because they are interested in how and why things are done, they resist being pushed to take action before they know how to do what has been asked of them. At work, they are usually the most reliable, hardest workers. Their primary behavioral characteristic is steady dependability.

People with the "Compliance," or "C," tendencies also like to go along with things, but they are more concerned about the why than the "S" people are. Asking why is one of their favorite questions, which reflects their concern about going by the book, and they ask questions to know what the rules are in a situation. They do not like surprises, and they want to know what is happening around them. They like to be told that they are doing things correctly, but they ignore other messages. They also are the most complicated and complex of the four behavioral categories. They are compliant to their own standards.

Now that we have previewed the four behavioral categories, let's look at specific highlights of each category to gain a clearer perspective of each dimension. As you read this, remember that these are highlights, or general tendencies.[3]

"D" HIGHLIGHTS	"i" HIGHLIGHTS
High Ego	Emotional
Impatient	People-Oriented
Desire Change	Disorganized
FEAR—Being Taken Advantage of	FEAR—Loss of Social Approval
Need Direct Answers	Optimistic

"S" HIGHLIGHTS	"C" HIGHLIGHTS
Loyal	Perfectionist
Family-Oriented	Sensitive and Intuitive
Possessive	Accurate
FEAR—Loss of Security	FEAR—Criticism of Performance
Slow to Change	Need Many Explanations

"D" Highlights

"D" people first of all tend to have high opinions of themselves. They are sure of themselves and are unafraid of showing their confidence. I once met a minister whose "D" score was very high. He related an incident that typifies the "D" attitude. He was considering taking responsibility of a new church, and the presiding bishop in the district began to warn him that his wife would have to discontinue wearing her jewelry to conform to the church's conservative bent. The minister listened carefully and then responded in a typical, blunt, confident "D" fashion, "If you don't like the way my wife dresses, I'll leave the denomination and start my own church."

The second "D" highlight is the quality of being impatient. "D" people do not care for details and a lot of fuss. "Lay it on me so we can get on with things" is their usual attitude. They want to get to the heart of the matter with a minimum of hassle. They do not care for a great deal of discussion about a proposed project or how it can be done. They want to get things moving, and they want to be in charge. This quality usually results in conflict with the high "C" person who asks lots of questions and wants to make sure things are done properly.

The third highlight is the desire for change. Within families and at work, "D" people often instigate changes, and they often do so without consulting those who are affected by the changes. Although this is fine for the "D," it can cause a great deal of trouble for those who have to live with the changes. For example, let's look at what happens if a boss who is a "D" changes the office furniture over the weekend without telling anyone. On Monday morning, he walks in, looks it over, and thinks, *It looks great!* The "i" is seldom in the office anyway, except to do a little talking and get some coffee. The "S" remarks, "I was just getting used to it." And the "C," after thinking about it for ten minutes, fusses, "I wonder who did it?"

Fourth, all people have areas of vulnerability related to their inner fear, whether the fear is conscious or not, and the fear has a definite effect on their behavior. The "D," "i," "S," and "C" all have their own particular fear that influences their behavioral style, as can be seen in the list of highlights above. Touching on people's fear can result in hostility, and if we can understand what their fears are, we can provide safe environments for them and minimize their hostility. The "D's" are afraid of being taken advantage of, which explains their quickness in taking charge. If they're in charge, they know what's going on, which reduces the possibility that someone will take advantage of them. When they sense someone else may unexpectedly be gaining the upper hand, they quickly go on the offensive to gain control. Their basic attitude is, "I'll get them before they can get me."

It is this fear that leads to highlight number five, the need for direct answers. The "D's" become impatient with lengthy explanations and too many details. They want to get to the bottom line. Of all the personality styles, "D's" respond best to a direct, pointed approach, which is often necessary to catch their attention and communicate the desired message.

It is evident from these highlights that the "D" people prefer to be in charge, which is a needed strength in society, trusting their own judgment more than other's opinions or feelings. They make effective leaders because they are able to overcome opposition without taking setbacks too seriously or personally. This strength, however, can become a weakness when they move too quickly without appreciating others' feelings and ideas.

Because they are action-oriented and spend very little time being introspective, "D's" are unlikely to struggle with hurts and inner frustrations as extensively as the "S" and "C" people do. This does not mean that hurts and conflict are absent from their lives. They handle their hurts in a more active fashion. If they have problems with their parents or with the church, they are more apt to rebel openly, take action to change the situation, speak up, or push their own hurt aside rather than submit and smolder in silence as the "S" and "C" people usually do. If you are a high "D" person, you will have experienced your own particular struggles, but they probably will not be identical to the ones described in this book.

In fact, high "D" people very seldom come to see me for therapy. When they do come, it usually is under pressure from a spouse or a family crisis, and they seldom acknowledge that they have any problems because they feel so good about themselves. "If my wife would just shape up, we'd get along fine," one husband told me with obvious disgust in his voice.

During a therapy session a high "D" wife remarked to me in a clipped fashion, "I didn't like that other counselor we saw. He wanted me to change. I know there is nothing wrong with me!" I could see what she was doing to cause trouble for her husband, but she obviously wasn't interested in my opinion.

Joshua, Sarah, and the apostle Paul are several Bible characters whose lives illustrate the "D" personality style.

"i" Highlights

First, the "i" people are emotional. They "wear their hearts on their sleeves" and show their emotions quite readily. In fact, they are often dramatic and expressive in their words and actions. Their feelings influence their decisions more than logic does, and they often are reluctant to do something if they are not in the mood. My wife has a high "i" friend who has trouble planning more than several hours ahead of time. This drives my high "D" wife to distraction because she likes to plan ahead and have everything organized. My wife's friend will never commit herself to something that is a week or even a few days away because when the time comes, "I might not be in the mood." Doing something when they are not in the mood can be very upsetting to high "i" people.

Second, the "i's" are people-oriented, which is their great strength. They love to be around people, and they often crave it the same way some people crave food. Spending time with friends is not only enjoyable but also rejuvenating and refreshing for them. A high "i" man who came to see me for marital therapy with his wife (actually, his wife brought him under threat of divorce) typified this very point. After his busy week as a salesman, his favorite evening weekend activity was not a quiet evening with his "S" wife but a rousing card game with several other couples. Sitting quietly at home quite literally felt like punishment to him, and if he did not see his friends for several weeks, he felt as though he were starving emotionally.

My daughter, who is a high "i," suddenly remarked one day as we drove past a lonely, deserted cemetery, "I wouldn't want to be buried there. No one could find me." This need to be around people makes it difficult for them to work in isolation. High "i" youngsters often will want to study with the radio or TV blaring as they sit at the kitchen table near the family.

One fellow told me he never understood why his wife waited until he arrived home from work to start cleaning the house. His puzzlement was cleared up when he realized his wife was a high "i" and needed to have people around before she could concentrate on housework. It is difficult for "i's" to spend time alone, and they will not voluntarily choose to live in an isolated country house or city apartment where they cannot see the neighbors. If they are isolated from people, they will use the phone to contact people, watch TV, or desperately search out some method of establishing contact with others. They very seldom go anywhere alone. They talk to almost everyone they meet, and they have a real knack for putting people at ease. Since they are uncomfortable in a group if there is silence, they quickly move to fill it. This quality, along with the fact that they have good senses of humor, makes them fun to be around, and they are a definite asset on committees because they keep the pace moving and generate enthusiasm. This strong interest in people often makes it difficult for them to be concerned with methods and details. This leads to the next highlight.

Third, high "i" people tend to be disorganized. A high "C" husband with a high "i" wife will often become frustrated because she functions differently from him. Enjoying people and being disorganized, she most likely will have had coffee with the neighbors and not had enough time to pick up the house, which does not seem that important to her anyway. The high "C" husband comes home, looks disgustedly at the clutter in the house, and asks, "Do you think we could make an aisle through here?" This disorganization is consistent with the quality of being influenced by emotion—it is hard to be organized when one's decisions are determined by impulse and being in the mood, because feelings are often quite changeable. Rather than have a concrete plan, "i's" prefer to wing it, adjusting their courses as they go along.

Fourth, the "i" people fear loss of social approval, and this has a definite influence on their behavior because it is their strong motivator. Recognition and approval are very important to them, which means they would rather have sophisticated titles and praise than pay raises. Being very quick to pick up on other people's moods, they are adept at reading people and understanding what they want in order to do what must be done to gain approval. This also explains why they do not like silence in conversations. Conversation gives verbal clues about what other people are thinking, and if the high "i" people know what others are thinking, they can take appropriate steps to gain or maintain approval. Because they like people and know how to please them, they are very good at selling themselves and getting other people to like them. They are also very concerned about how they look and generally have the best body image of any of the personality styles.

Last, they are optimistic, which makes them a definite asset to a group or committee. This optimism is a definite strength, but used to an extreme it becomes a weakness. They can easily overextend themselves and try to do things they are really not qualified or able to do. My daughter does this all the time. Anything that comes up, she knows how to do it—even before I show her, and even when I know she has never done it before. There are times when she ends up looking a bit silly because she really did not know how to do something. But in typical "i" fashion, she shrugs it off, often saying it was someone else's fault anyway.

The "i's" can have difficulty looking deeply at their feelings because they tend to skim the surface and are quick to use their highly developed verbal skills to talk themselves out of trouble or blame someone else when confronted with their mistakes. Abigail and the apostle Peter are good examples of high "i" tendencies.

If you are an "i" person, you do experience hurts, but unless your "S" or "C" factors are also quite high, you are able to bypass or at least not experience struggles with the same agonizing intensity as described later in this book.

"S" Highlights

The "S" people are first of all loyal. Ray was a quiet, steady fellow who kept his feelings to himself. He worked as a supervisor in a manufacturing company that had management problems. As the business lost money, it was sold to new owners who tried to shape things up by firing people and appointing new bosses. In reality, they made the working conditions abysmal. Many people quit or were fired, but Ray remained, plugging away at his job, and eventually he earned his twenty-five-year watch. The only reason he finally left the company was because it went out of business. Whenever someone tells me he has been at the same job for many years, I immediately figure he has definite "S" tendencies, whereas the "D's" and "i's" work with their hats on and are more likely to be job-hoppers. If the "S's" are not careful, their loyalty may prevent them from taking steps that would be good for them personally. In other words, they may be loyal when they really should be looking out for themselves. Similarly, they generally expect more out of themselves than they do of other people and will make sure they keep their commitments even though they have trouble holding others to theirs.

Second, they are family-oriented. They will have pictures of their families on their desk at work. Because they value being with their families, they will resist taking work home and resent it if work intrudes on their family time. They enjoy spending time around the house and having family gatherings. Since they have a need to belong, they often prefer to work in a large organization that becomes like another family where they can have a sense of belonging. Being an "S" myself, I have had a strong interest in my family tree and have spent hours asking my older relatives about the generations that have preceded me. I take loads of pictures of my own family and literally have a pictorial history of my life.

Third, the "S" people are possessive and have a definite sense of personal territory. One schoolteacher who was an "S" kept the school projector in her room and became very upset when others used it and did not return it immediately. She treated it as her own, even though it belonged to the school. This sense of possessiveness is equally evident in territory issues. Several years ago I was working as a psychologist at a small clinic. The offices had a common air system, which meant that if a person smoked in one of the offices, it eventually filtered into "my" air space. Since I had developed a deep dislike for smoke because it gave me a headache when I was working, I told the clinic supervisor that the smoking really bothered me, but he stubbornly refused to consider my feelings. Whenever the smoke began to seep gradually into my room, I felt as though I were being personally violated, and my inner helpless anger began to burn so strongly I could scarcely stand it. Absolutely at my wits' end, I finally took the only solution available to me. I moved all of my furniture into the vacant office that had the thermostat on the wall. Whenever I smelled the smoke coming silently through the air ducts, I turned off the ventilation system to keep the smoke out of my office and let it accumulate around the person doing the smoking. Imperfect as this approach was, because the smoke never totally cleared out before I turned the system back on, at least I felt I had some control over what was happening.

Fourth, the "S" people fear loss of security in both concrete and emotional senses. Having food and shelter is very important to them, as well as feeling that they belong. This is why they typically prefer to belong to large organizations with which they can identify. This desire for security also causes them to save things. As an "S," I have all sorts of things from my past: papers from early school years, books, magazines, and the box in which my stereo was packed when I bought it in 1971. As I tell my wife, who is a "D" and saves almost nothing, "I never know when I might need something." It's easy for me to become sentimental as I look through my memorabilia, but my wife tells me that even though I'm saving it all these years, she'll throw it out after I die.

This need for security can cause various complications, however. The "S" people have difficulty speaking up for themselves. They keep their own commitments but have trouble insisting that others keep theirs in return. As a result of being naturally fear-prone people, preferring stability, keeping things the same, and needing to feel safe, they avoid conflict as much as possible and withdraw under pressure. In doing so they keep their feelings to themselves (speaking up might cause trouble) and harbor their hurts. In other words, just as they save objects from their past, they also save hurts and have a hard time forgiving. The "D's" and "i's" forget quickly, and when the "S" brings up something the "D" or "i" did in the past, the more dominant types are amazed because they either do not remember what the "S" is talking about or react in stunned protest, "That happened three years ago!" To the "S," it might as well have happened yesterday. If you are an "S" person, you will recognize this tendency in yourself, and you can see how it begins to point the way to inner struggle. This point also illustrates why the "D's" and "i's" have different struggles; when they get hurt, they forget it and don't hang on to it.

Finally, "S" people are also slow to change. It is very difficult to ramrod anything past them because before they make a move, they want to understand what is going to happen, why it needs to be done, and how it is going to affect them. When you understand their need for security, it is easier to accept their need for slow, planned change. I know when someone tries to push me, I balk and prefer to do nothing until I understand the situation. Being slow to change is one of the strengths that makes "S's" steady and dependable, but as with other strengths, it becomes a weakness when it is overextended. That is, they don't change when change really is in their best interest. "S's" are generally able to work well with the other styles because they are adaptable people.

Abraham and Hannah exemplify the "S" behavioral tendencies.

"C" Highlights

"C" people are first of all perfectionists with extremely high standards for themselves. My daughter Molly exhibits her ''C'' quality in her artistic work. When she draws, she loves to embellish her pictures with flowers, a variety of colors, and other details that her high "i" sister doesn't even consider. Usually, the papers she brings home from school are very neat, so when she brought home some work that appeared unusually sloppy by her normal standards, we asked her about the change in quality. "Well," she stated firmly, "the teacher didn't give us enough time to do it the way I wanted to, so I didn't even try." "C's" quickly feel guilty if they don't live up to their personal standards, yet they strive to meet them and become angry with themselves when they don't live up to them. This often results in disappointment with themselves, personal dislike, low self-esteem, and proneness toward self-pity, depression, and a martyr syndrome.

Their high standards can become a weakness when they expect too much from others and insist that others perform to their specifications. One husband was quite insistent that his wife wash on Monday (he checked the laundry basket when he came home from work to see if she had complied), use a certain towel for drying dishes, and stack his underwear in the drawer according to its age. His standards frustrated his wife who did not feel free to be her own person.

Second, high "C's" are sensitive and intuitive. This is an especially important point to keep in mind when dealing with these people because they are very sensitive to others' comments and are easily hurt. (Note that this sensitivity has to do primarily with one's personal feelings—being hurt—not others' feelings.) My profile includes this factor, and I have lived with this sensitivity for years. When you criticize high "C" people, be sure you are right, and even then, do it with love. Their intuition can sense dishonesty, inconsistencies, dislike, and rejection. Being so sensitive, they often sense subtle vibrations that others, particularly "D's" and "i's," overlook, and then they feel foolishly alone because others wonder what on earth the sensitive individuals are talking about. They also tend to remember hurts rather than quickly to forget them.

The fact that they are so sensitive and intuitive is often experienced as a curse. I see it all the time in the people who come to me for counsel, and I am convinced that the sensitive people, the ones whose feelings are easily stirred, have a harder time in life because they feel so much—often more than they care to feel. These stirred-up inner feelings have to be handled, which is no simple task because people often think their feelings are wrong or should not be there, or it is "not Christian to feel this way." If you experience this, I am sure you will readily agree.

Third, "C" people are also accurate, which is consistent with their perfectionistic quality. When they do something, they want it done accurately. They make good quality control people, and they fill useful roles on committees because they have little tolerance for shoddy work. They like guidelines and prefer going by the book. This is a very important quality in many occupations such as engineering, accounting, and medicine. I certainly would want the surgeon doing open-heart surgery on me to go by the book rather than wing it as the high "i" person prefers to do. This desire for accuracy can also lead to excessive caution and procrastination because they may fear making a mistake. This hints at the next quality, which is their motivating fear.

Fourth, "C" people fear being criticized for their

performance because they take such criticism very personally. It is as though their personal worth were being attacked. For this reason, as well as their intense sensitivity, criticism directed toward a "C" person must be correct and delivered in a manner that makes it easy to accept. To avoid the criticism that feels personally painful, they search for the "right way" to do things and want things done perfectly so there is no need or opportunity for others to criticize them. Although they like to be praised, they are also suspicious and mistrusting of it because their sensitive intuition tells them that the person giving the praise may have ''something up his sleeve."

Finally, the "C" people need many explanations. They are analytical thinkers who do not fly by the seat of their pants, so in order to satisfy their deep need to know, they ask lots of questions. This can be annoying to the "D's" and "i's" who like to move things along and not take time to pay attention to such details. If the need for information is not met, "C's" become uneasy and reluctant to participate in the proposed project.

I once met a fellow who was the director of a Christian organization, and as he discussed his program and personal leadership style, it became obvious that he was proud of his "D" qualities. Instead of appreciating the weaknesses in his leadership style that could cause him to be too ambitious, he deliberately selected other "D" people for his board of directors because he knew they would support him. With misguided boasting he stated, "I do not want 'C' type people on the board." He knew the "C" people would ask questions and slow down his ambitious projects. His strategy was his eventual downfall, because discontented staff finally contacted the board of "D's" who simply had been trusting the director, unaware that the small organization had an immense debt and was in serious financial trouble. The director found a job in another state, and a new "S" fellow was appointed as director to rebuild the shaky program. The ambitious director was guilty of not having enough "C" people on the board who could have asked the right questions and averted the financial disaster.

"C" characteristics are evident in the lives of Moses, Esther, and Jonah.

Harvey and Linsey

Remember Harvey in my Sunday school class, the fellow who said he wished he did not have to think about things and simply had a list of rules to follow? It is now clear that he is a "C" person who wants to avoid criticism by doing the right thing and does not want the personal responsibility of having to decide what the "right thing" is. For him, thinking and making decisions without specific guidelines is risky business—a risk he prefers to avoid. As you might expect, he married a "D" wife who is more comfortable assuming responsibility for issues in their relationship than he is.

Linsey, the talkative latecomer to the class, is a typical high "i" person who would rather talk and socialize than think and analyze. Her optimism and spontaneity bring enthusiasm and sparkle to the group even though she occasionally puts her foot in her mouth. Needing social approval, she is always searching for ways to please people and gain their approval.

Fortunately for her, her husband is a "D" person who can take care of himself and does not have to rely on her fun-loving, disorganized style for his own support.

Understanding the behavioral principles described here makes it easier to understand some of the reasons that people do things. As you have read through the DiSC highlights, I'm sure you could begin to recognize yourself. But there is another important point I want to make about the differences in people.

The Strong and the Weak

Because the "D's" and "i's" usually are in the limelight of leadership and our society admires people who are achievement-oriented, self-confident, and in charge, the "S" and "C" people often feel that their way of doing things is inferior, and it's easy for them to feel personally inferior as well. Paul Tournier places all of this in a perspective that has been very valuable in helping me understand people in spite of their outward actions and differences.

The truth is that human beings are much more alike than they think. What is different is the external mask, sparkling or disagreeable, their outward reaction, strong or weak. These appearances, however, hide an identical inner personality. The external mask, the outward reaction, deceive everybody, the strong as well as the weak. All men, in fact, are weak. All are weak because all are afraid. They are all afraid of being trampled underfoot. They are all afraid of their inner weaknesses being discovered. They all have secret faults; they all have a bad conscience on account of certain acts which they would like to keep covered up. They are all afraid of other men and of God, of themselves, of life and of death. . . . What distinguishes men from each other is not their inner nature, but the way in which they react to this common distress. . . . among human beings there are two opposing types of reactions to the same inner distress: strong reactions and weak reactions.

The strong reaction is to give ourselves an appearance of assurance and aggressiveness in order to hide our weakness, to cover up our own fear by inspiring fear in others, to parade our virtues in order to cloak our vices. The weak reaction is to become flustered, and thus to reveal the very weakness we want to hide; it is to allow our consciousness of our weakness to prevent us from bringing into play the concealment-reactions which permit the strong to dissimulate their weakness. . . . In reality we all react strongly or weakly, according to circumstances, but in varying degree.[4]

In several short paragraphs, Tournier sweeps across all personality styles and places everyone on the same level with identical fears and needs—the only difference is the way each of us handles his fears, and this is what gives color to our world of personality. Quite obviously Tournier's concept of the strong parallels the "Dominance" and "influencing" patterns, while the "Steady" and "Compliant" patterns yield the weak reactions. With these thoughts in mind, let's look at why certain personalities experience difficulty growing up in the Christian home. As you read this, try to keep your own personal style in mind.

The Basis for Struggle

Although the risks and dangers present in growing up Christian are similar for all children, I have noticed that some people seem to grow up and live Christian lives relatively free of inner struggle and pain, whereas others have gnawing, persistent struggles. The people in this second group are the ones who are quite sensitive by nature, and they are usually born with an extrasensitive emotional and physical system that responds quickly to pressure, criticism, fear, stress, and even noise. Whether these people like it or not, and often even if they try, they are unable consciously to stop their bodies from responding with stomach-gripping tension in a nerve-wracking situation. Their sensitive, responsive nervous systems react and give them so many feelings to handle that they often must concentrate first of all on their own feelings. These are so strong and immediate that it is difficult for them to focus on the anxiety-producing external situations with any significant clarity of mind.

Some people are more prone than others to struggle with their Christian lives. These are the ones who are quite sensitive by nature.

Due to the rush of internal feelings, the sensitive people spend considerable time and energy thinking about their stirred-up feelings, which often makes the feelings even stronger and the hurts harder to forget. To avoid more hurt, they try to avoid conflict and live cautiously by the rules so others do not criticize them. The net effect of this is a more inhibited and complicated emotional life for the sensitive people because they have more stimulation to handle than the less-sensitive people do. The most critical effect, particularly in light of the discussion in this book, is their vulnerability to influences, remarks, and actions of others, especially people in positions of authority such as parents, teachers, ministers, Sunday school teachers, and so on. It is this deep vulnerability that causes many growing children and adults to have trouble in the evangelical community because they perceive and interpret what they hear in an intense manner, which means their experiences in the home and at church have deep and long-lasting effects on their lives. If you happen to be one of these sensitive persons, you know exactly what I mean.

On the opposite side from the sensitive people are the ones with stronger reactions. These people typically do not comply with the environment as the sensitive ones do, but instead are active toward the environment, trying to shape the world in the direction that makes them more comfortable. They see problems as challenges and do not mind conflict because their physical and emotional systems are less sensitive to being stirred up. When they are in the middle of nerve-wracking situations, their stomachs do not churn, their hands do not sweat, and they do not feel the rush of inner feelings as the sensitive people do. Not having to think about a jumping stomach or a trembling voice, the strong can devote all their mental energy and thoughts to the task at hand and say whatever comes to mind because they are not afraid of conflict. Again, I want to emphasize that the strong do experience hurts and have struggles, but they respond differently from those who have weak reactions.

The strong are constantly striving to move ahead, to make things happen, and this feels normal to them because it is. They struggle and are mystified when other people become upset with their aggressiveness and try to stop their "normal" behavior. They can be hurt at this point, but here is where the difference takes place. Rather than retreat in pained silence, as those with weak reactions do, they regroup and go after their goal again and again. They do not sit and smolder and resent—they use their energy to act. The "D" people will try to prove you are wrong, and the "i" people will do a lot of talking to explain why it is not their fault. Since the strong say what they think, they do not store their hurts and are able to recover quickly and move on to the next day. Some of them have trained themselves to not experience their feelings, and others have developed the ability to push them aside.

In comparison to the weak, they are less vulnerable to the actions of their parents and others in authority because by nature they have more faith in themselves than they do in others, so they reserve the right to pass final judgment on what will affect them. This is another way of saying they are slow to feel guilty. The weak or sensitive people, by comparison, are affected by whatever happens to them whether they like it or not and have a difficult time being selective about which things will bother them. This means they feel guilty easily, keep their feelings to themselves, and do not resist. They take an inactive approach. In light of these points, you can begin to see why two people are able to listen to the same hellfire sermon, and each can leave the service in a different frame of mind. The strong are usually not bothered at all, and the weak feel guilty and fearful.

People with strong personalities usually
do not hang around the church and struggle.

People with strong reactions usually do not hang around the church and struggle. Either they rebel quite openly against their parents and the church and eventually develop a meaningful faith, or else they simply turn the other way and reject the church altogether because they do not see a place for themselves to fit. Reacting to life in a robust fashion, they make room for themselves if there is none, while the sensitive ones linger and hold back, fearful to move too quickly for fear of inciting either God's or their parents' wrath. Feeling uncertain and having many internal questions, but afraid of voicing them or reacting openly against them as the strong ones do, they halfheartedly resist. Yet out of fear and obligation they attempt to live Christian lives in spite of their inner feelings, and thus they become reluctant Christians.

If you struggle in your own Christian life, you are probably one of yesterday's sensitive children who grew up in Christian homes and evangelical churches that did not appreciate their vulnerable natures and handled their tender hearts with fear and intimidation. If so, this has paralyzed you, making it difficult for you to experience the abundant life and joy that you hear described in the pulpit. With this background information about people in mind, let's now look at the specific dangers in the home and the church.

PART TWO

Common Dangers
in Christian Homes
and Churches

C H A P T E R 4

Dangers in the Christian Home: Part One

Terri is a twenty-eight-year-old woman who came to me for therapy, filled with hurts that she could barely express. The oldest of four children, she was born to Christian parents who attended church regularly. Her father was a respected man in the church, having served on consistory (called church board in some churches), being involved with the music committee, and so on. Terri was treated horribly by her father, and my best explanation for his behavior is that he wanted his first-born to be a son.

Unconsciously, he hated Terri. Unfortunately, she was an extremely sensitive, vulnerable child. He consistently yelled at her to keep her mouth shut and told her not to express any feelings. He slapped her repeatedly across the face; he regularly used his belt to whip her around the body and head. For additional punishment, he forced her to spend hours locked in their totally dark, old-fashioned cellar. One time, hearing the rats scurrying through the cellar, Terri climbed the few stairs leading to the slanted, folding cellar doors and tried to push them open, knowing ahead of time she would be unable to move them. Unable to escape the darkness, and with the sound of rats approaching, this eight-year-old, sensitive little girl crouched as high as she could in the narrow space between the stairs and the cellar doors, screaming at the top of her voice in sheer terror. So piercing was the experience that much of it has been forced out of her memory. She can't remember being let out of the basement and can't even remember why she was being punished.

To make matters worse, the next child, another daughter, could do no wrong in Dad's eyes and became his favorite. When the sister misbehaved, she was never punished; Terri was. In fact, Terri was consistently blamed for anything the sister did. During their early adult years the favored sister died unexpectedly from cancer. People said to Terri, "It's too bad your dad's favorite died." At the funeral home as the family was in the receiving line to greet the people coming to offer condolences, Dad turned to Terri and curtly snapped, "Go to the other end of the line. You don't belong in this family anymore!"

Needless to say, her father's attitude has had a profound effect on Terri, and it has permeated all areas of her life. We'll return to Terri in a moment, but with her experiences in mind, let's examine several important points to gain perspective.

Psychological Foundations for Spiritual Life

Adult spiritual life has psychological foundations that are established in the home, and these foundations are developed in the day-to-day relationships between parents and children. The child participates in some of the relationships and observes others, and each relationship contributes a different piece of the foundation eventually formed in the child's life. The danger point where many things can go wrong exists within this relationship area, and sensitive children with weak reactions, or "S" and "C" personality patterns, are the ones who are most vulnerable to negative family patterns because they keep their hurts inside and don't assert themselves on behalf of their own viewpoints.

This certainly was true of Terri, who was a sensitive child and lacked the inner strength to withstand her father's treatment. The youngsters with strong reactions do not give in easily and in spite of their hurts continue trying to move through the mass of parental and church restrictions. Stronger children feel more comfortable picking and choosing what they will believe, whereas the sensitive ones try to believe everything and are unable to discount those points that are contradictory in the church and in their parents' behavior.

In our early relationships with our parents, we develop patterns of acting and thinking that continue into adult life and influence our decisions, often in subtle, unconscious ways. When a person comes to see me for personal therapy, I always spend time at the first or second visit inquiring about the family. What were Mom and Dad like? Who were the other children? How did Mom and Dad get along? How did they treat the children? What was Dad's personality like? Mom's personality? What were the prominent feelings present as a child? Understanding the way the family worked helps me understand the person sitting before me.

If family relationships are warped,
they can create silent, often unseen
barriers to adult spiritual development.

There are relationships in the family that parallel spiritual relationships, and if these family relationships are warped or distorted, they can create silent, often unseen barriers to adult spiritual development. Before those of us who have experienced such barriers are able to progress spiritually, we must first understand and clear out the emotional issues that block emotional growth as well as spiritual growth. Dealing with these issues is often complicated for those of us who have grown up in Christian homes because we have been taught by specific instruction or by implication that questioning or challenging our parents is either "sinful" or dangerous.

Earthly Father and the Heavenly Father

In the New Testament, Jesus often compared human fathers to God the Father and encouraged His listeners to use their everyday pictures of their fathers to understand God as well. Although I can understand this, I have always been mystified by it because Jesus seems to have assumed that fathers are always decent people and children always have positive relationships with their dads that they can easily transfer to God.

> "You men who are fathers—if your boy asks for bread, do you give him a stone? If he asks for fish, do you give him a snake? If he asks for an egg, do you give him a scorpion? [Of course not!] And if even sinful persons like yourselves give children what they need, don't you realize that your heavenly Father will do at least as much, and give the Holy Spirit to those who ask for him?" (Luke 11:11–13 TLB).

Bread, fish, and egg represent basic needs the son might ask his father to meet in daily living, and I believe these needs include emotional ones: an encouraging word, time spent together, hugs, and "I love you." It makes sense that people whose fathers meet their needs will have a positive foundation from which to view God as a Father who also meets needs and cares about feelings.

People with fathers who did not meet their needs will have trouble viewing God as a Father who meets needs and cares about feelings.

How does Jesus view the person who does not have a good relationship with Dad? What do people do when as children their dads gave them stones and snakes? And what about the many children growing up today in single-parent homes with no father at all? I have worked with people from such homes, and their total concept of father is simply a blank hole—they can't picture even one bit what a father is. They have no father concept to transfer to God, and although this also creates problems, it may not be as bad as having a bad father image to overcome. It is especially sad when Christian fathers treat their sons and daughters in emotionally unkind ways, building deep, unnecessary flaws into their children's emotional foundation. People who have not had an actual father in the home may need to experience a relationship with an older man who serves as a substitute father. In this way, they can at least develop a partial concept of a father.

J. B. Phillips sheds some light on this for us:

> When Christ taught His disciples to regard God as their Father in Heaven He did not mean that their idea of God must necessarily be based upon their ideas of their fathers. For all we know there may have been many of His hearers whose fathers were unjust, tyrannical, stupid, conceited, reckless, or indulgent. It is the *relationship* that Christ is stressing. The intimate love for, and interest in, his son possessed by a good earthly father represents to men a relationship they can understand, even if some of them are fatherless![1]

Let's return to Terri and her experiences with her father. One day as Terri sat in my office, struggling with a major disappointment in her life and wondering why God would allow her present dilemma, I slowly observed, "It almost makes God seem . . ." I paused, searching for a word, and was about to say "unfair" when into the silence she blurted, "Like my father!"

The spontaneous forcefulness of her remark startled me. "I can think of Jesus Christ the Son, the Holy Spirit the Comforter, but when I think of God as Father, I think of injustice, beatings, and a lot of fears. So I think of Jesus Christ as Son, Holy Spirit as Comforter, and God as Creator, but that makes Him seem so far away," she explained with sadness in her voice. "Last Sunday was Father's Day," she continued. "I just couldn't bear to think of it. Tears were streaming down my face during church. My husband asked what was wrong, and I said, 'Nothing.' Then I realized the minister was talking about love, compassion, and caring—all the things I never had from my father. What I have is a big, empty spot that hurts."

Terri's adult spiritual life is complicated and hindered by the rotten piece of psychological foundation that her father built into her life. She is unable to gain comfort from her heavenly Father because her intense feelings stemming from her dad's treatment instantly block her. He gave her stones and snakes, not bread and fish. "Terri's is an extreme case," you say. In some respects, perhaps, but other Christian fathers have sexually molested their children, and I believe such abuse is more common in the Christian community than most people realize. Parental actions do not have to be this severe to cause problems. With a sensitive child, a cross look or an inconsiderate attitude can be more devastating than physical abuse.

Some children who have had negative, abusive fathers grow up without being affected, and children with differing personalities can grow up in the same home and be affected quite differently from one another. A fellow who had spent most of his adult life as a minister had grown up with an abusive father. As we discussed his experiences at home, he told me that before he entered the first grade, he knew he wanted to be a minister. From that point forward he had worked single-mindedly toward his goal. The fact that his father was a negative, mean person never affected him, and even as a child he was able to look beyond his father and not take his actions seriously. He also spontaneously observed, "This business about your father affecting your concept of God as Father never happened to me." In my estimation, he has definite "D" or strong reactions in his personality that enabled him to strike his own course independent of his father's actions.

He also explained that his older brother took a different approach. The brother was a more sensitive person who did not pursue his personal goals because he did not feel support from his parents. Following the typical pattern of the "S" personality style, he withdrew and took an inactive approach to the obstacles at home.

My father worked very hard to meet the needs of the four growing boys in his family. For example, he never asked us to do any work on the farm that he was unwilling to do; in other words, he did not shove the dirty work on us kids as has happened on some farms. To help us become comfortable around water, he bought a small lakefront property and helped us construct a floating raft from which we could dive. Going for a cool swim was always a treat after a day in the hot July sun making hay. He shared his love for travel with us and expanded our horizons by taking us on various trips, including New York City, Washington, D.C., the Smoky Mountains, the western U.S., and part of Canada. Now that I am an adult with children of my own, I especially appreciate his effort because he did all this with four boys riding in the car, and there were no interstate highways at the time. I don't think I could do that!

My most meaningful need that he met was probably more difficult for him at the time than I realized. When he was a farm boy, the work was done with horses, and for some reason he absolutely disliked them. On the other hand, I have loved horses for as long as I can remember. When I was in the eighth grade, a truck unexpectedly pulled into our driveway while we were eating supper. Naturally, we all walked out to see what was happening. No one said anything as the truck driver slowly attached the livestock ramp to the truck and then disappeared into the animal cargo area. To my surprise, he emerged leading a large brown-and-white pony down the ramp. He brought him to me and said, "His name is Tony. He's yours." My dad had secretly arranged the whole thing. I could hardly believe it. In spite of his personal dislike for horses, he even furnished all the feed, and later he let me buy Ginger, my favorite, high-spirited mare. When he gave me the horse, he gave me bread because it met one of my deep needs. Having my horse was a special part of my adolescence. In contrast to Terri's father, my dad put effort into building a positive foundation for my growing concept of God as he worked to meet my needs.

Our family, like yours and other families, was not perfect, and there were things about it that I did not like. I have decided as an adult that hurts are a part of life and will take place in the best of families; the critical point is how we handle them. Being a person with definite sensitive qualities, I reacted to the family incidents that caused me pain and made the mistake of saving them just as I saved all sorts of other things from my childhood. Fortunately, my childhood hurts have turned out to be an asset, but that's getting ahead of my story.

My father was slow to give praise and quick to criticize and point out flaws. This often gave the impression that he did not care, even though he did. He and I have talked about this after I was grown, and he explained his reasoning. "If I didn't say anything, that meant what you did was okay. I only said something if it wasn't." He also was concerned about the family image. Although I never was sure what the family image was, this concern influenced many of his decisions and actions. Consequently, I think he saw the family (primarily us boys) as a collective group that had the potential to make or break the family image, so personal feelings we had as individuals were usually subordinated to the greater good of the family.

As I have talked to people through the years, I have learned that this is a common attitude in many families. One woman exclaimed in exasperation, "What will the neighbors think? What will the neighbors think? I got so sick of hearing my mom say that all the time!" She said her parents based many family decisions on what the neighbors might think. Fortunately, my parents never used that particular phrase. As a corollary to this, individual successes received very little personal recognition. Just as the whole family image supposedly suffered when we did wrong, so also the collective family took credit when any of us did well.

As with all families, mixed in with the positive things my dad did were some things I didn't like and an area of our relationship that I had trouble handling. The expression of personal feelings wasn't encouraged, and we didn't have open, family discussions about things. Our family was also reserved in the display of affection. From my point of view, Dad repeatedly made decisions that affected me without taking my feelings into consideration. The deepest hurt of my teenage years was an instance of this.

Keep in mind that Indiana's "Hoosier Hysteria," the love for basketball, is a nationally recognized phenomenon, and I was no exception in my love for the sport. I mounted a backboard and hoop on one of the beams in the barn and practiced as often as I could, mentally visualizing myself as the star player at school with everyone counting on me for the big play that would win the game. But my dad did not share my enthusiasm. I faced a dilemma. As a sophomore in high school, I decided I wanted to play basketball to gain social recognition and win back my girlfriend, who had fallen for one of the fellows who was a basketball player.

Although I was facing a deadline to sign up for basketball, the very thought of asking my dad if I could play brought terror to my heart.

Every morning while my dad and I were milking the cows, I mentally rehearsed what I would say to him and tried to determine when the most opportune time would be to ask him. I decided I would ask him while he was in the milkhouse washing out the milking machines. But morning after morning as I approached the milkhouse, my throat felt choked, my heart began to pound, and fear gripped my stomach. In spite of my desire, my fear overcame me morning after morning until so much time had passed that I could not be eligible for the season opener.

Finally, I realized I had to do it, no matter how hard it was. Simply forcing myself, I asked him one morning, but he did not agree. I approached him two more times, and then he said with reluctant disgust, "Well, go! If your grades are down and if you aren't playing half of the time by Christmas, you've got to quit. Is that okay?" At that point I felt compelled to agree to anything.

My actual playing time was limited, and I did not become the instant star I had hoped to be. Nonetheless, it was a dream come true for me. But it was destined to end. Shortly before Christmas, Dad said I had to quit the team. He said he couldn't milk the cows all by himself, and my place was at home. It didn't seem to matter that I had one brother three years older or that my younger, ten-year-old brother was simply fooling around in the house during chore time. He didn't do any chores in the barn, and I had started milking cows morning and evening when I was eight years old. This didn't seem fair to me.

The most painful scene of all is etched in my memory, and I find no record of it in my diary, perhaps because it was so painful and I never knew who might read what I had written. It was a Sunday afternoon within a week or so after I was forced to quit. My folks had invited some people over for dinner that day, and in the afternoon as we sat in the living room with the visitors, the subject of basketball came up and someone asked how I was doing. I quietly replied, "I'm not playing anymore." At that point my dad laughed and said, "Tell them why you quit, Don!" His public statement struck like a knife to the deepest regions of my being, but I remained silent, the obedient youngster afraid to speak.

Many years later as I struggled with my confused, angry feelings toward God and toward my dad, I suddenly realized that the feelings I had in my relationship with my dad were identical to my feelings toward God. I felt as though my dad didn't care about my deepest feelings, and I didn't feel that God cared, either. This feeling was further reinforced at church by sermons that said what I wanted or cared about didn't matter. Overlooking the good things my father had done for me, I had become stuck in my hurt, thought he didn't care, and then transferred the feeling to God.

Before Terri will be able to look at God as Father, she must first deal with her feelings about her earthly father. I had to work on my own attitudes as well. If you also are experiencing trouble seeing God as a caring, loving Father, the first area you will want to examine is your relationship with your own father to see if you have become stuck in the hurtful area of the relationship. This will be discussed in more detail later in the book.

Father's Relationship with Mother

A couple who had grown up in a conservative denomination described to me part of their personal search for their niche within the church community. For a time, they ventured away from the mainline denominations and attached themselves to various small, independent churches.

One church in particular heavily emphasized—even insisted—that the man was to be the head of the house. This hierarchy of male domination was the backbone of the church organization, too, with the minister being the man at the top who gave ironclad directions. As the couple described the minister, he sounded like a "D" personality who had certainly overextended his strengths into the weak area.

The most striking point the couple made was the minister's insistence that the man in the home be the head and the woman had to submit—no questions asked or else church discipline was started. "My wife and I both had full-time jobs, and we have several children," the mild-natured husband stated. "I was told at church that it was my wife's duty to take care of me, and as her husband I was expected and supposed to demand that she do things even if she were tired. In the evening I sat in my chair while she fixed dinner and did the dishes. She was supposed to put the children to bed by herself, bring me coffee, or anything else I wanted. All of this finally got to me. I just couldn't live that way, so we decided to leave that church." What the Bible actually says is this:

> For a husband is in charge of his wife in the same way Christ is in charge of his body the church. (He gave his very life to take care of it and be its Savior!). . . . And you husbands, show the same kind of love to your wives as Christ showed to the church when he died for her (Eph. 5:23, 25 TLB).

As children watch how
Dad treats Mom in daily living,
they are subtly, without realizing it,
developing a concept of how
Christ relates to His church.

Although the apostle Paul didn't mention husband and wife as parents in these verses, it's obvious that children in the home are front-row observers of their parents' relationship. As children watch how Dad treats Mom in daily living, they are subtly, without realizing it, developing a concept of how Christ relates to His church. This becomes another foundation stone for later adult spiritual life and another danger point for personal development. If a youngster sees his father treating his mother as Christ treated the church, it becomes easy to transfer this concept into the spiritual realm with comfort and significant meaning. If Dad is a domineering tyrant, however, even in the name of God, a simple transfer of his father's character to Christ is impossible because Christ was not a tyrant. The observing youngster has to get rid of a set of false ideas of how a man should relate to his wife in order to see Christ more clearly.

The best explanation I have heard of this passage has been one I learned recently.[2] The Greek term for "head" (which the KJV uses in Eph. 5:23 rather than the TLB's "in charge") described the actual center of control of the body, and it was the same term used for the controllers of organizations. Paul took this well-known Greek term, turned it upside down, and used it to describe a relationship that was service-oriented. Indeed, Christ's relationship to the church has been giving and sacrificial in nature; He died for the church and, as its head, exists to serve and give life to the body—not govern it like a dictator.

It is this type of relationship Paul is advocating for husbands to have with their wives—not dominating or bossing them around, but supporting them as their own bodies and even sacrificing for them if necessary. This type of giving and caring provides an example children can use to understand the mystery of Christ and the church. Failing to develop this positive concept in the home simply adds another burden to be overcome as growing youngsters attempt to develop positive spiritual lives. What a responsibility and opportunity this is for fathers!

Mother and Grace

In our country there have been the patriotic, homey concepts of the flag, Mom, and apple pie. There is something about mothers that is basic to human life. I've never heard a football player or a professional boxer on TV yell into the camera, "Hi, Dad!" It's always, "Hi, Mom! Look at me!" There also is the saying that "he's so ugly only a mother could love a face like that!" The implication is that when no one else cares and the world is cold, at least "Mom who carried me into the world will love me!"

Just as mothers and "Mother Earth" are basic to human life, so grace is a fundamental element of Christianity that permeates the Christian life. Although there are various technical, theological definitions of grace, I am referring here to the "concept of kindness bestowed upon someone undeserving thereof. Hence, undeserved favor, especially that kind or degree of favor bestowed upon sinners through Jesus Christ. . . . Grace, therefore, is that unmerited favor of God towards fallen man."[3] The key word in this definition that relates to our discussion is *unmerited*, the favor God gives that we do not deserve. Doesn't this sound like the type of love we usually expect a mother to feel for her child, to accept and bestow favor on her child simply because of who the child is without setting up a series of hoops for the youngster to jump through before the favor is granted? The person who has felt this deep acceptance from Mother will find it easier to accept God's grace than the one who does not know what it feels like to be loved and accepted just for being. The mother-child relationship in the family can build a powerful foundation for positive adult spiritual life, or it can create untold complications that are difficult to overcome.

The person who has felt deep acceptance from Mother will find it easier to accept God's grace than the one who does not know what it feels like to be loved and accepted just for being.

What if Mom doesn't love her child? The psychological literature is filled with information about the mother-child relationship and the potential for either positive or negative effects. I have seen people who have not been loved or at least have not felt loved by their mothers, and it has had a profound emotional effect on them. If a person has to earn love and approval from the mother who brought him into the world (incidentally, earning approval in this manner is an unending task because the sought-for approval never comes), how can he suddenly turn to God and turn off all psychological habits to bask in God's love? If someone feels he has to work to earn God's love, he probably had to earn his mother's love as well.

I don't believe people have to encounter severe or total rejection from their mothers to have difficulty in this area. One young woman who had grown up with a very spiritual mother, told me through her pain, "I was never able to be good enough. She always found something wrong with what I did. Now I don't believe anyone will care about me unless I give them a reason." A person with this attitude will have a hard time accepting God's unmerited favor without trying to earn it, which is an impossibility.

My relationship with my mother was similar to that of many other Christians who have talked to me. Perhaps you will see similarities to your mother. Raising four boys on a farm is a lot of work. I recall helping my mom run the clothes through the ringer of the old-style washing machine in the basement. Certainly, lugging all those clothes up and down the stairs was hard work, and since there were no clothes dryers in those years, she had to hang the wash outdoors all year around. Even with today's conveniences, few people find fulfillment in such work. But in this and many other ways, she was meeting our needs. On hot summer days, for example, she always made a big pitcher of cold lemonade and brought it out to the barn where we were putting hay in the mow. Between Dad and the four boys, it didn't take long to empty the pitcher.

One of the ways my mother paid special attention to my desires was to fix certain foods. Every Saturday, she made bread dough from scratch and baked cinnamon rolls, pies, cakes, and so on. Everyone else in the family liked nuts except me. I simply didn't like to have crunchy walnuts in rolls, cupcakes, or anything. So even though it was extra work, my mom often left a corner of the cake clear of nuts or made nut-free cupcakes that were "just for Don." That always made me feel special.

My mother has always been a strong Christian, and she wanted her sons to share her faith. To this end, she poured a lot of herself into the family. Although I can fully agree with her intentions, my sensitive nature had trouble with some of her methods.

Many of my efforts at self-assertion were often stifled either directly or indirectly by statements that made me feel guilty. Whenever I did something she didn't like, I can never recall hearing her say, "I don't like what you're doing!" Instead, she took an indirect approach. "Aren't you ashamed?" she asked accusingly—her favorite phrase. "Aren't you just so ashamed?" she repeated. Then I had to sit in a chair "until you can say you're sorry!" This requirement cast me into great inner conflict. I generally wasn't sorry for what I had done because I didn't see what the big deal was, but I was definitely afraid to express my opinion to my mother. My conscience knew that if I reported being sorry when I honestly wasn't, then I was lying and headed to hell for sure. With a torn heart I sadly took my place in the designated chair, and with fearful determination I tried to forcibly change my views until I could at least feel a little bit of guilt in my stomach. Then I hurriedly reported my "sorriness" to my mother in a subdued tone before I lost the little bit of regret I had been able to muster.

My mother's second-favorite phrase was stronger. If I had done something that she really didn't like, she asserted, "What would Jesus say if He saw you do that?" As a young boy I didn't know what Jesus would have said, and my mother never said what she thought He would say, either. It was clear, however, that I was in definite trouble. For some reason I had the feeling that she loved me only when I was behaving or doing the right thing. Later, as an adult, I realized that my sensitive nature had remembered her reprimands more than her loving actions, and that in doing so I was having trouble dealing with God's love as well.

Cathy is a thirty-eight-year-old woman who is the third of five children. Her growing-up years were characterized by feelings of being different, low in self-worth, and inferior. At age seventeen she became pregnant by a boyfriend she didn't love, but since she didn't have an open, conversational relationship with her mother and feared more rejection if her mother learned her secret, she decided to marry her boyfriend, hoping her marriage would hide the truth from her mother. The marriage ended in disaster. Her husband abused her, took advantage of her, and ran around with other women. Eventually, she became involved with a man who treated her very well—so well that she didn't like his thoughtfulness because she felt she didn't deserve it. Her nervousness and anxiety increased to the point that she was afraid to ride over bridges even as a passenger in a car, so she seldom left her home.

As we discussed her situation and family background,

several important facts came to light. From Cathy's childhood to her adulthood, Cathy's mother treated her differently from her other daughters. She was consistently critical and rude and even told Cathy she was excluded from her will. Cathy's child was treated similarly and did not receive gifts from Grandma when the other grandchildren did. This always troubled Cathy, and she consistently wondered what she could ever do to make her mother like her. Even though she often went out of her way to please her mother and gave in to her wishes at her own expense, things never changed.

Before Cathy was born, her parents were having marital conflicts, and Mother was considering divorcing her husband who was in the army. When her husband came home on leave, Mother became sexually involved with her husband against her wishes and became pregnant with Cathy, a pregnancy and a child she did not want, by the man she wanted to divorce. As we discussed this, Cathy recalled hearing her mother say that she had not wanted her. Mother's actions through the years supported her statement. Obviously, this has had a profound effect on Cathy, who took her mother's actions seriously and decided that "I am a no-good person. I can't please my mother. No one else can care for me, either. I have no right to want anything for myself."

This negative self-concept affects everything Cathy does and ties her up in knots. Her mother never wanted her and communicated this in subtle ways through the years to Cathy, who now can accept love only from her small daughter. Cathy is a Christian but does not attend church because she feels so sinful compared with all the people at church, unworthy to attend. In spite of my best efforts, it has been difficult to help her change these deep, negative feelings about herself. With these feelings, it is difficult for her to experience God's grace and concern for her. No one else has cared. She can scarcely relate to honest human love.

Cathy's situation is similar to that of many other people who have talked to me about their struggles, and it illustrates the important role of mothers in their children's lives.

Looking Ahead

Let me add that the critical point here is not only what our parents may have done, but what *we think they have done,* or our interpretation of what they have done. It is a fact of human nature that we act upon what we believe is real, whether it is real in fact or not. Consequently, distortions can easily slip into our thinking.

It is important for those of us who struggle to realize that even though certain struggles appear to be spiritual ones, they often have a recognizable emotional origin in our early family experiences as illustrated here. If we don't understand this, we can spend a lot of time and energy believing we have a spiritual problem because we don't feel secure in God's love, for example, when in reality it is an emotional issue that started with our parents at home. We need to examine our psychological foundations that have developed within the home, separate the emotional from the spiritual, and realize that we have to work on the emotional areas first. To have a positive spiritual life, we must clear up our emotional distortions as much as possible. Later chapters will discuss this process in more detail and provide you with specific suggestions that you can apply to your own life.

CHAPTER 5

Dangers in the Christian Home: Part Two

Nate was a pleasant fellow, kind and generous. I became acquainted with him in college. He had grown up in an evangelical Christian home, and as an adult he was genuinely serious about his faith and his relationship with Christ. After graduation from college, he landed a good job and married a Christian woman. Children began to appear, and the family grew. Being concerned about his role as a Christian father and desiring to pass his love for God to his children, Nate endeavored to teach them his faith. He and his wife joined an evangelical church and attended faithfully: Sunday school, Sunday morning church, and Sunday evening worship. Of course the children were regular attenders as well.

I often stopped by to visit when I was in the area where he lived. As Nate and I were talking one day, he discussed his spiritual goals for his children and concluded emphatically, "And my most important goal for them is to know the exact day and hour that they get saved!"

After our conversation, Nate's words rang in my ears. But as I watched his family develop, I noticed that he did not buy his kids a swing set (every other youngster on his street had one) or make them a sandbox (such things would clutter up the yard), and he rarely allowed them to play in the yard. The toys they had were few, and they had to play in the driveway, the street, or someone else's yard.

In fact, the children were told by the parents that they could play on the neighbor children's play equipment. As for Sunday observance, Nate would not allow the children to play on Sunday, and I never saw either Nate or his wife out playing with the children. When I went with them on picnics, the food was handed out sparingly as though it had to last for years. The potato chips were counted out several chips per child (who can eat just three?), and then the bag was put away, still in open view, while the youngsters struggled valiantly to restrain their hunger and maintain composure.

As the years passed, the children began to demonstrate more of their own personalities, and I noticed that they all had bad attitudes. They were grabby, selfish youngsters. Being mean to other kids was everyday behavior as they sauntered around the neighborhood with sad and surly faces. In fact, neighboring parents gradually began to prohibit their children from playing with Nate's children because they were so negative and destructive, striking other children and breaking toys.

Everyday Attitudes

As I pondered all this, comparing Nate's spiritual goals for his children with his everyday treatment of them, I saw how his children appeared to be turning out. I saw, too, the operation of a more generally striking truth that I had also seen in the lives of struggling Christians who have come to me for therapy. That truth is the basic point of this chapter: the way parents treat their children in daily living has more impact on their children's eventual spiritual development than the family's religious practices, including having family altar, reading the Bible together, attending church services, and so on.

Perhaps you're wondering if I'm saying that regular family spiritual activities are not important. No, that's not my point. They are important, but the way parents treat their children in everyday living can subtly undermine all their lofty spiritual aspirations. When the children become adults with bitterness and resentment toward the church and their parents, the well-intentioned parents are totally devastated and mystified. I believe many evangelical parents are similar to Nate; they have good intentions and positive spiritual goals for their children. In their minds they have followed worthy objectives without realizing that Christian principles can be undermined by poor relationships within the family.

The way parents treat their children
in daily living has more impact
on their children's eventual spiritual development
than the family's religious practices.

There are a number of specific errors I have seen parents commit that create danger points, and although there is insufficient space to thoroughly cover all of them here, I do want to mention several to give you a clear understanding of what I am saying. These danger points, occurring in the relationships between children and parents, are specific actions that fit in with the major points discussed in the previous chapter. As you read through this chapter, keep your own childhood in mind to see if you find any similarities between your parents' actions and the points discussed here.

Children's Feelings and Opinions

Too often, well-intentioned Christian parents treat their children as though the kids' opinions and feelings have little, if any, worth. Perhaps this is not totally the parents' fault because even psychologists didn't recognize that children have emotions until well into this century. This concept is akin to the previously mentioned notion of meeting children's needs. Children have feelings, too, and even though their little opinions may not seem important compared to adult concerns, they are immensely important to the children. By the very act of listening to their children's opinions, parents communicate that children have worth. By allowing children to express their opinions and feelings, parents help them learn that such expression is appropriate and permissible. This also helps children become comfortable with emotions, a lesson that is very helpful later in life.

Evangelical parents who do not listen are creating danger points for their children because they are communicating through their actions that they do not care about their children at a personal level. This contributes to a negative self-concept in the child. When parents unexpectedly yell at a child, hit a child, or even ignore a child, the child feels responsible for causing the parents' action. A child is not developed enough to reason, *Mom is crabby because she had a rough day* or *I know Dad really loves me, even though he never plays with me; he puts in lots of overtime so we can have a nice house and I can have nice toys.* Instead, a child thinks, *I must be a bad kid since Mom never wants to hear what I have to say,* or *I must be a bad person because Dad never spends time with me.*

These early thoughts are natural responses for children, and unfortunately they usually take root at an early age and become part of our individual self-concepts that persist into adult life and cause us to act and feel as though we really were bad people. And many of us believe that our *feelings* are wrong for the same reasons. This conviction makes us hate ourselves for having such terrible, unacceptable thoughts and feelings.

Years ago a minister friend was describing an aspect of his child-rearing practices. He had made a rule that his son could not use the word *hate*. In effect, he banned it from the approved household vocabulary. He did not want his son to hate anything, and he described disciplining his son when he happened to say something relatively innocent, such as "I hate this pair of pants." In no uncertain terms, the son was told he could say "I don't like this pair of pants" or "I don't want to wear these pants," but he could not use the word *hate*. As I listened to my friend, it occurred to me that something was missing in his approach: he was banning the word, but he was not teaching his son how to handle the underlying emotion, which would remain regardless of the word used to describe it. What was the boy supposed to do when he experienced a strong negative emotion, as all of us do? Should he not feel it? That certainly was implied. Or was he simply to think of it as something else just by changing the label on it?

All the dad did was make a ridiculous rule that closed off an area of expression for his son without teaching the boy the real lesson of dealing with hateful feelings, emotions that are certain to develop because they are part of sinful human nature. Consequently, the son was kept from an area of personal growth that could have strengthened him.

Parents' Hypocrisy

An old adage says, "Your actions speak so loudly I can't hear what you're saying." Nowhere is this more true than in parent-child relationships, and evangelical parents who do not live what they preach are setting up danger points for their children. Just the other day a fellow told me that when he was a child his parents dropped him off at Sunday school, but they did not attend. As a youngster, he wondered silently what was going on: *If Sunday school is so important for me, why can't my parents stay, too?* This double standard caused him to take Sunday school less seriously than he otherwise would have.

Many adults who have grown up in Christian homes have told me about their mixed feelings of bewilderment and anger because their parents promoted positive Christian values and regular church attendance and enjoyed outstanding Christian reputations in their communities but behaved quite differently at home. Remember Terri's father from the preceding chapter? "People in the church wouldn't believe it if I told them how my dad acted at home," she told me. "Everybody at church thinks my dad is a really good guy." Another person reported about his mother who had an upstanding Christian image in the neighborhood, "You ought to hear my mom swear. She can turn the air blue!"

Related to this is the inability of some parents to admit to being wrong, ever. "I can show my dad in black and white, and he still won't admit he doesn't know what he's talking about!" said one client. It takes a mature person to admit to being wrong, but it certainly gives more credibility to parents in the eyes of their children. If parents can't admit they're wrong, who else is left to take the blame besides the children? More input for negative self-image results, and children are prevented from seeing their parents as real people, an important point that will be discussed later.

Scripture and Personal Protection

In my opinion, one of the most harmful practices in evangelical homes is parents' use of God and Scripture to control children, avoid personal responsibility, and justify negative child-rearing practices. One of the verses many children hear from parents is Paul's injunction in Ephesians 6:1 that children should obey their parents. Many mothers always quote this verse when they need extra weight to support their arguments against their children's behavior. One fellow told me, "Once I was old enough to read the

Bible myself, I noticed that a few verses later it told fathers not to make their children angry, something my father did repeatedly. But my parents didn't pay attention to that verse."

One of the most harmful practices
in evangelical homes is parents' use
of God and Scripture to control children,
avoid personal responsibility, and justify
negative child-rearing practices.

A minister remarked to me about the common use of Jesus in monitoring children's behavior. He said that many Dutch homes in the Midwest have the following motto on their walls:

Say nothing you would not want to be saying when Jesus comes.
Do nothing you would not want to be doing when Jesus comes.
Be nowhere you would not want to be when Jesus comes.

He concluded his observation by saying, "What a guilt producer on a young child!" Relative to this type of thinking, another minister commented, "I don't think I'd like to be taking a bath, either, when Jesus comes."

Nadine, during her therapy, said her mother told her that not only must she obey her parents, but she also had to "obey them in the Lord," which meant that "I had to do things with gladness and a happy, grateful heart in the Lord." Consequently, she had two problems. She had to do whatever her parents wanted, and she also had to muster up some sort of positive feelings about the situation so she could at least do it partly for the Lord. There was no room for her true feelings.

Linn grew up in an evangelical family and had a slight handicap that made her self-conscious. During Linn's early teens, her mother died unexpectedly, and her father needed her to assume more household duties. She dropped out of school and became quite devoted to the tasks at home, although she tried to push aside her honest resentment at having to give up her own life. Psychologically, to protect herself, she plunged into evangelical beliefs and overlaid everything in her life with some type of spiritual interpretation, thereby obscuring her true feelings. She had a verse to explain every incident that happened; everything was "God's will," and she could avoid being responsible for something that did not work out because obviously God had not wanted it to.

After Linn grew up, married, and started a family of her own, she did not relate to her children in a personal way because she always placed God or a verse between herself and them. When things did not go her way, she used guilt to gain control. As I worked with several of her children in therapy, it became obvious that this good Christian mother had systematically and unknowingly taught her children to be dishonest with themselves emotionally. She had not allowed them to express personal opinions unless they were in agreement with hers, and she had induced relentless guilt until they agreed. To gain the love they needed, they had to act as though they did not believe or feel what they actually felt.

Later, during the course of therapy as her children tried to talk to her about some childhood feelings, they found it impossible because Linn refused to relate on a feeling level. Following her habitual pattern, she quickly turned the conversation into a recitation of Bible exhortations, admonitions, and guilt-producing statements—never expressing her own feelings or opinions. Hiding her own anger and pain behind a facade of spirituality (she was dishonest with herself), Linn insisted that her children play the same game. She used God and the Bible to protect herself and get her own way.

Linn's grown son recounted to me the hour-long family altar over which his mother reigned daily after the evening meal. The spiritual benefits of this exercise were lost not only because it was so long and tedious but also because Mother totally ignored his personal feelings, obviously certain that the greater good was being served by family altar. The son was an excellent athlete who dearly loved sports, and it was a regular neighborhood tradition that by 6:30 every evening the guys began lining up players for the nightly baseball game. Unfortunately for Lester, choosing teams took place while he was stuck at the supper table in the middle of family altar. With a sinking heart he listened to the phone ring unanswered, knowing that a friend was calling him to play ball, but he was not free to do what he wanted. As he listened to family altar and watched the clock, he knew he was missing more and more baseball. The result was a tremendous mixture of anger toward Mom, deep hurt, and (of course) guilt, not only for being so mad at such a "good Christian mother," but also for being unenthused about God and family altar. Fortunately, Father intervened occasionally, telling Lester he could leave family altar early to catch the game. This was a breath of fresh air because he recognized that "at least my dad understood my feelings."

In using spiritual concepts for her own protection, Mother made herself a god of sorts, demanding total loyalty to her wishes and requiring her children to sacrifice themselves on the altar of her personal needs, throwing aside anything they wanted for themselves if they expected any affection from her. Without realizing it, she was demanding selflessness in them, but she was totally selfish in direct contradiction to her stated beliefs. Unfortunately, such behavior is common in evangelical homes, and it is often easy for mothers to use God and the Bible to control their children out of their personal needs. If this has been true in your experience, you realize how devastating it can be.

Train Up a Child

"Train up a child in the way he should go, / And when he is old he will not depart from it" (Prov. 22:6). This is a verse I have heard repeated for years, and "spare the rod, spoil the child" was usually close behind. The general notion seemed to be that it was necessary to be tough, not put up with any nonsense, and pound the truth into children's heads. Although this may have resulted in quiet, well-behaved children, it certainly did not consider the youngster's personal feelings.

Many parents have remarked to me that "kids today sure are different from when I was growing up! My dad would never let anybody disagree with him. What he said was it! I see all these kids nowadays—I don't know where it's all going to end!" In spite of their apparent longing for the "old days" when family relationships were more structured, I always sense some resentment and hurt because such people inherently understand that their feelings were not important to their parents.

If your parents worked against the grain of your natural personality style, they created danger-point conditions for you. Look at the examples cited earlier, and you can see this principle in each one. Terri was a sensitive, vulnerable child, and her father was rejecting and physically abusive. Lester was a high "i" person who needed lots of social approval, but his mother cut him off from his friends and an opportunity to gain social approval; she was not meeting his needs. Cathy was a sensitive child, and her mother told her she was unwanted. Working *with* a youngster's natural style communicates all of the positive values mentioned earlier and encourages positive faith toward God instead of creating obstacles that interfere with adult faith.

I believe there is value in the Christian home, and I am totally convinced that the parents mentioned in these examples had good intentions. I have never met a parent, no matter how bad, whose goal was to raise a messed-up child. I am deeply concerned, however, about the subtle dangers that creep into the homes of well-intentioned Christian parents who are doing their best to pass their values to their children but who in doing so create conditions that can undermine the benefits of their good intentions.

C H A P T E R 6

Dangers in the Church

The two-thousand-seat auditorium in Detroit's Masonic Temple was packed for the Saturday night YFC rally, and as always, excitement was electric in the air. Our own singing group, The Teen Singers, and their back-up band were hot, and the kids showed their appreciation with repeated, rousing ovations. The club time was a regular rally feature in which the YFC staff performed a skit that was a crude forerunner of today's "Saturday Night Live" sketches. At this particular rally just before Thanksgiving in 1966, we had brought two live turkeys on stage with various pieces of clothing and had recruited several volunteers from the audience to participate in a contest to see which teen could "dress" his turkey first. It was a screaming success, and then the program moved toward the serious part of the rally, the message. Jacques, our director, began to set the mood as he introduced the speaker, Joey Z., a former Hollywood-show-business type who had become a Christian several years previously.

As the house lights dimmed and the spotlights followed Joey's confident stride to the center mike, the audience hushed in eager anticipation. Joey's black, slicked-back hair glistened in the glare of the spotlight as he snatched the mike from the stand with a practiced flourish. "It's great to be in Detroit tonight! You're a wonderful crowd! That music—wasn't it terrific? I haven't heard anything that good since I played in Vegas five years ago! You know, even though it was exciting to stand on the stage of Caesar's Palace and do the introductory act for Frank Sinatra, nothing can compare to the thrill of knowing Jesus Christ as my Savior. You can add up all the Hollywood thrills, gold records, fancy parties, the whole works! But the night I accepted Jesus Christ was the most exciting of all."

As a YFC staff member, I was stationed at the left rear of the auditorium to keep an eye on the crowd and watch for hands during the invitation. But as I listened to Joey Z.'s message in the semidarkness, I silently compared his remarks to my own experience and found a tremendous gap between the two. As he continued to speak, my mind drifted away in conflicted thought. Actually, opening for Frank Sinatra sounded more exciting than any experiences I had had with Christ. Guiltily, I wondered what was wrong with me. Somehow the Christian life had never been as automatic or thrilling for me. Mine was more of a struggle. What did Joey Z. have that I didn't? I'm sure that many of you have had similar experiences as you have listened to positive, evangelistic speakers.

Christian Examples

Experiences such as this have puzzled and bothered me for years. Even though I went to almost every available church service through the years, I can't recall hearing sermons on the struggles of the Christian life. Listening to this veritable parade of speakers, ministers, and evangelists shaped my perception of the Christian life and what it should be, but when I began to be honest with myself, my experiences did not match what they were saying. I had grown up believing that whatever a minister said must be true, especially if he had Scripture to back it up, and they all did. Therefore, if they were right, the problem had to be in me.

In the last few years I have begun to understand more clearly the role that personality plays in the lives of church leaders, and this has helped me put Christian speakers, evangelists, and ministers in a little different perspective. I trust it will be helpful to you as well.

Psychological studies of how people choose their jobs tell us that people usually select a vocation that is compatible with their individual personality styles and that meets personal needs. For example, a high "i" person who by nature likes to talk and be around people will be more attracted to sales than to a position as a research chemist in an isolated laboratory. A high "D" person will choose a job that allows him to be the boss—not just one of the workers. A high "C" person will choose a job with specific guidelines and a need for accuracy, such as engineering or quality control. And usually, but not always, the people who go after the leadership positions in society, in Christian as well as secular organizations, are people with strong reactions, the "D's" and "i's" with the dominant personality styles. When I applied these insights to the church, I saw several things that constitute danger points for youngsters growing up in the church.

Danger Points in Teaching Style

I suspect that many of the highly visible speakers, especially evangelists, who are publicly teaching about the Christian life have limited personal experience with struggle. Their lack of struggle may be due to their personality style, or since they are in a leadership or teaching position, they may not feel comfortable with struggling, so they attempt to avoid it. In either case, they expect others to follow their example. Yet it is the nature of people with weak reactions to doubt themselves and feel inferior. As they try to follow the examples they hear from the pulpit, they attempt to have Christian experiences that are contrary to their nature, interpreting their failure to succeed as further evidence of their spiritual weakness and lack of faith. This creates a potentially deadly trap for many youngsters growing up in the church. This is the first danger point in the church.

In retrospect, I decided Joey Z. was a high "i" person who was naturally emotional, easily excited, quick to be optimistic, and very good at talking excitedly about anything, whether it be Christ or a used car. In other words, a definite part of his meaningful salvation experience was due to his particular personality style. But in his well-intentioned enthusiasm to share his experience, he implied that everyone else ought to feel the same way he did, not realizing that only other high "i's" could duplicate his experience. My problem that night as I listened to him was that as an "S" I was feeling pressured to duplicate the experience of an "i" in my own life—a psychological impossibility. I am my own unique person, and Joey is his own unique person, so our experiences will be different.

Many of the people who are publicly teaching
about the Christian life
have limited personal experience
with struggle, yet they expect
everyone to follow their example.

The pastor at a church I attended had a definite "D" personality, but he spoke often about struggles in the Christian life, even his own, from the pulpit. It was refreshing to hear such supportive statements, and I learned from others who had known him before I arrived at the church that his preaching style had changed drastically as the result of an earlier, serious encounter with cancer. Incidentally, such a hard-hitting experience is often necessary to help the "D" person open his eyes to points he has been ignoring due to his naturally high level of self-confidence.

"Not all ministers are 'D's' or 'i's,'" you say. You're right. I know many ministers with other personality styles, but it is a point we need to keep in mind. We will look more specifically at the role of personality later in this chapter.

Danger Points in Leadership Style

There is a second danger point that is related to the personality style of people who seek leadership within the church, and I have also observed this principle in human service agencies as well as private business. Most leadership positions in our society involve pressure and potential tension that are often greater than the sensitive personalities want to bear. Since the strong lack this sensitivity, they enjoy the challenge without necessarily experiencing the pressure as negative, and many of them like to be in control of things as well. Naturally, being the leader puts them in a position of control and power, so they gravitate toward leadership positions. Generally, however, they lack the level of sensitivity toward others that would help them take others' feelings into consideration. The wise leader who is aware of his leadership deficiencies compensates by selecting people with complementary strengths to advise and assist.

Several problems can develop. It is easy for personalities who desire power to use the socially sanctioned role of minister to take charge over others. In other words, they can feel in control because "you don't challenge or question the minister." And if someone does, what better retort than to spiritualize the issue and intimidate the questioner with scriptural logic or even fear and guilt? The listener may feel that to resist the minister is fighting God Himself, when in reality the minister may be using God to defend his own views or actions.

This point hit me unexpectedly one day as I was working on a psychological report. I was using one of the manuals that provides interpretation for the Minnesota Multiphasic Personality Inventory (MMPI), a widely used personality test. According to the manual, one common adult profile consists of anger/rebellion in combination with feelings of alienation from people, or not fitting in with people. Such people have usually learned at an early age to distrust the world because as children they perceived other people as hostile, rejecting, and dangerous. However, they have also learned that they can protect themselves and reduce their fear of being hurt by striking out at others before others strike out at them; in addition, they are most comfortable when inspiring guilt and anxiety in others.

It is easy for personalities who desire power
to use the socially sanctioned role of minister
to take charge over others.

As I was preparing my report, the following words suddenly leaped from the page: "Such people may end up in jobs where their behavior is socially approved, e.g. law enforcer, school disciplinarian, or *over-zealous clergyman*" (emphasis added).[1] What a deadly combination. As I read it, I suddenly began to see the hellfire ministers I had heard in a new light. *How many of them were using the Bible to carry out a personal need to inspire fear in others?* I wondered to myself. As I pondered this new insight, my emotional reaction quickly flitted from relief to shock to anger—anger that I had been subjected to such needlessly inspired anxiety and guilt as a youngster.

As my initial reaction passed, I began to have second thoughts about how my new insight applied to my experiences in growing up because in the psychology field it is well known that the MMPI is pathologically oriented, meaning it measures serious emotional problems instead of normal personality characteristics. The fact that all the hellfire ministers I had heard were seriously disturbed seemed highly unlikely, but the general thought remained in the back of my mind.

Months later, as I read material describing the DiSC system that Dr. Geier developed to describe normal behavioral styles, I found the following remarks describing a personality style that he entitled "Inspirational":

> They enjoy the friction that occurs in antagonistic situations. Inspirational persons welcome the challenge of confrontation when only one winner is possible. Quick in thought and action, they like to match their wits and skills against others. . . . Inspirational persons seek positions that command more influence and power than they presently have. Their goal is most likely to be a position of authority which is officially sanctioned. . . . [They] most enjoy having authority over people, but will also work to control monies or materials. . . . [They] influence others by controlling them. Their control is magnified if they are in authority positions, but it is a force even when they are not. Inspirational persons consciously attempt to modify the thoughts and actions of others through the manipulation of motives toward a predetermined end. In short, they know what they want and how to get it. They are quick and astute in identifying the motive structure of those around them; they know what other people need or want. They use this knowledge to elicit the desired response. Even if an individual's needs are not conducive to obtaining the desired help, Inspirational persons are skilled in creating the need. . . . Whatever the motivation of the individual, the Inspirational person holds out the carrot—fulfillment of the need—to obtain the desired response. . . . If directives are

insufficient, Inspirational persons tend to resort to intimidation. They can use it on either a psychological or physical basis or a combination of the two. In essence, they tap people's fears or threaten their self-concepts. Inspirational persons can be skilled in such practices as prolonging the waiting time for an appointment, allowing the conference to be interrupted by numerous phone calls, or using their command of language to place the other person in an inferior position.[2]

Although not identical to the material in the MMPI manual, this narrative describing a personality style has striking similarities, and it applies to "normal" people, which means it has broader application than the problem-oriented MMPI. After pondering this subject, I have decided that many of the ministers who preached hellfire sermons while I was growing up were not actually cut out of this personality cloth; they were simply doing what they had been taught or what they had seen others doing. However, I do believe there are many people with this personality style in the ministry as well as in other professions. Since personality style affects practically everything we do, and personality plays a crucial role in the way the organized church handles its business, the role of personality in church leadership constitutes a potential danger point for developing Christians. It is something each of us needs to understand. Let's examine the role of personality more closely.

Role of Personality

The person who is drawn to a leadership position often has a *need* to control, to have power, and enjoys the challenge of the leadership pressure. In order to do this, the person cannot be too concerned about pleasing people and being sensitive to others' feelings or else he will feel soft or weak. If the pastor has a personal need to control or have power, he is unlikely to encourage his parishioners to think for themselves because they might think differently from him and he would have less power in the church. I have known many insecure people who were not open to new information that might challenge their ideas, and if a person is psychologically closed, he will be theologically closed as well. Generally, a person must be mature to allow independence in others, and if a minister can't accept psychological openness to himself, how is he going to accept and encourage either psychological or theological openness in his people?

In essence, the psychology of ministers (and others as well) precedes their theology and influences their theological interpretations and applications. Before ministers can tell people it is okay to think, ask questions, and struggle, they themselves must believe it and be secure enough with their own feelings to let their parishioners enjoy the same freedom. The minister who personally likes things to be "black and white" will emphasize biblical issues in a black-and-white fashion, while those ministers who are psychologically open will encourage psychological and spiritual openness in their congregations. One minister told me he gradually realized that whenever he was personally depressed he consistently selected sermon material from the minor prophets in the Old Testament.

Many ministers are unaware of the role personality styles and needs play in their theological interpretations and church-related decisions. A friend of mine wishes ministers would say, "This particular scriptural interpretation suits my personality best." I believe this is what happens with most people, including ministers, anyway, so why not admit it openly? Otherwise why would there be so many different denominations and varied scriptural interpretations?

Lest I be misunderstood, let me add that basic scriptural tenets are not equally open to different interpretations. Certainly, salvation, Christ's death and resurrection, and so on cannot be changed without destroying the essence of Christianity. But other topics *can* be interpreted in many ways depending on the person and his particular level of maturity at the time. I believe that most ministers who are rigid, critical, and slow to let others have their own views are naturally this way as people, so they present God in a manner that is consistent with their personality style. Those who are psychologically relaxed, open, and confident will convey God in a warm, accepting fashion.

A friend of mine who serves as a consultant to Christian leaders throughout the country calls ministers God's point-men,[3] and I believe he is totally correct. I believe they are crucial to the church and set the tone for its members. Perhaps that is why I want them to be the best they can be. I don't want you to think I'm trying to stamp out ministers or personality. I do recognize that all of us, ministers included, must meet personal needs through our work. But this point is more critical in the church than at the factory—or even in politics—because people look to ministers for direction regarding the eternal destiny of their souls, which is a weightier issue than nuclear arms, the prime interest rate, or who is foreman at the shop. Obviously, ministers' personalities are going to affect what they do, but it is a dangerous situation when a minister is unaware of how his individual personality influences his theology and how he may be using the ministry to meet personal needs in the name of God.

An extreme example of this is Jim Jones and his People's Temple, since out of his own needs he controlled people for his personal advantage in God's name. This extreme type of behavior is more likely to occur outside the major denominations because they have safeguards to prevent seriously unbalanced individuals from entering the ministry; Jim Jones was turned away by several denominations before he started his own church. The small, independent churches that are under the total control of the pastor are more likely to be vulnerable to self-serving and domineering leadership.

In addition to psychologically screening candidates for the ministry, many denominations have published a schedule of doctrinal points that pastors are supposed to include in their sermons over a three- or four- or even five-year period. This is to ensure that parishioners are exposed to all the appropriate theological beliefs of the church, and it reduces the possibility of a minister's simply preaching on his favorite theme or out of his own personality needs.

Personal Conclusions

From all of this I have drawn several conclusions that have been helpful to me, and I trust they will help you, also. Most importantly, I have come to realize that ministers are people, too, with their own emotions, motives, struggles, and needs. They are not the perfect, infallible people that I thought they were when I was growing up. I now realize that my failure to recognize this concept has contributed to my struggles because I trustingly believed whatever I heard in church, particularly the sermons using fear as a motivating influence.

Let me add, however, that God certainly is not limited by the personality or even the motivation of the person who is preaching. A listener can be blessed or spoken to by the Holy Spirit in spite of apparently negative circumstances or less-than-pure motivation. Paul made this point quite clearly:

> Some, of course, are preaching the Good News because they are jealous of the way God has used me. They want reputations as fearless preachers! But others have purer motives, preaching because they love me, for they know that the Lord has brought me here to use me to defend the Truth. And some preach to make me jealous, thinking that

their success will add to my sorrows here in jail! But whatever their motive for doing it, the fact remains that the Good News about Christ is being preached and I am glad (Phil. 1:15–18 TLB).

God's ability to turn twisted motivation into eventual usefulness is also evident in Joseph's life. After Jacob's death, the brothers feared that Joseph would finally seek revenge against them, so to forestall his anger, they sent him a message: "Before he died, your father instructed us to tell you to forgive us for the great evil we did to you" (Gen. 50:17, TLB). But Joseph was not interested in revenge and replied, "As far as I am concerned, God turned into good what you meant for evil, for he brought me to this high position I have today so that I could save the lives of many people" (Gen. 50:20 TLB).

One of my psychology professors taught me that understanding a person's theory requires understanding his personality first, because theories develop out of a person's personality and experiences. I keep this truth in mind as I listen to ministers, also. Presently, when I hear a sermon, I try to determine the minister's personality style, examine possible reasons that explain why he is emphasizing his particular points, wonder about his personal background, and assess how much he understands people and the psychological processes through which they have to go toward maturity. I also speculate about the minister's own Christian experience. Basically, I ask myself how similar the minister's personality is to my own, and if his is different, I try to figure out why his experience is meaningful to him. Then, I have to adjust it to my own personality style, if possible.

We have the freedom and responsibility
to think and decide.
We don't have to be passive listeners
who accept everything we hear.

Now that I see the person in the minister, I am much more careful about how seriously I take messages from the pulpit, and I put more personal effort into evaluating what I hear to determine if it fits with Scripture as I understand it. I also realize that we have our own responsibility to think and decide, and we do not have to be passive listeners who accept everything we hear. You may consider my method a psychologist's way of thinking, of course, but it helps me spiritually, and you might also find it useful.

Weakness vs. Perfection

There is a related point that deserves comment. Too often ministers and church members alike expect ministers to be perfect, which puts a strain on both minister and congregation. I realize that some ministers like to promote this view (for their own psychological needs), but we need to see ministers as imperfect human beings who have been called to a special ministry. That does *not* make them perfect saints or authorities with the last word on everything. Although many ministers feel they must present themselves as perfect examples to their congregations, the congregations must make it possible for the ministers to step down from this pedestal.

The notion that ministers are perfect and that they expect perfection from others often discourages people from going to their pastors for help with their struggles. Many Christians come to see me because their hearts are full and they can no longer contain their feelings. After sharing a painful secret with me, they have often sighed, "I could never tell my pastor what I just told you." Often when troubled Christians do meet with their ministers, they don't tell their entire story, usually omitting their sexual sins. Although hiding part of the truth may protect them from the minister's possible judgment, it also keeps them from receiving the fullest extent of his help. So they come to see me, believing a psychologist, unlike their pastor, is going to accept them in their imperfect state. Some have had affairs, and others are angry with God for personal difficulties they must face in their lives. Others are tired of being walked on and wish they could speak up on their own behalf, but they fear that doing so would not be Christian behavior. Most of them are afraid of struggling with the ever-present reality of their feelings, and they believe they must somehow push these feelings aside in order to smile on Sunday and be the excited Christians their minister exhorts them to be.

Actually, it seems to me that most people, or at least the struggling Christians, can relate to weakness better than to perfection. Several years ago I heard about a prominent minister in a small community who was arrested for a sexual offense. He subsequently resigned from his church with the news of his indiscretion prominently displayed in the local newspaper. A friend of mine later became acquainted with him through their mutual place of secular employment, and the former minister told my friend he could not believe how many Christians from his denomination approached him about similar and other problems after his public downfall. This tells me that those hurting people felt comfortable baring their souls to him because his image of perfection had been stripped away, and they knew he couldn't judge them in their own weaknesses. From his vantage point, I am sure his opportunity to minister was *increased* as a result of his problems.

Sin—the "Master List"[4]

The third major danger point in evangelical church practices is related to how the issue of sin is defined and handled. I am referring here to the everyday definition and not the official statements found in major theological creeds. Sin in the evangelical church is generally defined in two ways. One is a specific "master list" of sins, and the second is vague and implied, generally precluding anything that is "selfish" in nature or "just for me because I want to." The second definition seems to be a catchall for whatever is not specifically on the master list and has been a source of great difficulty for many sincere Christians.

When I was growing up, the master list of forbidden things included tobacco in any form, alcohol (especially when consumed in taverns, as they were called back then), dancing, bowling alleys, movies, cards, and of course such standard things as lying, stealing, and not going to church. Other sinful items included jewelry, flashy clothes, open-toed shoes for women, short hair for women, and so on. Television was a developing phenomenon at the time and was often referred to as a "tool of hell."

It is interesting to observe the changes in the list of sins during my lifetime and the changes in the attitudes of people who help develop or promote such lists. As a boy, I remember hearing my mother exclaim in utter exasperation to my father, "Why—I never would have thought it of Esther! I saw her today and she had shoes on without toes and heels." Today my mother wears open-toed shoes without a second thought. People who would never have set foot in a theater years ago now watch programs on TV that have worse content than anything they refused to see in the theater. A friend of mine once told me how he prided himself in not sinning by shunning the movies, and one day as he was watching TV, he realized that the very program he was watching was the same movie he had self-righteously avoided several years previously.

Danger Points

The way in which we define sin creates a danger point not only for growing children but for adults as well. Too often we define sin in terms of specific behavior to be avoided instead of conveying the broader concept that sin is a state of being that falls short of God's glory (see Rom. 3:23), and that this state of being manifests itself in certain behaviors. When sin is defined primarily in terms of behaviors to avoid, the groundwork is laid for a dangerous self-righteousness. This sets the stage for a hierarchy of spiritual success within the church. The saints are the ones who have mastered the list, and the stragglers are the ones who still have a long way to go. In this context, distance is created between Christians because it is easy for the saints to look down on the stragglers while the stragglers feel inferior to the saints. One fellow told me that the church he attended had such a list, and as a young person he never mastered the list sufficiently to even join the church.

The trouble is that any list can be followed no matter how severe it is because it does have an end to it and can be mastered.[5] A person who follows the list begins to believe it is possible to reduce the inner sinful state by reducing certain external behaviors. In other words, the focus is on the *manifestation* of sin (the list) and not on the inner state of being.

When sin is defined primarily in terms
of behaviors to avoid, the groundwork
is laid for a dangerous self-righteousness.

This focus was clearly the point of conflict between Jesus and the Pharisees who meticulously followed the law (their master list) and saw themselves as quite self-righteous. In fact, Jesus' statement that the person who commits adultery in his heart is as guilty as the person who actually commits adultery in the body (see Matt. 5:28) was designed to tear away the self-righteous facade from the Pharisees, who were focusing on outer behavior.

Defining sin in this manner also sets a trap for sincere Christian parents as they train their children. Focusing primarily on behavior, parents try to teach their children to avoid certain actions, and as the children succeed in doing this, they fail to develop an appropriate awareness of their inner state of being. Instead, they develop strong guilt if they cross over the line, so they live in constant fear.

My mother exerted her best efforts to put the fear of God into me so I would not participate in her list of sins. At the same time, I was regularly hearing frightening, hellfire themes at church, and all this seemed to tell me that to sin or even to think about it was to risk God's awesome wrath, something I did not want to chance. Consequently, *my attention was directed toward my outward behavior to the neglect of my inner emotions and my inner state of being.* By "behaving," I imagined I could avoid punishment.

All this, however, was somewhat puzzling and never made a great deal of sense. There I was, being carefully monitored by my parents so I did not engage in any of the major sins (they even prohibited me from seeing a puppet show at school when I was in the second grade), and at the same time I was told at church that I should be so very grateful that Jesus died to save me from all my terrible sins. What sins? What had I done? My experience was that Jesus took away more than He gave. Because of Him I was prohibited from doing many things that seemed both attractive and harmless.

It is also easy for the definition of sin to reach such narrow proportions that personal naturalness is stifled and guilt is strengthened. Several years ago I discussed this issue with a woman who had grown up as a minister's daughter. Her experience relative to the definition of sin was no better than mine. Her godly grandmother had repeatedly drilled into her the verse in James, "Therefore, to him who knows to do good and does not do it, to him it is sin" (4:17). She said this verse had a deep effect on her, and she described how it influenced her life in even very small, insignificant situations as a youngster. Whenever she walked through the house and was tempted to pass some lint on the carpet without picking it up, for example, this verse came into her mind, which immediately threw her into conflict. She knew picking it up would be the "good" thing to do, and therefore simply walking past it would obviously be sin. But she honestly did not feel like picking it up. Therefore, the lint on the carpet became a choice between obedience and sin. This is a heavy and unnecessary issue for a growing child.

A woman in her thirties told me she feels guilty using scissors on Sunday morning to trim a loose thread from her daughter's dress because that's working on the Sabbath. In fact, until several years ago, when she did use scissors on Sunday she selected a pair that had plastic-wrapped handles that could insulate her hand from the lightning that might strike her as she sinned. Although she knew rationally that there would be no lightning, she took the precaution anyway.

Barrier to Forgiveness

This leads to another subtle danger point in the Christian life for those of us who have grown up with the "master list" definition of sin. A young man who was raised in a close Christian home sat with me in my office. He felt torn. When he was honest with himself, he felt extremely angry with his father, but his Christian teaching told him he should not be angry. He must respect his father and honor and obey him. Even though he really was angry, he tried to deny his anger, to push it aside and pretend it really wasn't his. He tried this for several years, but as he sat before me I could tell by the look on his face that his efforts hadn't worked.

He was trying to avoid the struggle and the even worse "defeat" of admitting his true feelings. "They are unacceptable!" he insisted to me. "Don't speak up to your parents, that's disrespectful and you might get angry. If you get angry, you're sinful and bad. Avoid the argument and smile anyway. That's how I've been taught."

He was burdened and will continue to be burdened as long as he tries to live up to the master list rather than accept his anger. His denial also prevents him from obtaining the very forgiveness he so desperately needs. "If we say that we have no sin, we are only fooling ourselves, and refusing to accept the truth. But if we confess our sins to him, he can be depended on to forgive us and to cleanse us from every wrong" (1 John 1:8–9 TLB). Once he faces his true feelings head-on and can honestly say, "Yes, I really am angry and the anger is mine," then he will be in a position to take his anger to God and receive forgiveness. In other words, trying to be self-righteous and holy when we really are not leads us away from forgiveness, away from an attitude of gratitude, and away from a more positive Christian life.

Trying to be self-righteous and holy
when we really are not
leads us away from forgiveness
and a more positive Christian life.

Job is the clearest scriptural example of a person's struggle with angry emotions and frustrations in reaction to devastating personal losses and suffering. He didn't hold back his feelings, and he didn't deny his frustrations as he spoke to God:

I am weary of living. Let me complain freely. I will speak in my sorrow and bitterness. I will say to God, "Don't just condemn me—tell me *why* you are doing it. Does it really seem right to you to oppress and despise me, a man you have made; and to send joy and prosperity to the wicked?

Are you unjust like men? Is your life so short that you must hound me for sins you know full well I've not committed? Is it because you know no one can save me from your hand?" (Job 10:1–7 TLB).

He definitely spoke his mind as he struggled with the meaning of sin and suffering, but God did not desert him or turn on him as he vented his feelings. God waited patiently and demonstrated a readiness to listen. In time, Job resolved his anger, and God blessed him above his original state. Doesn't God also listen to our complaints? Isn't He ready to listen as we cry out?

Good News?

Sadly, it seems to me that instead of the New Testament message's being the good news that we can face our imperfect inner nature without fear because Christ has paid the penalty for it, we have turned it into a continuation of the Old Testament rules. A subtle foundation for later conflict in adult spiritual life has been neatly laid in an unsuspectingly innocent fashion, and the notion of fear that weaves its way through these principles only serves to complicate the struggle to free ourselves.

Serve God or Else:
Fear in the Future

It was a Wednesday evening, the fourth night of special spiritual emphasis meetings in my home church. The evangelist, a young, energetic, articulate man, stepped up to the pulpit and prepared to present his sermon. His Scripture reading was Jesus' narrative about the rich man who had rejected salvation and from the torments of hell asked Abraham to send prophets to his living relatives to warn them of eternal damnation. The rich man also requested, to no avail, that he be given a drop of cool water on his parched tongue (see Luke 16:19–31).

Fear—the Basic

Upon completion of the Scripture reading, the young evangelist began his sermon with a disclaimer, "The subject I'm preaching about is not a pleasant one because it deals with a fearful, dreadful reality. Yet, I feel God has laid it on my heart, and I must preach the full Word of God." Having said that, he proceeded with amazing enthusiasm to deliver a magnificently graphic and frightening description of hell and the dangers of rejecting salvation. In fact, he seemed to enjoy the fiery sermon in spite of his earlier disclaimer to the contrary. I, of course, as a young person, responded with appropriate fear and trepidation because, after all, he was a minister and was preaching from the Bible.

This sermon is typical of the many sermons I've heard through the years in the evangelical church, and I'm sure that many of you have heard identical or similar sermons. If you're a sensitive person, I'm sure that such sermons have left lasting, fearful impressions on you and complicated your Christian life.

When a person is serving God out of fear, the Christian life becomes a series of duties to perform in order to avoid punishment.

Fear and desire are the two most powerful motivators in dealing with people,[1] but fear can have devastating effects when used improperly or inappropriately. When fear motivates us, tremendous energy is expended in a defensive fashion to avoid the object feared, and personal creativity, joy, and fruitfulness are difficult to achieve. When we are serving God out of fear, the Christian life becomes a series of duties and obligations to perform in order to avoid punishment, and it is very difficult to have a joyful, thankful heart under these circumstances. It has always amazed me how often ministers use indiscriminate fear to scare people into the kingdom, and then they wonder why the converts stand around like scared sheep.

When fear is used to motivate people, especially sensitive children, in the name of God, it is a grave mistake and constitutes one of the biggest dangers and difficult obstacles that young people have to overcome in order to live happy, fruitful, adult Christian lives. Fear can run deep in a person's life and nip incessantly at one's heels in spite of efforts to reduce its influence. It is especially damaging to those persons who have strong "S" and "C" personality components because they are naturally sensitive to criticism and loss of personal security. Fear locks a person up and prevents the open discussion that could help reduce the inner anxiety.

The point that concerns me is that fear is so pervasive in the sermons preached from many evangelical pulpits. It's even a thread that's woven through many of the messages and lessons presented to children. And to make matters worse, no one ever talks about the fear and how we are supposed to deal with it.

To my chagrin, I must confess that I have done my share of dishing out fear to motivate others toward Christ. I take small comfort in the fact that I was only copying other prominent evangelistic speakers. At a national YFC convention at Winona Lake in the late fifties, I listened to a well-known YFC leader preach on Hebrews 9:27. His sermon began with a graphic description of the personal panic he experienced when a plane on which he was flying almost crashed. He used this to lead into the notion that after one dies, the Judgment must be faced, as stated in the text. As a young person, this sermon impressed me as a good one, so several years later I used the same concept when I presented the gospel to young people at a Detroit YFC meeting.

I substituted the plane crash story with an experience from my life that took place while I was a sophomore in college, living and working in a funeral home. During my first week at school, I attended a new church on Sunday, and later in the week the same person I had witnessed leading the Sunday school was lying dead in our funeral home, the victim of a car accident. As I looked at his corpse, I reflected on the brevity of life, the sermon text, and filed the experience away for future use. I can still remember standing before a handful of young people at the Detroit YFC camp, hammering away with this message. Now let's look at major sermon topics that use fear to motivate people.

Hellfire—the Unavoidable

Hellfire was a fearful reality that was graphically portrayed on a regular basis in my home church. It seemed to be particularly useful and present at evangelistic meetings, during which I sensed there was a bit of strategy involved in addition to the Lord's leading of the evangelist in choosing the sermon material. It usually was after a number of services had passed with few people being saved that the evangelist felt God laying on his heart the fact that he should preach the full Word of God, which consistently meant he was going to preach a hellfire sermon and "shake the trees." I clearly remember overhearing the pastor and the evangelist consoling each other after one evening service when the altar call went unheeded. Said the one man to the other in a tone straining for optimism, "Man sows, but God gives the increase." Both were obviously trying to avoid feeling as though they had failed.

When hellfire was the topic, the usual Scripture was Jesus' account about the rich man and Lazarus. And as I described earlier, the evangelist really seemed to enjoy the sermon in spite of his disclaimer that the subject was a fearsome reality. The rich man. His parched tongue. The wide gulf between him and Abraham's bosom. The flames burning his body. The endless agony, worsened knowing it will never cease. The utter misery and fear of it all. As the minister became emotional, his voice would rise in increasing crescendo, bordering on becoming hoarse, and then fall to a quiet, soft pleading. He spent twenty-five minutes frightening everyone, and only five minutes showing the way out.

Some ministers are even more dramatic. A number of years ago a newspaper article described an ingenious evangelist who set himself on fire with gasoline (without injuring himself, of course) during his sermon to graphically illustrate "what a man in hell looks like."

The picture of the suffering rich man was so graphically etched on my mind as a youngster that it frequently returned to me in living color when I went to the milkhouse on a hot summer day to drink the cold, refreshing water that gushed from the hose attached to the water faucet. As I enjoyed the cool water splashing liberally against my lips, an image of the rich man flashed into my mind, and I pondered his request for one drop of cool water for his parched tongue. He would have traded a million dollars of his wealth for one drop, and I was drinking all I wanted.

Following this image came a second one—seeing myself burning in the flames with the rich man and remembering my days back on the farm when I could drink cold water from the hose in the milkhouse. Briefly, I tried to etch into my memory the experience of the cold water in my mouth, wondering if the memory would help assuage my suffering in the event I landed in hell. The fearfulness of it was too much, and I had to push it out of my mind. Even now, as an adult, these images often return when I drink from a garden hose.

Through the years I have heard many people comment about the fearfulness of such hellfire sermons during their youth and how their personal fright has caused them to stay away from church. Perhaps your feelings are similar to those of one woman who somewhat jokingly, but with a certain seriousness in her voice, reported, "When I was growing up, it seemed like getting saved was a form of fire insurance."

Altar Calls—the Avenue

Closely related to the topic of hellfire sermons is the altar call that is usually a regular component of evangelical church services, although more in some denominations than others. After an appeal for salvation, personal dedication, or whatever else has been emphasized in the sermon, the altar call is conducted as the avenue through which remedy can be sought. Fear also is prominently evident in this altar call.

There is a certain predictability to the altar call. The minister usually asks the congregation to bow their heads and close their eyes as the pianist softly plays "Just as I Am." Then he asks those who have felt some sort of conviction to hold up a hand so he can pray for them. In large meetings, the evangelist usually has spotters placed strategically throughout the auditorium in the same manner as an auctioneer has spotters looking for bidders.

"I see that hand! And another in the balcony! And the young man in the back!"

After he has prayed for the raised hands, the altar call proper begins, usually with everyone singing "Just as I Am." As a young person, I always knew it was going to be a long altar call if no one responded to the first or second verse. The evangelist usually was pretty sure someone was "holding out," and he halted the singing to speak entreatingly to those who had raised their hands but had not come forward. If this didn't work, he told a story about an evangelistic meeting he had held recently (most of the evangelists had a similar story) where a young man sat in the back pew with his friends and was obviously under conviction, yet didn't answer the altar call in spite of earnest pleading. After the meeting, according to the story, the young man sped away in his car and was killed instantly when a train ran into him less than a mile or two from the church. Leaning into the microphone, the evangelist warned with a stern, calculated tone, "And he was ushered instantly into an eternity of hell. Do you want this to happen to you?" And this generally was frightening enough to make several compliant, insecure people so unsure of their salvation that they walked down the aisle.

As a young boy growing up in the church, I often got tired of standing and listening to all the stories and threats. And invariably, just as I thought it was about to wrap up, someone went forward, which fueled the evangelist's hopes for more seekers. He would happily cry out, "Sing another verse, Wilma! They're still coming!" And then we sang all four verses of "Pass Me Not, O Gentle Savior."

For some reason, altar calls seemed to go against my grain. When I was fourteen years old, I clearly remember one bright, sunny August Sunday morning. Special meetings were being held, and I knew that I would have to face the intense pressure and guilt of altar calls that day. To fortify myself, I saddled up my horse and rode to an isolated field on the farm carrying a small green New Testament that had "helps" in the front and back. I carefully reviewed the plan of salvation and the written sinner's prayer. As earnestly and sincerely as I could, I repeatedly closed my eyes and prayed for Christ to save me from my sins. I wanted to be sure that I was a Christian so I would not have to go forward to the altar that day. Having done as much as I knew how to do, I rode back to the house, hoping I was adequately prepared.

Altar calls at camp meetings were particularly unsettling, especially at the Sunday night meetings when the crowds were extralarge and evangelistic fervor was at its peak. The tabernacle was a large structure with steel beams supporting the roof, which was raised in the center and front and sloped to the sides and rear. There were wooden panels on all the surrounding sides. These were raised and held open with chains to allow ventilation during the muggy Indiana August evenings. The benches were made of two-by-fours and two-by-sixes. In my early years, the main aisles were concrete, but the seating area was dirt covered with wood chips. The odor of the wood chips, the muggy air, and the mass of people all combined to create an impression that is indelibly printed on my mind along with the heavy seriousness of salvation and other eternal issues.

While the evangelist had the people close their eyes and raise their hands if they had a need, ministers strolled through the aisles looking for hands. Then, during the invitation, the serious business began. The hot evening air had just been heated even hotter by the fiery, hellfire sermon, and the atmosphere was heavy with the weight of eternal destiny, the pleading singsong of "Just as I Am"; perspiring women quietly fanning themselves with palm-leaf-shaped woven rattan fans that had "Leinhart Funeral Home" stamped on both sides; an occasional baby's cry; and the crunching of someone walking on the gravel outside the tabernacle's raised side panels. By this time I usually wished I were so fortunate as the fellow walking outside.

With fear coursing through my veins, I sang along with the congregation, hoping I could escape the wrath that was so ready to fall. As the invitation progressed, the ministers who had been looking for hands began to slowly repeat their stroll through the aisles, gazing intently at the rows of standing people. If a minister spotted a person who had raised a hand but had not gone forward, he often physically approached the person, sometimes climbing over three or four people standing in the row to reach the resistant sinner. Occasionally, the person responded immediately by going forward, and other times I observed a few minutes of heated discussion, with the minister's finally persuading the person to go forward, or else he left in defeat. It always amazed me that anyone could have the audacity to refuse this persistent pleading in light of such serious consequences. *Will they die on the way home tonight?* I quietly wondered to myself. It also seemed to be an embarrassing thing for a minister to do to someone, yet I knew that if a person's soul was at stake, momentary embarrassment was insignificant in comparison to an eternity in hell.

Whenever I saw one of the ministers heading in my direction, my heart began to pound, my palms became sweaty, and with terror in my heart I tried to appear as "Christian" as I could by seriously focusing on the hymnbook and looking the other way.

Perhaps you didn't grow up in a church that had altar calls and so haven't had identical experiences, but young people from covenant theology homes report comparable experiences that may be similar to yours. Their ministers seldom use altar calls on Sunday evenings, but most of the tactics of fear and intimidation are still evident. Some of them warn that being in the church is no assurance of salvation. They speak of "the elect," referring to people whom God has predestined for salvation, but they proceed to insist that God's electing must be confirmed by each individual's willful choice. They warn about the unpardonable sin of resisting God's grace. They usually use the same plane crash or car accident stories to drive home the point of a missed opportunity.

Shying away from altar calls in the literal sense, covenantal preachers nevertheless call for personal decisions in their sermons and offer "to talk with anyone in my study right after the service." Many impressionable young persons, too afraid to meet with the pastor individually, go home with a heavy load of guilt and fear.

Covenant theology churches, in which I have spent part of my life, are also keen on sending children and young people to youth camps for a week each summer and to weekend retreats, where the formal topic or theme is seldom personal salvation. The leaders and guest speakers may talk about sexuality, dating, spiritual gifts, getting along with parents, or whatever. Sooner or later, however, the kids all realize they're falling short of "redeemed behavior." The speaker uses this recognition to create the fear that "if I'm not living as a Christian, then perhaps I'm not a Christian after all." At the very least, the leaders try to obtain commitments to Christ of those newly discovered sinful areas of life or promises to give Christ some years of dedicated service.

The Second Coming—an Imminent Certainty

The second coming of Christ is a familiar evangelical theme that was able to inspire dread in me at an early age. It all sounded so dramatic, dreadful, and sudden in its swiftness—so sudden, in fact, that I had to maintain an ever-watchful eye lest I unknowingly be caught in a momentary sin and be sent straight to hell.

The effects of Christ's coming have been described to me in graphic and terrifying ways. When I was five or six years old, I experienced a children's sermon that I have never forgotten. The woman directing the meeting was talking about the Second Coming to a group of children who were all about my age. To dramatize the point, she had a mock newspaper with headlines describing the panic and fear among the citizens who had been left behind on earth after the Rapture. For example, the newspaper had a story about a commercial airliner that was suddenly left pilotless when the pilot was taken in the Rapture, and it subsequently crashed. Secular society, consisting of nonbelievers who had been left, was stunned and at a loss to explain the sudden disappearance of the pilot and many other people.

When I was a little older and attended a Bible program, we made a large clock with pictures of various Bible events representing the hour numbers on its face. Again, to drive the point of fear home, we were told to place the hands of the clock five minutes away from midnight because we were nearing "the end times." My paper clock, at least two and one-half feet high, hung on my closet wall as long as I lived in my parents' home. Each time I looked at that clock, a shiver shot up my spine as I saw the hands close to midnight. I probably would have felt too guilty to remove it from the closet wall so I wouldn't have to look at it.

The point seemed to be, "The world is going to end soon, so don't make many plans for yourself or other personal goals. Forget yourself, try to save as many people as you can. And be really careful that you don't get caught in an act of sin."

The "five minutes to midnight" warning pretty much cuts across denominational lines and faith traditions. Theologically, as I have since learned, trying to predict Christ's return is unbiblical. Jesus clearly said, "The Father sets those dates . . . and they are not for you to know" (Acts 1:7 TLB). His description of the end times in Luke 21 has tempted many preachers to assert that theirs is the end time, although these conditions have been present in every century since Christ.

Some Christians believe numerically and dispensationally that history must end in this century or soon after the year 2000. Beyond this biblical analysis, they can currently point to threats of exploding populations and nuclear weapons to enhance the sense that the end is near. Those whose biblical interpretation is not dispensational also face these population and weaponry threats, and they have always been able to preach "now is the hour" of salvation. Regardless of the underlying theology, it seems the threat of impending judgment and doom is present.

This teaching influenced me when I was debating whether to leave YFC in Detroit to attend graduate school, because I sensed that pursuing more education was taking time out from the real work of the kingdom. I feared this would be unacceptable to God in light of the shortness of time. As I discussed this concern with the president of my college, he related similar feelings when he was going to college in the 1930s. "I seriously considered going further with my education," he began, "but I sensed the urgency to get to work for the Lord because we seemed to be near the end times. I have often regretted not going on to school. I believe I would have been better prepared for my work if I had." It was at least consoling to hear that I was not the only one struggling with the church's teaching.

Sermons highlighting the Second Coming always seemed to emphasize the biblical account of two men sleeping in a bed; one would be left, with the other going to heaven (see Luke 17:34). In growing up I always shared a bed with my older brother, so the story had special personal significance with which I could identify. Taking what I heard quite literally, I was sure that if Jesus came I would be the one left in bed—alone and terrified. Somehow the frightening stuff in the Bible always applied to me.

It also amazed me that the ministers often prayed, "Come quickly, Lord Jesus!" I honestly couldn't say that. I hoped He would wait, because I wanted to grow up and do things in my life. Somehow His coming signaled the end of any personal meaning or fulfillment for me. But I never said anything. My wish for Jesus to hold off His return did not square with what the minister said, and my honest feelings called into question the very legitimacy of my own salvation. If I didn't want Jesus to return, did that mean I wasn't a Christian?

When I was a junior at our church college, several of the fellows in my dorm were planning to be ministers and had grown up hearing the same messages I had heard. I remember one particular topic of discussion that came up frequently—sex. Two of the ministerial students were within months of being married and had not experienced the joy of sexual intercourse. Somewhat jokingly, but also with an underlying seriousness, these fellows both hoped that Christ's coming would take place *after* their weddings. They didn't want the Second Coming to keep them from tasting the pleasures of sex. I, of course, being nowhere near the point of being married, was in total agreement, and I wondered silently if I would ever be afforded enough time to eventually marry and participate in that longed-for ecstasy.

When I was a youngster, the imminence of Christ's return also conflicted with my frequent desire to masturbate. My sexual feelings were strong, but the fear of Christ's return was permanently etched in my mind, and when I finally gave in to my sexual urge, it was a bittersweet experience. Not only did I feel as though I were sinning, but my enjoyment was also tempered by the fear that I had better hurry up and do it so I could repent and ask for forgiveness before I heard the bugle signaling Christ's return.

I am very aware of the Scriptures that refer to Christ's coming "as a thief in the night" (2 Pet. 3:10), "as the lightning comes from the east" (Matt. 24:27), and so on, but in considering the sermons I have heard, I wonder if the ministers were explaining the verses properly when they used the "unexpectedness" of Christ's return to scare people away from sin so they would not be caught in the act. Now as I read those same verses, I sense a spirit of carefulness about one's attitude toward life being advocated, not a sense of cowering fearfulness. More specifically, we are urged to be alert to the true meaning of life and not become so caught up in the daily routine that we lose perspective of ourselves in relationship to God (see Matt. 24:37–39).

Paul urged people to "comfort one another" with the knowledge of Christ's return, which is inconsistent with living in fear of it.

When tragedy strikes close to home, we are reminded of the brevity of life and how quickly our lives can change. At such times we often observe, "I need to do my best today while I still have my health, and I need to be grateful to God for my family and the good things He has given me instead of worrying about all those things that don't make any difference anyway." It is this type of attitude, or the notion that we should live each day as though it were our last, that we are supposed to have relative to Christ's second coming. In fact, Paul urged people to "comfort one another" with the knowledge of Christ's return (see 1 Thess. 4:18), which is inconsistent with living in fear of it.

In spite of my present views as an adult, the fear that was pounded into me as a child surfaces unexpectedly. One time several years ago I was working in the yard, and when I entered the house, my wife and daughter were not there as I expected them to be. The house was silent. Linda, my wife, had not told me she was leaving. Where was she? Automatically, a shock of cold fear surged through my body. *The Rapture has occurred and I've been left! Oh, no! Now what?* I thought as I was overcome with panic. To my great relief, Linda soon emerged from the recesses of the basement, and I realized I had been spared.

This panic experience has happened many times, and it continues to flash inside me whenever I find myself unexpectedly alone. When it happens, I hurriedly search for someone who I'm sure is a good Christian, and if the person is present, I reassure myself that the Rapture hasn't taken place. Is this the type of Christian experience God wants you and me to have?

The Judgment—the Inevitable

The Second Coming is presented as an ever-present reality that could happen at any time; the Judgment is more distant in the future, yet equally fearful and certain. Sermon after sermon depicted for me the fearsome events of the Final Judgment in which God was at His awesome best. I always pictured crowds of people milling around, waiting for their numbers to be called so they could go in and hear their fates. Of course, if a person had strong enough faith, he had no worry because his salvation was secure. My sensitive nature tended to fear the worst, and I had often read Jesus' warning that some who think they are saved will be turned away (see Matt. 25:31–46). That could include me.

Ministers described a big book, the Lamb's Book of Life, in which names of the saved were written down. They said each person will step up to the bench with fearful, bated breath and announce his name. God will then turn the pages of the book, running His finger down the list to see if the person's name is written there. If the name isn't there, God will angrily announce with ultimate finality, "Depart from Me. I do not know you!" Then God's angels will haul the condemned person away to deposit him in the eternal fires of hell as he screams in helpless, utter terror. Of course, all the onlookers will also be struck with terror as the departing lost soul points to Christians he has known and angrily accuses them of never telling him the news of salvation that could have prevented eternal condemnation. Ministers used this final point of fear to inspire people to witness: "Do you want others pointing their fingers at *you* as they are sent off to hell?"

I was also taught that all of men's secrets were going to be opened up at the Final Judgment, apparently for public scrutiny. It sounded as though God had a film crew making videotapes of everything I did, and when I was working in Detroit, several friends and I discussed this very issue with nervous humor. We even turned and waved at the imaginary cameras, figuring we would someday be watching ourselves on God's huge projection screen when He rolled out the projectors and put our lives on display for the whole world to see. I always wondered if it would show us in our most intimate and private moments.

As I ponder these thoughts, I wonder if I am remembering only the fearful portions of the sermons and forgetting the rest. Did the minister describe the fact that when God is ready to put my life on the screen, Jesus will step forward and say, "Now in this case, You'll have to play the video-tape of My life because I took Don's place"? When Jesus' tape is played, the only picture on the screen is His sacrificial blood, which washes the sin from your life and mine. This is the essence of atonement as I now understand it, but for some reason the fearful description of the Judgment is more prominent in my memory than the reassurance of salvation.

Not only was fear prominently displayed in these major sermon topics about future events, but it was also evident in the everyday topics. Let's look at this second use of fear in the next chapter.

C H A P T E R 8

Serve God or Else: Fear in the Present

My first experience of being saved took place when I was eight years old. As usual, we were having special meetings at church, and it was a Sunday morning. A husband-wife team was handling the musical portion of the services, and as usual, this particular service was culminating in an altar call. As the hymn was being sung, the pastor walked down the aisle to the third or fourth pew from the front on the left side of the sanctuary where my older brother, Dale, and I were standing. Dale was next to the aisle, and the minister took him by the arm and whispered in his ear. I never knew what he said, but he led my eleven-year-old brother to the altar where they knelt.

Within minutes, my mother, seeing Dale at the altar, came down the same aisle with tears streaming down her face. As she passed by my pew, she reached out for my arm, and without resistance I accompanied her to the altar. I laid my head down on my arms, which were resting on the dark, varnished altar rail. I can't recall any deep feeling of conviction at the time, but I certainly knew what was going on.

As was customary, within a few minutes the wife of the evangelistic team approached me and the other seekers at the altar. The woman knelt on the platform in front of me, and since the platform was higher than the floor on which I was kneeling, she had to bend low to be on my eye level.

When I heard her voice, I raised my head, and within inches of my face was a full view of her cleavage. Captivated by this unusual view, I hardly heard her as she quietly questioned, "Do you believe in Jesus the Savior?"

Of course I did. I thought that was a dumb question. Didn't everybody? But I answered quietly and obediently, "Yes."

"Do you believe He saves you from your sins?"

Another dumb question. "Yes, I do," I said as I continued to stare. And that was it! They told me I was saved, and my name was automatically added to the list of people who were to be baptized at the next baptism.

Salvation—the Only Goal

If all the fear in evangelical teaching has a purpose, it is to keep people from sin and motivate them toward salvation. Being saved or born again was one of the primary emphases of my church. It seemed that the whole object was to be saved and sanctified, and after that, it just somehow all worked out—just how, I never knew. No one said much about day-to-day living.

Having grown up learning about God and Christ from my earliest recollection, and hearing my mother's constant use of Jesus to shame me, I knew that salvation was necessary, but it was not particularly clear to me. It seemed as though God were giving me an offer in *The Godfather* movie sense of the word, that is, one I could not refuse. It was, "You are doomed for hell, son, and the way to escape it is to be saved!" That makes it tough to turn down salvation, but the motivation was always fear, a negative.

My next experience of being saved took place when I was about eleven years old, and it was a private, more meaningful experience. Beginning in the third grade, I milked cows twice a day, and my dad always had a radio in the barn that played while we milked. One program that he often listened to came on at 6:00 A.M., and I believe it was called the "Cadle Tabernacle Hour." It originated from the Cadle Tabernacle, which had been founded by Howard Cadle in Cincinnati, if my memory is correct. The opening theme was "Take Time to Be Holy." I enjoyed listening to the program and often felt guilty about not speaking to the Lord more often. My dad also had a book written by Howard Cadle, which I began reading. The specific content of the book escapes me, but as I read it I began to feel an inner stirring and conviction. I invited Christ to come into my heart in an honest, sincere manner that seemed to result in an inner sense of feeling different. I didn't tell anyone of what I had done, but it was my most meaningful salvation experience.

It was never clear to me how salvation was supposed to actually work or feel. Most ministers made it sound quite automatic. A verse I heard a lot was "old things are passed away; behold, all things are become new" (2 Cor. 5:17 KJV). I never felt that I had very much "old" that had to pass away, and certainly everything didn't seem new to me. I didn't even feel like a sinner.

As mentioned earlier, I had been carefully monitored by my parents so I did not engage in any of the major sins, and at the same time I was told at church that I should be so very grateful that Jesus had died to save me from my sins. *What sins?* I thought. What sins had I done? With sin being defined in terms of behavior to avoid so God would not become angry at me, it seemed that Jesus took away more than He gave. Besides, sin was "out there," not inside me.

Those of us who have grown up in a Christian home with this type of experience can find it difficult to have a deeply meaningful salvation experience, because so many things get in the way. We find it difficult to serve God out of gratitude when our primary experiences consist of fear and obligation.

In order to fit into the church as a good Christian,
it's easy to fall into the trap of
going through the motions and repeating
the acceptable phrases without realizing
the superficiality of it all.

In order to fit into the church as a good Christian, it is easy to fall into the trap of going through the motions and repeating the acceptable phrases without realizing the superficiality of it all. This was most apparent in our Wednesday evening prayer meetings when it was testimony time. We had "popcorn" testimony time, which means we were supposed to "pop up" to testify. All the testimonies, even the adults', were variations of the same theme, and no one seemed particularly concerned because we were all apparently saying the "right thing." One after another we each parroted, "I'm so glad that Jesus saved me, and I want to follow Him all the days of my life." And then we sat down with a feeling of smug satisfaction that we had done our duty.

Sometimes youngsters had to really search themselves to find a basis for a meaningful testimony, particularly if they had not had extensive "sinful" experience. One young fellow in a YFC meeting was trying to illustrate the changes in his life as the result of being saved. Since he was only about fourteen at the time, he had a limited background from which to draw, but he did his best in line with the concepts he had heard at church. "I used to be a really bad kid before I met Christ," he began. "When I was seven and eight years old, I did really bad things. At school I threw spitballs at girls and stuff. But now I know Christ, and my life is really different."

The sad thing is that this is often the extent of a person's spiritual experience, and it seems to me that many churches inadvertently keep people at this level of spiritual development by emphasizing salvation instead of helping people actually live a Christian life and face day-to-day, practical situations.

Is Salvation Certain?

On my first day on the job with Detroit YFC, I had an unexpected conversation with several of the staff. Our office was on the second floor of a building across from a neighborhood store. The city Campus Life director, who was a Bob Jones University graduate and a believer in eternal security, posed the following question to me and several other fellows as we stood by the window and gazed in the direction of the store. "Suppose a fellow who is a Christian goes into that store across the street and holds it up. As he runs out of the store and starts across the street, he is hit by a car and killed. What happens to him? Does he go to heaven or hell?"

"Why, he goes to hell, without a doubt!" was my instant reply.

"I'm not so sure," my director slowly replied. "Only God knows what's in his heart, and I'm not so sure God would treat him that way."

I was shocked. To me, according to what I had been taught, it seemed so black and white and so very certain that such a misdeed would result in loss of salvation. I listened to the ensuing staff discussion and was definitely in the minority. My home church was of the Arminian persuasion, which meant we didn't believe in *eternal security,* a term I had never heard until I was in college. We were taught that one was saved by faith, but it was also possible to backslide to the point where one could lose salvation and end up in the oft-described fires of hell. Although it was never really clear what would cause ultimate loss of salvation, it always seemed like risky business to push one's luck to find out. Better wisdom dictated playing it safe rather than taking a chance and being eternally sorry. Not only was fear lining the path to salvation, but it was also an ever-present hedge along the Christian road. As I listened to the staff airing their views, I had to admit that their point of view had some appeal; it certainly allowed more slack than my narrow view did.

Not only does fear line the path to salvation,
but it's also an ever-present hedge
along the Christian road.

Through the years, as I've had more discussions with my eternally secure friends, I've come to believe that we often are looking at opposite sides of the same coin. Even though we may start out from theological positions that appear contradictory, we arrive at the same practical conclusion. When I said that a person's behavior merited loss of salvation, my Calvinist friends said the person could not have been a Christian in the first place or he would not have acted as he did. So he did not lose his salvation; he never really had it in the first place. To my way of thinking, it doesn't make any ultimate difference if he had it and lost it or never had it at all—he is still lost either way.

Emotionally, the eternally secure people have some of the same concerns that I've had. I have often said jokingly but with some seriousness to my Calvinist friends, "You had it made. Being eternally secure, you could do whatever you wanted (in growing up) and not worry about losing your salvation the way I did." Most of them have given me a puzzled look because that is not how they have felt. Whereas I've feared losing my salvation, many eternally secure people are worried about the legitimacy of their salvation. They know they can't lose it if they really have it, but they worry if they really have it or not. Again, we arrive at the same emotional point of concern and conflict. We fear and worry for different reasons, but the resulting anxiety that needs to be overcome is identical. One group emphasizes God's sovereignty, and the other emphasizes the human responsibility to choose righteousness. Both groups, however, provide avenues of fear for sensitive or insecure young people.

Evangelism—a Duty

Securing our own salvation is given top priority in the evangelical community, and a corollary to this is, of course, making sure that others are saved as well. When I was a youngster, no one ever told me how to lead someone to Christ, but it certainly was expected. There seemed to be, especially as I grew older, a continuous sense of responsibility and duty to witness to anyone I saw. This reached its most intense level during my years of full-time Christian work in Detroit.

In witnessing, as well as in securing salvation, fear was the motivating force in my life. If I didn't try to save everyone, not only would something dreadful happen to the unsaved person, but God would deal harshly with me, too, because I would be responsible. As mentioned earlier, I was clearly told that the people I hadn't witnessed to would accuse me at the judgment seat as they were ushered away to eternal damnation and torment. In Detroit, I found myself being reluctant to strike up a conversation with the fellow as he gassed up my car (it was not self-serve back then), because I felt that even if I had a little bit of a relationship with him, I would be obligated to somehow confront him with the gospel. So if I didn't really know him, I felt less obligation.

This guilty burden of obligation was with me almost continually. Somehow I discovered stock car racing and just loved to drive to Flat Rock (south of Detroit) to watch the

Saturday night races when I was free from my YFC duties. Inwardly, I had to justify going to the races because I was doing it purely for fun, which felt a bit wrong because I was doing something for myself (remember the implied definition of sin). I also felt that I should be out saving the world rather than enjoying the races. After all, wasn't that my calling as a YFC staff person? Or perhaps I could partially make up for enjoying the races by witnessing to people at the track, which would give me some justification for being there other than for personal fun. As I recall, I simply made the best of it, not witnessing, but thinking up good reasons why it was permissible to have fun at the races anyway.

For me, witnessing was not an act of love for the other person but an attempt to save my own skin. I didn't have clear, positive experiences to sell, so I had to use the same approach that was used on me; scare them first so they'll want salvation. I sadly shake my head as I recall a witnessing experience I had late one night in a suburban Detroit self-serve laundry. Being single at the time, I had to do my own wash. I usually went to the laundry late at night because my innocent modesty was embarrassed at having to wash my underwear in full view of women.

One particular night, near midnight, a young woman in her late teens or early twenties came in to do her wash. Because I had this fearful burden that I had to witness to save my own skin, I figured God had sent her into the laundry so I could lead her to Christ. I struck up a conversation with her and presented the gospel the best way I could. For some reason she wasn't interested. I can't remember why, although now I can understand that a young woman alone late at night in a laundry in Detroit *should* be skeptical of a stranger trying to peddle anything. Of course she was in a bit of a predicament. She couldn't really escape me because she didn't want to flee into the night without her laundry, which was in the machines.

With the Final Judgment scene pictured in my mind as described earlier, I saw my chance to reverse the situation. Here I was, witnessing to a person who was turning down God, the reverse of the condemned person being dragged off to hell by God's angels and accusing me of not witnessing to him. *Someday,* I thought to myself, *I'll stand at the judgment seat and see this poor woman sent off to the fires because she is refusing salvation at this very moment.* With this scene in my mind, I said with all seriousness and stern certainty to the woman, "Someday [I didn't explain how or when, but I was picturing the Judgment scene], you and I are going to meet again, and you're going to remember this talk here tonight. And you're going to regret it. So remember it for when you see me again."

I really thought I was doing God's work and left the laundry with a joyful heart because I had witnessed and carried out my full Christian duty. Now I shake my head in embarrassment and realize the insensitivity of my remarks to that young woman. I wonder how much unnecessary fright I caused her. It certainly was not a loving, Christian thing to do, but it seemed to fit with the way the church was presenting the gospel to me and how I thought I should live. I fear that this same type of thinking continues in the church today.

Sometimes we try to collect spiritual scalps
to gain acceptance and influence
in God's army rather than witness
out of a genuine concern for other people.

Some of the people I knew at that time who were actively successful at soul-winning did not quite ring true with me, and I now believe that their motivation was no better than mine. One summer at Detroit's YFC camp, a college graduate who had been involved with another Christian organization came to spend time with our staff in hopes of joining the team. He was an unathletic, pudgy, physically unattractive fellow, but he was committed to witnessing. I recall repeated occasions when he left the YFC camp and spent the hot summer afternoons at the nearby state park beach. Upon returning to camp, he proudly announced, "Well, I had five people make decisions today." Of course everyone was pleased to hear that, and he received appropriate praise, which is what he wanted in the first place. I countered some of my hidden jealousy at his success by telling myself that he was only doing it to overcome his inner feelings of inferiority so the staff would see him as a worthwhile person. It seems to me it is very easy for witnessing to become a self-centered experience; we can try to collect spiritual scalps to gain acceptance and influence in God's army rather than speak out of a genuine concern for other people.

Sanctified—Once and for All

Sanctification was a regular topic of sermons in my home church and was called the second work of grace, while being saved was the first work of grace. I had enough trouble mastering and maintaining salvation, so sanctification was quite another issue. It was difficult for me to understand what it actually entailed, in spite of the numerous sermons I heard. Later discussions with my Calvinist friends led me to realize that their notion of total dedication was very similar to sanctification, but by another name, and they didn't emphasize the "not sinning" part. For them, it was mostly a matter of putting Christ as Lord over one's life and the lifelong process of spiritual improvement that follows conversion.

In my church, one had to be saved as a prerequisite to sanctification, and it usually sounded as though sanctification didn't come easily. One had to seek it. It required a great deal of prayer, and somehow, when it happened, it made the Christian life much easier. In addition, it had something to do with not sinning at all. To be "sanctified holy" meant that one rarely, if ever, sinned and that the roots of the sin nature had been uprooted and destroyed like a farmer tearing out a rotten apple tree by the very roots.

Sanctification meant purity of heart, or at least purity of intentions, although it was allowed that people in spite of their intentions would slip. But these were called mistakes, not sins, thus maintaining the sanctified state of purity, or sinless perfection, as it was called.

By the time I graduated from college with a B.A. in biblical literature and a minor in theological studies, I was convinced that Christians rarely, if ever, sinned, and that all sin was removed from people through the second work of grace. I can't recall how I actually squared all this with my own experience because I never had a sanctification experience similar to ones described in the pulpit. The overwhelming notion from the pulpit, however, was that sanctification was crucial and almost as necessary as salvation itself. "Follow peace with all men, and holiness, without which no man shall see the Lord"(Heb. 12:14 KJV). This was a common supporting Scripture that added credence to the seriousness of the search for holiness. Through the years, I have noticed that many of the Christian writers I enjoy are from the Calvinist persuasion. The fact that they don't expect perfection from me has been a welcomed message and a relief from a fearful burden.

Heaven and Eternal Life

Since my earliest recollections and throughout my growing years, I have repeatedly heard about the magnitude of heaven and eternal issues in comparison to life here on earth. This teaching, in addition to the heavy emphasis on fear, has had a deep effect on me. I mention this because I believe that a number of you have had similar feelings, but no one talks about it at church. Heaven (this almost sounds heretical to say) has never been a source of comfort for me, yet some people can't wait to arrive at the pearly gates. When I hear eternal life discussed so glibly at church, I find it incomprehensible that everyone sitting in the church is very excited and has no fear. It is something totally beyond my comprehension.

Streets of gold, choirs singing, strange-looking beasts standing around the throne, as described in Revelation, and such have had absolutely no appeal, even though I know they are all symbolic. Actually, the Indians' concept of a "happy hunting ground" with horses and beautiful, open country has always been something to which I could more easily relate. A significant part of my struggle related to this has been the deep, persistent fear of living forever. It just somehow has seemed like an awfully long time doing who knows what, and it has given me a deep sense of helplessness and sheer terror that I'm still unable to escape, particularly in the quiet of night. For years I have inwardly shivered with fear whenever the hymn "Amazing Grace" is sung at church. One verse says,

> When we've been there ten thousand years,
> Bright shining as the sun,
> We've no less days to sing his praise
> Than when we'd first begun.

At a deep level, I realized in my twenties that life was not something I had learned to enjoy. Life seemed like a burden to bear; I was a player in a game I did not ask for. Living forever has never seemed like any treat to me. I have sat in amazed puzzlement as I listened to Christians talk about the peace and joy that having eternal life has given them, because that has not been my experience at all.

Such concerns have never been discussed in my presence in the church, and I mention this with some reticence because it continues to be a source of tremendous consternation for me. The intense inner feeling is that since the real essence of existence is in eternity and not in this life, what I want here has to be of minimal importance; it is only a preparatory stage where I prove myself or, in a more literal sense, write my own ticket for not only the location but also the manner in which I "spend" eternity.

The practical consequence of this has been a definite feeling that self-assertion is wrong or, more specifically, wanting much of anything simply because I want it is wrong. A corollary to this is the feeling that during my life on earth, I at least have the freedom to make some of my own decisions and pursue some of my own goals, although possibly at my soul's risk, but then the Judgment seems distant in the future and a bit vague. When eternity starts, then it seems God takes total control, and there is forever after no clear concept of me as a person with any particular freedoms or specific personal ability to affect my own future.

If such feelings are not present in your life, you are fortunate, but my work with people in therapy has helped me to see that many Christians struggle with such fears.

Thread of Fear

This thread of fear that is woven through many of the evangelical messages often creates a conflicted, problem foundation for those of us who are sensitive by nature and vulnerable to such heavy, fear-inducing methods. Such an approach in presenting Christianity sets the stage for many personal complications not only in childhood but in our adult lives as well. We will look at some of these complications in Chapter 10, but first let's examine one of the most critical implications of these danger points.

Self-Denial Is Only
Half the Story

Nadine paused, cast her gaze past me, and looked out the window in my office as she pondered her next remarks. She had grown up in an evangelical, covenant theology home, the youngest of four children and the only girl. We were discussing her early family and church experiences to trace their influences on her life. She continued, "I never really thought much of myself as a girl. I was always kind of fat and shy. It always seemed that if I wanted to fit in, I had to do what my parents wanted. And it seemed like God was always looking over my shoulder. I remember we used to sing this little Sunday school song, 'Be careful little feet where you go! / Be careful little eyes what you see! / For your Father up above is looking down in love, so be careful little feet where you go.' I was always afraid that God was watching down on me to see if I did anything wrong. And now, I feel like I have never really been free to be the real me. Inside this fat body I feel like a slinky, pretty woman, but I don't know if I can be that. It sounds so selfish, and I keep reading in magazines about the 'me generation,' and I don't feel it is right to be part of that."

Assert or Deny

Nadine's struggle is typical of that of many Christians who have talked to me about the overwhelming issue of self. Where do we fit in? And if we do anything for our-selves, is it selfish? What is the difference between selfish-ness and proper self-interest? Is it wrong to speak up if we don't like something, or does God want us to put up with it and suffer in silence? This issue of self with all its ramifica-tions is one of the most crippling consequences of the dan-ger points in the evangelical community, as Tournier notes: "How many mediocre personalities are there in our churches—people who have not the courage to live full lives, to assert themselves and make the most of them-selves, and who look upon this stifling of themselves as a Christian virtue, whereas faith ought to create powerful personalities?"[1]

In the minds of many people, including my own as I grew up, the principle of self-assertion and the biblical truth of self-denial were seen as opposites and mutually exclusive. I was taught quite clearly that I couldn't have both and that to assert myself could bring deadly conse-quences because it would be sin. I remember a Sunday school song we sang that quite clearly taught where I fit into the picture. It was a song about joy. According to the song, the way to spell *joy* is to "put Jesus first, others second, and yourself last." This idea, along with my mother's control and the minister's hellfire sermons, certainly made it seem dangerous to want anything simply for myself. Nadine's struggle had been identical to mine.

Many Christians see the principle of self-assertion
and the biblical truth of self-denial
as opposites and mutually exclusive,
but they're both necessary.

There is no doubt about the biblical concept of renuncia-tion or giving up something one possesses. Jesus talked about the principle of denying oneself, turning the other cheek, and going the second mile. A person must also be ready and willing to turn his back on his parents for the gospel's sake. Paul advised that we should be content regardless of our state in life (see 1 Timothy 6:6–8 and Hebrews 13:5). This theme of renunciation is a prominent one in evangelical teaching, but I question whether it has been placed in proper perspective.

This issue of self-denial was clearly brought to my attention a few years ago after my first daughter, Amanda, was born. A family friend, in an effort to provide appropriate Christian literature for Amanda, gave us a children's book. It was the type of book that parents read to small children. Inside the cover was the stated purpose of the booklet series: "Eight educational booklets for the nursery-age child, giving him a solid, basic conception of God's love, His creation, and conduct that pleases God. These are conveyed to impressionable 2's and 3's by colorful pictures and two or three lines of rhyming copy."[2]

Notice that the author's intent is to impress on "2's and 3's" the "conduct that pleases God." To accomplish this purpose, the booklet contains a series of pictures depicting Julie, the main character, doing various actions on someone else's behalf, with each action justified and supported by reference to Scripture. In one picture she is standing by a tree, smiling, as she watches another little boy using her swing. The rhyme is:

> Why does Julie with a smile
> Let her playmate swing awhile?
> Because Jesus says, "Love one another."

In another picture she is seen wiping her feet at the back door:

> Why does Julie wipe her feet
> So Mommy's floor is clean and neat?
> Because Jesus says, "Obey your mother."

Other pictures show her sharing her toys with friends, helping her brother who has fallen, bringing a drink to her working, perspiring father, eating what's good for her, going to sleep without a whine, and so on. She does each of these things because "Jesus says, 'Love one another,' and 'Obey your mother.'" The final verse sums up Julie's experience:

> Why is Julie glad and gay?
> A happy girl throughout the day?
> Because she loves Jesus and what he says![3]

As I read the book, I was struck by several things. First, I suddenly realized how closely the booklet's contents paralleled my evangelical upbringing. But more importantly, as a psychologist I was disturbed to realize that throughout the entire booklet the total thrust of Julie's behavior was for other people. From both a psychological and a theological point of view, the book taught only renunciation, or giving up. In every picture she was depicted renouncing her own desires in order to give to other people, including her parents, her friends, and her brother. And not only did she do all this with a smile (contrary to normal two-year-old children I have known), but her total selflessness made her a "happy girl throughout the day."

In addition, each action was supported by invoking Jesus' commands with the direct implication that doing otherwise would be acting contrary to Jesus. Not once in all the pictures did *anyone* give to Julie. She was not pictured receiving, and not one picture illustrated Julie doing anything for herself. She never enjoyed her swing, wore nice clothes, said no to carrots, or in fact acted as a normal two year old who by nature is going through the stage of "the terrible twos" on the way to developing normal independence. The stated purpose of this book was to *directly contra-*

dict this normal childhood development in the name of God who designed children and their stages.

This booklet about Julie illustrates, in my opinion, the general evangelical approach to self. The direct and indirect statement is to put self last, don't consider your own needs to be important, don't be assertive in achievement. If a person does any of these things, the implied definition of sin comes into play: "anything for me is wrong." As Nadine lamented, "It sounds so selfish, and I keep reading in magazines about the 'me generation,' and I don't feel it is right to be part of that." As a side effect of her Christian training, she even feels guilty about wanting to lose weight and improve her appearance for fear she will be acting self-centered. Many "Julie's" who have had this type of training have sat in my office, guilt-ridden because they do not like what is happening in their lives, and yet they believe, as they have been taught, that it is wrong for them to assert themselves to improve their situations. Perhaps you also are a "Julie" or a "Nadine" with similar feelings and experiences.

For years I tried to live by this philosophy, believing that personal goals such as being successful or doing what I wanted were wrong. Somehow if success or money "happened" to come my way—in other words, if it was not the result of personal, "sinful, willful" determination—that was acceptable. I could assert myself on behalf of God's work, but not for my own benefit. I secretly wanted a nice house with a farm and horses, but I was convinced that God wanted me to deny myself and forsake any wishes of my own. For many years, but especially when I was working for YFC, I believed that the poorer I was, the more spiritual I was. Consequently, I lived in a sparse basement room that cost ten dollars per week, and I never bought a TV, stereo, or any other amenities that most people obtain when they live on their own.

The Role of Self

Within the church, there appears to be a lack of consensus about what constitutes proper perception of self and how the sense of self fits into the Christian life. The concept of self-esteem for Christians has been popularized in recent years by Robert Schuller through his books and television programs. In comparison to the messages I heard growing up, his ideas are a refreshing breath of fresh air because they bolster my self-worth.

Some people take exception to the idea that Christians should have good self-esteem because they equate positive self-esteem with sin. Recently, I was discussing this point with a prominent layman. In response to his statement that Schuller's notion of self-esteem is sinful, I asked, "Do you mean I should say that I'm a worm?"

"Of course!" was his instant reply.

"Whether you call it self-esteem or self-worth, it is plainly the foundation of Christian love for others."

Although I don't intend to resolve this complicated issue here, I believe many people are confusing self-esteem or self-image, a part of our psychological equipment, with our inability to earn salvation, a spiritual concept. I can have good self-esteem and still recognize that my righteousness is "like filthy rags" (Isa. 64:6). Conversely, calling myself a worm is not going to earn any spiritual points, either. Often I see Christians beating themselves on their heads, putting themselves down, and treating themselves horribly in the name of God. As author David Seamands says with great wisdom:

145

The truth is that self-belittling is not true Christian humility and runs counter to some very basic teachings of the Christian faith. The great commandment is that you love God with all your being. The second commandment is an extension of the first—that you love your neighbor as you love yourself. We do not have two commandments here, but three: to love God, to love yourself, and to love others. I put *self* second, because Jesus plainly made a proper self-love the basis of a proper love for neighbor. The term *self-love* has a wrong connotation for some people. Whether you call it self-esteem or self-worth, it is plainly the foundation of Christian love for others. And this is the opposite of what many Christians believe.[4]

Abby is a middle-aged Christian woman who learned several years ago that she is diabetic, but even though she knows enough about diabetes to write a book on it, she fails to eat properly or take her insulin regularly. On one occasion she began a diet that she knew could lead to an insulin reaction, and even her physician advised against it. As a result, she became quite ill at work when her sugar dropped to a dangerous level, almost requiring her to be hospitalized. Her doctor referred her for psychotherapy because her eating habits were potentially dangerous for her physical health. As we discussed her life, it became obvious that she had a low sense of personal worth.

She had become a Christian at the age of thirteen at an evangelical church, and their training along with her non-Christian mother's constant criticism affected her self-image. She didn't really care if she died, although she had no intentions of killing herself. Consistently, she put everyone else ahead of her own feelings or needs since she enjoyed doing things for others. After listening to her, I remarked, "Instead of loving others as you love yourself, you treat other people better than you do yourself. For you, we should turn Jesus' statement around and tell you to love yourself as much as you do other people."

I am convinced that teaching children to give up things before they have learned to possess them (renunciation), or to put themselves last before they have mastered self-assertion, creates feelings of low self-worth. Carried to an extreme, this restricted upbringing can cause some people to even doubt their existence, let alone experience worth, as Tournier points out.

> It is by daring to express his desires, tastes, and opinions, and through feeling that they are respected, that the child becomes aware that he exists, of being a person distinct from other persons. It is a violation of the person of the child to try to direct him in everything according to what his parents think best, without heeding his own preferences. He comes to the point where he no longer knows what his desires, tastes, and opinions are, and an individual without any personal desire, taste, or opinion does not feel that he exists, either. This can be observed in families with high moral or religious pretensions. The parents are so sure they have a monopoly of absolute truth that any other view than their own can only be a grievous error in their eyes. They are so sure of their judgment in all matters, that they impose it on their children—for their own good they think.
>
> This often goes along with the teaching of self-abnegation. While still young the child must learn to forget himself, to disregard his personal desires, to behave in accordance with the requirements of others, seeking always to please them rather than himself. Of course the parents head the list of the "others" who must be pleased and have constant service rendered to them, whereas they themselves scarcely ever bother to gratify any of the child's pleasures which they look upon as mere selfish whims. And they accuse him of selfishness if he manifests any personal aspirations.[5]

Church leaders and ministers often treat Christians in the same fashion as the parents in this quotation treat their children. They do not allow the parishioners to ask questions or assert their own opinions. The implication is that only the minister or the parent is capable of making correct decisions, while the parishioner or the child is inferior and must be told what to do. As a result, a sense of low self-worth is promoted, and an incorrect concept of self-assertion inhibits people from fully experiencing and knowing themselves.

"It is a violation of the person of the child
to try to direct him in everything
according to what his parents think best,
without heeding his own preferences."

The irony of this is that in the name of God well-intentioned parents and ministers lay a foundation that makes Satan's work easier. Says Seamands:

> Satan's greatest psychological weapon is a gut-feeling of inferiority, inadequacy, and low self-worth. This feeling shackles many Christians, in spite of wonderful spiritual experiences, in spite of their faith and knowledge of God's Word. Although they understand their positions as sons and daughters of God, they are tied up in knots, bound by a terrible feeling of inferiority, and chained to a deep sense of worthlessness.[6]

Self-Image as a Personal Thermostat

This sense of personal inferiority is especially damaging because the self-image definitely influences how we act. In other words, we live according to how we feel about ourselves, not according to our actual personal qualities or abilities.[7] In the past I was often puzzled whenever I saw a very attractive girl dating an unattractive guy. She could have any boyfriend she wanted, I thought to myself. Why did she pick someone who looks so different from herself? It all made sense when I realized that the fellow's appearance was identical to the way the girl *felt* about herself. She had picked a guy who fit her self-image, not her true beauty.

Because our actions are consistent with our self-images, it's hard for us to change how we act without changing our self-images first. For example, a golfer who is accustomed to having a score in the high 90s suddenly realizes on the first nine holes that he is doing better than usual, and that if he continues, he will end up in the high 70s. Since he doesn't see himself as a 70s golfer, his low score is inconsistent with his self-image, which makes him uneasy. His self-image thermostat kicks in to bring things in line, meaning he begins to miss putts, lands in sand traps, and so on until his score returns to the 90s range that fits his self-image. Then he can relax. His behavior is now consistent with his self-image.[8]

This same principle is present in all areas of life, not just sports. A fellow who feels that he is a born loser will act like a loser, which not only makes success elusive, but he repeatedly makes life situations turn out in a losing way, thus confirming in his own eyes the fact that he is a loser without realizing the role he plays in it. If by chance he begins to be successful, he becomes anxious because success is contrary to his self-image. As did the golfer, he will unconsciously do something to stop his success and thus end his anxious discomfort.

Two Movements

It wasn't until I discovered Paul Tournier's book, *A Place For You*,[9] in 1969, two years after I had left YFC, that I learned there is much more to the issue of renunciation and self-denial than I had learned at church. Tournier points out that in reality self-assertion and renunciation are two sides of the same coin, with the contradiction being "more apparent than real, theoretical rather than practical."[10] He describes self-assertion and renunciation as two alternating movements, not opposites. Before a person can renounce something, he must assert himself to possess it. Before he can give to another, he must receive. Tournier likens the process to the rhythm in nature, where the trees burst into bloom in the spring and give up their leaves when the fall season arrives. Only the leaves that have grown in the spring are able to fall in the autumn. He writes, "Thus there is a rhythm between attachment and detachment. One must first receive, in order to be able to give. One must first possess, in order to be able to give up. . . . One must first have a place before leaving it. One can abandon only what one has got. One can only give up what one has received."[11]

As he continues to explain this rhythm, he quotes Teilhard de Chardin:

> "Which is better for the Christian, activity or passivity? Life or death? Growth or diminishment? Development or curtailment? Possession or renunciation?" And as a priest he replies: "Why separate and contrast the two natural phases of a single effort? . . . Develop yourself and take possession of the world *in order to be.* Once this has been accomplished, then is the time to think about renunciation: then is the time to accept diminishment for the sake of *being in another.* . . . First, develop yourself."
>
> He recognizes that books about the spiritual life "do not generally throw this first phase of Christian perfection into clear enough relief."[12]

It's obvious, at least from my perspective, that the evangelical church has been emphasizing the second of the two movements and not only neglecting the first stage, but trying to keep people from ever entering it in the first place. In many instances, parents and ministers even use God to block the door to the first stage of self-development. This, of course, also prevents people from growing into the second stage where they can freely and genuinely give.

Tournier uses the term *premature renunciation* to describe the type of Christian training that Julie received. In other words, Julie was taught to put herself last before she was actually ready to do so—thus prematurely. This also describes the general approach used by the evangelical church in regard to the role of self. In this light, Tournier points out, "It would be absurd and unjust to urge detachment upon a man who had never received the thing in question. Unfortunately it is often done."[13]

Under the guise of spiritual training, growing children are taught and allowed to experience only the second movement of giving things up, which makes the sensitive ones develop into crippled adults burdened by fear and guilt, not powerful personalities who can step out in faith. Even a "D" person once told me, "When I was growing up in the church, I used to think God had put me together all wrong because I was naturally aggressive, and I kept hearing how wrong it was to be aggressive and go after things."

Heart of the Problem

This brings us to the heart of the problem that we face in growing up as second-, third-, and following-generation Christians. Because we are surrounded by Christian traditions, because fear is threaded through the church's teachings, and because sin is listed clearly in terms of specific actions to avoid, those of us who are sensitive become timid, afraid to move for fear of either sinning or making someone angry with us. So we concentrate on following the rules, avoiding the master list of sins, and living a life of renunciation without ever having possessed ourselves. Our lives become restricted and hollow as we live by traditions and beliefs without making them our own. Our Christian experience is not vital, meaningful, and personal because we're simply going along with our parents' ways.

By following the rules and abstaining from the proscribed sins, it's easy for us to develop a sense of self-righteousness that is deceiving, but also in this process is an important emotional point. To maintain this righteous self-image, we must avoid evil behavior, and we must not think or feel it, either. This means that any thought or emotion that contradicts our self-righteous image has to disappear.

During their childhood, many sincere Christians began to store away or push aside from their minds emotions and thoughts that contradicted the image they believed they should have. They began to stuff inner emotional closets full of hurts, anger, sensual thoughts, guilt, resentment toward parents, and so on. They hoped that the old saying "Out of sight, out of mind" would apply as they sought to rid themselves of their negative feelings. As time went on, and time does go on because this process can continue for years, they gradually lost touch with many of their feelings and became superficial shells of people with a nice external spiritual image. They always do and say the "right things," winning spiritual victories with ease because they have most of their problems stuck in the closet. They even become the envy of the more honest strugglers who are unable to do it all so easily.

Tournier summarizes this situation in a clear manner and highlights the crucial difference between first-generation Christians and their children:

> A child brought up in an environment like that [an evangelical type of environment], in which all worldly pleasures are frowned upon, will forswear dancing, flirtation, theatre-going, alcohol, tobacco, nice clothes, and any interest in good food. He will retain perhaps for the rest of his life the idea that everything pleasurable is forbidden, and a

sin. One day I shall have to tell him that enjoyment is permitted! But I am unlikely to have any success. All enjoyment, even before the idea of it rises to the surface of his conscious mind, awakens in him the distress that is characteristic of the violation of a taboo, and his pleasure is spoilt.

A negative education of this kind destroys a child's self-confidence and pushes him into neurosis, because it blocks the spontaneous force of life within him. . . . Many people do not like life. Their upbringing has left them with a prohibition inside of them, which says: "Living prohibited." . . . To put a brake on this vital impulse on the excuse of teaching the child wisdom or Christian humility, is to fail to understand the rhythms of Nature implanted by God.

Do not blame his parents for having put constraints upon him. He has followed their example freely. He wants to be able sincerely to repeat with them the words of St. Paul: "For his sake I have suffered the loss of all things, and count them as refuse, in order that I may gain Christ" (Phil. 3:8). His parents had found the "pearl of great value" (Matt. 13:46), and in exchange for it they had joyfully sacrificed all this world's pleasures. And so for them it was a true renunciation, the sign of a liberating experience. The child, for his part, was giving up nothing, since he had known none of the things he was giving up. He heard about Jesus Christ from the cradle, so he could not be a new discovery for him. And so the Christian life appears to be for him an impoverishment, a dispossession, instead of a blossoming and a fulfilment.[14]

"Living prohibited!" What a message to learn in the name of Christ! And what a contradiction it creates. It is as though we have to live, but in such a careful, fearful manner that we are not really living at all. And at the same time, we're supposed to be the picture of joy and Christian happiness that will let others see the abundant life in us. The Christian life for the second and third generations can easily become a burden to carry instead of a liberating experience.

Revolt Denied

Many Christians who have grown up in the church, especially if they don't have a strong amount of "D" in their personalities, remain in the stage of premature renunciation because the key to moving past it lies in revolt or rebellion that leads ultimately to assuming responsibility for oneself. Such self-assertion will involve risk because many in the church will not understand it.

The sad part is that the evangelical church seems to have completely ignored the role of self-assertion in human development. In fact, anyone who has studied human behavior knows that the key to building a solid person is the self-assertion against constraints that develops the inner sense of being a real person. Parents have known the two year old who defiantly yells, "No! I will do it myself!" This is the child's first step, assertion, so vital to his personhood, and then after the youngster has stated his position, he is willing to "renounce" and let Mom start the jacket's zipper anyway. But in order to accept the help, the child first had to refuse it.

The danger of growing up in a Christian home
is that parents and ministers will interfere
with the God-designed movement back and forth
between self-assertion and renunciation.

Most Christian parents can accept this self-assertion in a two year old, but when a youngster reaches adolescence, parents and the church quickly become less understanding. Perhaps this is because teens can get into bigger trouble than the two year old who insists on tying his own shoe. The adolescent stage of life is so critical because it is the bridge between childhood, where decisions are made by others, and adulthood, where young people become responsible for themselves. To become independent, autonomous adults, young people usually have to go through the adolescent phase of rebellion, throwing aside what they have been taught in their childhood, questioning their values, and trying new ways of acting. As Tournier says,

> To allow them to grow up in complete liberty and in ignorance of the moral and spiritual exigencies of life would be in fact to deprive them of the opportunity of the rebellion, or at least the crisis of adolescence, through which they must pass before finding a more personal faith. But when that crisis comes, it is important to respect and accept it as the first movement that is the necessary preliminary to a return to the faith and a more thoughtful adherence to the ineluctable exigencies of life. The child will surmount his crisis only if he is free to express his doubts and his rebellion, to reject what has been inculcated in him. But then it will be seen that not all the seed sown in his mind has been sown in vain. . . . The first movement is a guide, a preparation. Whether it be a matter of an imposed morality, at the age when the child still needs it; or self-assertion and revolt at the approach of the age of responsibility; or the testing-time of illness and the questions it raises; or, finally, the self-discovery and self-acceptance which form part of a course of psychotherapy—these are all experiences which prepare the way for another, the experience of abdication, an experience which is much greater, much longer lasting, but which would not be possible if it were not preceded by those other experiences in the first place.[15]

The danger of growing up in a Christian home is that parents and ministers will interfere with this God-designed movement back and forth between self-assertion and renunciation, or giving something up. As Tournier points out in this quote, "The child will surmount his crisis only if he is free to express his doubts and his rebellion, to reject what has been inculcated in him." But such freedom is rare if not totally absent from the church. To the contrary, evangelicals try to *keep* their people from going through this phase, apparently unable to see that it is the path of preparation for a more solid faith. It is no wonder that so many young people are leaving the church today. The church is stifling their development.

Consequently, the people with the "D" dimension in their personalities are apt to look at the hypocrisy, the tradition, and the nonvital Christians in their church and say "Who needs it?" The more sensitive ones either drift away slowly or else out of guilt stay in church, not because it attracts them, but because they're afraid to leave. They remain, living unhappy lives of renunciation, going through the motions, silently struggling, but never really understanding why their lives are not more rewarding. It is because no one has explained their dilemma to them, and they live on the border between adolescence and adulthood. They are filled with someone else's values but are afraid to throw out what they have in order to develop their own firsthand, faith-giving experiences. That's because they've been told that to question or throw out what they have will bring deadly consequences. The result is a church with first-generation Christians who have a meaningful faith, and the rest are hand-me-down, duty-bound, following-tradition Christians who have never completed the adolescent phase of development. This is where reluctant Christians start and often remain.

Lucy, a cute, blonde girl, was one of the most devoted Christian teens in my YFC clubs. At the time, I was emphasizing the renunciation aspect of the two movements because that was all I knew. I counseled her to dedicate her entire life to God, and we dealt with it in specifics, including school, relationship with parents, personal future, and especially dating. All of this she did with a willing heart. After I had left YFC, I looked Lucy up when I was visiting in Detroit, and she told me how she had run unexpectedly into difficulty.

"You remember how we talked about giving every area of our lives to God?" she stated. "Well, at the time it was easy to give my dating life to God because I didn't have one! Then when I started dating and began to be aware of my sexual feelings, I realized that when I made my earlier commitment I didn't know what I was doing. I didn't really understand myself. It was a real shock, and I had to figure the whole thing out again. When I realized what it *really* meant to give God my dating life, it wasn't so easy because this time I *knew* what it was all about!" Lucy learned from her actual experience what Tournier states in his book; a person cannot truly give something to God that he does not fully possess.

Even as I write, my Sunday paper contains an Associated Press story[16] that illustrates the point of the two movements and how one lays the foundation for the next. I am sure that a person could use this story to tell people that they must forgive, but in his shortsightedness he might well overlook the first stage that made forgiveness possible.

According to the news account, a couple in Kentucky had an only child who was killed at the age of eighteen by a drunk driver in a car accident one mile from his home. The couple was outraged and "dedicated their lives to punishing the drunken driver who had killed their only child." Motivated by hatred, they observed his every court appearance and followed him to the county jail to ensure that he was actually serving his time. The court process was slow and did not punish the driver as severely as the mother wanted. "Every time it would be delayed, I would get more upset and my hatred for him would grow," the mother recalled to the reporter. After two years of this, the couple realized that their anger toward the driver was beginning to consume them and their efforts at revenge were only hurting themselves, so they decided to forgive him and help him rebuild his life. "The hate and bitterness I was feeling were destroying me. . . . I needed to forgive Tommy to save myself."

The ebb and flow of the two movements is clear in this story. Even though the period of active revenge was a painful, difficult struggle, its value was in preparing the parents for the more meaningful second stage. The first step was to assert themselves, to express their outrage through their actions, and to seek revenge, which was putting legs to their feelings rather than pretending to be forgiving when they really were quite angry. This allowed them the experience of learning firsthand about their anger.

Observing their intense anger for two years, someone may be tempted to say they were not letting God handle the revenge. However, in light of the entire situation, their angry period was a preparation for the second step of giving up their hatred. Forgiveness was a meaningful, liberating experience for the parents because they had lived out their anger in the first stage. Now they encourage the former drunken driver as he builds a productive life, and they have even taken him to their church, where he has been baptized.

Countless Christians are suffering needlessly because they were trained to believe and act as Julie was in the little booklet; they don't understand the proper role of self in their Christian lives. If you'll examine your own life and others' experiences, you'll begin to see the truth of the two movements. We will look at some ideas on dealing with this issue in Chapter 16.

PART THREE

Struggling with the Effects
of These Dangers

The Price of Trying to Be Perfect

Dixie is a young married woman who has struggled with many of the issues outlined in the preceding pages. During her therapy, as we discussed some of her early experiences, she recalled how dangerous it was for her to exhibit any sense of normal femininity in the home. Her father totally forbade her to wear any makeup, and her mother demanded that she wear her skirts to a defined length even though she looked out of place with her peers. She also had to avoid the appearance of having any affection for boys in order to escape her mother's displeasure.

An Alert Conscience

One particular teenage incident made a deep impression on her. She said, "Behind our house were some small hills with a railroad track going through them. One day I was out walking along the tracks with a boy and we were holding hands, when I suddenly saw my older brother come out of a small wooded area with his girlfriend. It shocked me to see him, but even worse, I was sure he had seen me and was afraid he would tell Mom. If he did that, I knew I was in really big trouble. So, I left my boyfriend and ran home as fast as I could. I had to get to my mother before my brother told her. So I told her this big story that I really didn't like this boy, and he had made me hold hands with him even though I didn't want to. I said I had no intentions of doing that with him, and didn't know for sure how it had all happened. I was really scared at the time, and it still upsets me to think about it."

Growing up in an evangelical environment can make it difficult to be spontaneous, fun-loving, and comfortable with oneself, because the predominant message often is "Living is prohibited!" Having to contend with God, church, and parents, as well as his own inner feelings, the growing, sensitive, evangelical child has a limited number of options from which to choose. Obviously, as was the case with Julie in the children's book, training at home and church is being done in the name of God, and resisting it or fighting back is not only sinning, but inviting God's judgment as well.

Since love has become closely tied to behavior, or how well we perform to the evangelical tune, we learn to be on the alert for any potential action or emotion that might displease the dispensers of love.

The natural focus for a sensitive personality is to develop a strategy, as Dixie did, that avoids the wrath of both parents and God. The only sure way to do this is to be or at least appear to be a model child, selfless in following all the rules. To accomplish this requires some unnatural effort, because a growing child normally wants to assert himself, explore his environment, and experience himself and his emotions. Since love has become closely tied to behavior, or how well he performs to the evangelical tune, however, he has to be on the alert for any potential action or emotion that might displease the dispensers of love.

As Dixie's account reveals, this requires an alert conscience that is able to keep track of the rules and quickly spot any emotions or situations that might cause trouble or look self-serving. In the process of maintaining this alertness to avoid the deep guilt that comes from crossing the forbidden line, it's easy to develop an overly critical and sensitive conscience, which adds to the crippling burden. Of course, persons with "S" and "C" personalities are more prone to such self-monitoring because it comes naturally to them.

When I was about thirteen years old, I was climbing in the large maple tree that stood next to the milkhouse, something I always enjoyed doing. My mother happened to pass by and yelled at me, "Don! Don't climb any higher than that!" My conscience quickly seized that command as another one to be added to the list, believing that her directive was good for the rest of my life and that to *ever* climb any higher was sin. To help myself avoid such sin and its heavy guilt, I quickly fished in my pocket for the knife I carried with me and carved a notch in the tree so that whenever I was climbing in the tree again, I would know where I was supposed to stop.

Attempting to follow the master list of sins wasn't particularly hard for me as a youngster because I was given little opportunity to do otherwise. Even normal adolescent curiosity was closely monitored by my strict conscience, which resulted in regular struggles with my frequent companion, guilt. Not once during my high-school years did I go to a movie, although every Saturday when my mother took me to Elkhart for my piano lesson, we passed the Elco Theater with its rows of blinking lights and brightly lit marquee. I always tried to peer into the lobby, wondering if I could see anything that would help me understand why it was so sinful. The scent of popcorn that seeped out the door was always so delicious, and I dearly loved popcorn. The local radio station had a regular music program featuring a fellow who played "the big organ in the Elco Theater." The music sounded all right to me and didn't seem sinful. What was so bad about the Elco?

When I was a senior in high school, our entire class went on a trip to Washington, D.C., and New York City. Part of the planned itinerary was Radio City Music Hall, which I knew was a famous auditorium. Out of conscience, several of my closest friends decided not to go. I wanted to go, but I knew it was highly questionable in terms of Christian propriety because the Rockettes were on the program in addition to a Liz Taylor film, *Cat on a Hot Tin Roof*. I decided to go, rationalizing that I was actually going to see the famous auditorium and I couldn't help it if they had other things on the program. To carry through with my thinking, I slumped low in my seat while the Rockettes were doing their high-stepping numbers, and I tried not to watch too intently because that would be giving assent to their sinful activity. My feelings during the movie were no better, as I repeatedly reassured myself that I was really there to see the auditorium and that I therefore could not be held accountable for the contents of the movie. I even sat back and closed my eyes, trying to feel tired and sleepy to aid in distancing myself from the fearful guiltiness of being in such a questionable situation.

When my father took us to visit the Indiana State Penitentiary, we were each given a complimentary bag of chewing tobacco that had been packaged by the inmates. That little bag intrigued me for many years as I kept it in one of my dresser drawers and saw it whenever I opened the drawer. More than once I wanted in the worst way to open it and take a hearty bite out of it to see how it tasted, but my fear of sinning always stopped me. Sermons at church had clearly described the sinfulness of tobacco, and one visiting evangelist had enjoyed telling a story about riding in a car with a number of men when they stopped to give a ride to one of the local "sinners" who happened to have a cud of tobacco in his mouth. The evangelist humorously recalled that he watched the tobacco-chewing sinner become visibly distressed when he learned the parson was in the car. The sinner was so guilt-stricken in the minister's presence that with great determination and effort he swallowed his cud, much to the minister's amused delight. I knew, therefore, that taking a bite from that chewing tobacco would be a mistake I would regret. So I resisted my inner urges and never did sample its mysterious pleasures.

Sunday evening social scenes with other fellows often resulted in conflict and guilt for me, so I tended to back away from them, not knowing how to handle the situations. I was certain that buying something to eat on Sunday was very wrong, especially something as frivolous and unnecessary as a cold mug of root beer at the Goshen A&W on a hot summer evening. More than once I died inside when the group I was with pulled into the drive-in after we had been to a special church program somewhere and the car-hop came to take our order. I slumped in the back seat with guilty fear, looked out the window, or tried to pretend I was asleep or tired. When it was my turn to order, everyone looked at me. "I don't want anything," I muttered.

"Aw, come on Sloat! Don't you have any money? I'll pay for it! What do you want?"

I wanted a frosty mug of root beer, but the sense of sin was so strong that I knew I should resist. And many times I did, never saying what my true feelings were. I sat there in misery, not enjoying myself because of the agony of my inner feelings, and not free to join the fun that the other fellows were having. Somehow having fun with them would mean I was sanctioning this terrible activity. All the guys were from the same community or even from my church, so it always amazed me how they could feel so okay about it. Didn't they realize how wrong it was?

My thinking on this topic remained unchanged until I moved to Detroit and had to eat out on Sunday because I did very little cooking for myself. Even as a senior in college, I never bought anything on Sunday, although Sandy's hamburger stand was across from the school. In fact, I was appalled that a fellow ministerial student had so little conscience that he bought his supper there on Sunday night as he returned to campus from his church assignment. He usually came to our dorm to eat his hamburgers, and I remember telling him that it was better for him to go without food at all than to buy his fries and hamburgers at Sandy's on Sunday.

Sex and Guilt

Many Christians have difficulty putting their sexual feelings in perspective and channeling them properly. Cal, a gentle, Christian man in his forties, had been referred to me for therapy. He wrung his hands nervously as he talked, and he frequently glanced away to avoid eye contact as he slowly and cautiously began to empty his burdened heart. Growing up as an only child had been difficult for him, especially since he had a vision loss that was undiagnosed until the second or third grade. At first his teachers thought he was retarded, but he was actually quite bright. Socially, he was shy, and he felt unloved at home.

As he grew toward adolescence, he began regular masturbation as a form of giving himself good feelings, but he was overwhelmed with guilt that he tried to assuage through extensive Bible study. As this cycle continued into adulthood, even though he married, his guilt about not being able to stop was creating more and more pressure on him. The suffering he felt was quite real. He told me, "I have never been able to tell anyone about this before. It is so hard to talk about. In fact, I never thought I would tell anyone." Ironically, as a by-product of his vicious cycle, he gained a more detailed understanding of the Bible that aided him in his service through the church.

My adolescent sexual feelings resulted in a great deal of guilt, as well as fear that Christ might return while I was in the act of masturbating. Consistently, beginning at a young age, I was overcome with tremendous guilt that often lasted for two to three days. During this period of time I mentally berated myself, and I felt worthless and ashamed. For comfort I repeatedly prayed for forgiveness and studied Psalm 51, making David's plea my own. Yet experience told me that my sexual urge would return and I would go down in defeat, sinning again and again. I was told at church that true repentance meant not only that I was sorry, but that I was sorry enough not to sin again. Painfully, I knew I would.

Hebrews 10:26–27 added immensely to my fear: "For if we sin willfully after we have received the knowledge of the truth, there no longer remains a sacrifice for sins, but a certain fearful expectation of judgment, and fiery indignation which will devour the adversaries." Since I knew I had received the truth, and I also knew I had willfully sinned, I assumed it must mean I had committed the unpardonable sin, something I had been warned about in church. I listened carefully to sermons to discern more accurately what the unpardonable sin was in order to lessen the agony of my fear. Whenever I saw books in Christian bookstores on sex, I eagerly looked up the section relating to masturbation, hoping to find someone who would say it wasn't a sin. No one ever did. I was too afraid to talk to anyone about it. Dread filled my soul because I couldn't stop myself.

Young people often protest, "It's not fair. Why did God give me these strong sexual feelings and then tell me I can't do anything with them until I'm married? I don't understand it." Young people who give in to their sexual urges out of curiosity, peer pressure, or some other reason often find themselves in another vicious cycle, and this is particularly true if they find their sexual experiences enjoyable. The excitement and enjoyment increase their appetite, but the more they indulge, the more guilt tags close behind.

This results in one of the most difficult dilemmas Christian teenagers and adults encounter when they find themselves committing "sins" they enjoy. They feel inwardly torn because when they are honest with themselves, they have actually enjoyed their premarital or extramarital relationships and do not regret them. They feel guilty for becoming involved, and guiltier yet for enjoying it. *How can something wrong feel so good?* they wonder. If those "wrong" activities weren't enjoyable, it would be easier for them to turn their backs on them in disgust and assert, "I'll never do that again." But often the race is on, with passion winning out over reason and personal values. This can have disastrous results both emotionally and spiritually if the underlying issues aren't faced openly.

Church Services

Besides inducing fear and guilt, church services weren't very useful in a practical sense when I was growing up. There was minimal emphasis on the everyday realities of life as they related to Christianity. Sunday school lessons typically involved an Old Testament character whom my friends and I experienced as boring and irrelevant to our lives. The general emphasis seemed to be on conforming rather than on thinking through our position on a subject.

The Wednesday evening prayer meeting for youngsters was a miniature adult service. We sang songs, followed by "popcorn testimony meeting." Of course there were only ten or twelve youngsters, so it was difficult for peer-pressure reasons not to participate. There were a few standard sentences that practically everyone used, and then we sat down with apparent satisfaction at having fulfilled our Christian duty. Whether or not any of us really understood our testimony was beside the point.

The general emphasis at church seems to be on conforming rather than on thinking through our position on a subject.

It was the same with prayers. After the testimony time, we all knelt at our chairs to pray after the requests had been taken. Again, almost everyone's prayer was cut from the same cloth. The prayers usually covered the minister who had to prepare the sermon, the missionaries on faraway mission fields, the leaders in government, and the sick. Often if I was not the first one to pray, most of the good topics had already been taken by the others, and I worried about how I could pray for the same topic without using the same words that had already been said.

We also were not to be "of the world," although it was never clear what the "world" really was. From what I could figure out on my own, it generally meant one should not try to be rich. If money or success fell into one's lap without willfully trying for it, that was okay, but trying to make money and deliberately trying to be successful seemed to border on sin. Having expensive clothes and a fancy car, telling funny stories, and having a good time all seemed to be wrong somehow. The primary emphasis was on being totally dedicated to God and maintaining a serious, sober view of life. Whatever I wanted was not important. Genuine self-assertion was acceptable only if it were done on God's behalf.

Vocational Choice and Dedication

The point of not wanting for oneself was especially evident when the subjects of dedication and vocational choice were under discussion. Our church emphasized dedication, and Romans 12:1-2 was often quoted. Many altar calls were devoted to dedication, and the emphasis was usually related to missions and mission work. As mentioned earlier, I now realize that my Calvinist counterparts faced many of the same principles as they were growing up.

The impression is commonly given
that full-time Christian work is
the only praiseworthy vocational choice
in God's eyes, but that is untrue.

One of my biggest fears as a teenager was that God would call me to be a missionary to Africa. This fear was compounded by my inner feeling that when people dedicated their lives to God, He tested their dedication by directing them into a vocation totally opposite to their natural preferences. Or if He didn't do that, He would cause them to be physically paralyzed (my worst fear) to see if they really meant it when they said, "Thy will be done."

It also seemed that God's primary vocational interest was in full-time Christian work, the mission field in particular. A constant stream of missionaries came to our church showing color slides of mud huts, thatched roofs, people with leprosy, calabashes, and rows of native students wearing blue uniforms. Invariably, the missionaries all said the same thing: "The fields are white unto harvest. Come and labor with us." Laboring with them was the last thing I wanted to do, but I was afraid to even think it for fear God would hear me and pick me to go to Africa as a test of my faith. Never once did I hear speakers say that God called or even wanted people to be businessmen, lawyers, farmers, or construction workers. Consequently, the idea that God valued certain occupations above others gradually crystallized in my mind, and going to Africa as a missionary seemed to head that list. In descending order were ministers, missionaries, and general full-time Christian workers. Then there was room for people who elected to stay at home, but garnered some of God's approval by being Sunday school superintendents, deacons, or song leaders or by filling some other type of church position. After He had selected the people He wanted for His preferred vocations, the remaining Christians were free to choose among the lesser vocations that held little importance in the job hierarchy.

From my perspective, looking forward vocationally was not a pleasant task. Certainly I wanted God's approval, but I also knew I didn't want to go to Africa to get it. Being a minister didn't appeal to me because most ministers I knew were solemn, drove four-door sedans with blackwalls, and wore old, baggy suits. I desired more flash than that. From my vantage point on the farm, the only other vocational possibilities were teaching school, farming, or "working in town," whatever that meant.

I remember one particular dedication altar call at the conclusion of a missionary rally. It was a typical hot Indiana August afternoon, and I hadn't wanted to go in the first place. It seemed like such a waste of a perfectly good summer day when I didn't have to do farm work and would have preferred doing something fun, like riding my horse. My parents, of course, prevailed, and I reluctantly attended the service. At the close of the rally, intense pressure was put on the young people to go forward to at least make themselves available should God want to draw from the labor pool. In other words, going forward didn't mean I was promising to be a missionary, only willing to be. Giving in to the social pressure, I reluctantly went forward as I held my breath and secretly hoped that God wouldn't notice me. As the youthful crowd surrounded the altar, the speaker added to the pressure by asking adults in the congregation to come and stand behind each young person to symbolize support for the teen willing to go to the mission field. Instead of feeling supported, I felt as though I were being squeezed tighter and tighter into a choice with no alternative. With a great deal of relief, I survived the ordeal without being called to Africa, and I left the service hoping the matter wouldn't come up again.

Since that time I have come to what I think is a much healthier understanding of vocation. The Bible emphasizes that more important than the specific job we have is the type, or quality, of people we are. God wants us to love Him, love others, follow His leading, and be our own unique selves as we develop the particular talents He has given us. The vocation we have is only the setting in which we display our special qualities; being missionaries to Africa is not going to win God's favor if we aren't the right quality of people in the first place. I believe God wants quality people scattered throughout all areas of society and work, and He will guide those who are open to His leading.

False Self-Righteousness[1]

We usually can be fairly successful in mastering our particular church's list of sins, which gives us a false sense of being "pretty good" people. At one point in my life I was even certain that I seldom, if ever, sinned anymore because I thought I was behaving so well.

When we have focused on our external behavior at the expense of our internal being, we experience conflict when a thought, action, or feeling suddenly emerges that contradicts our self-righteous image. A "good Christian" suddenly finds himself in the middle of a sexual affair. A kind, self-sacrificing Christian woman unexpectedly lashes out in vicious anger toward her spouse. Stunned, she can't imagine the source of her intense emotion. We often are in utter shock when this happens, and the fight is on to overcome the negative feelings or thoughts because they threaten to tarnish our righteous self-image or, worse yet, push us into the pit of hell. Usually, we try to pray them away without success. Then we doubt our faith and feel we must be worse Christians than we originally dared believe because now our faith isn't working. We read the Bible for reassurance, but the only verses that stand out are the ones about lack of faith, the evil effects of anger, and the five virgins who didn't make it into the feast (see Matt. 25:1–13).

With no relief forthcoming, the vicious cycle continues. Either we repress and conceal our inner despair so that we can be enthused Christians, or we live very frustrated, depressed, conflict-filled lives.

Many of us Christians don't see the church as a source of healing, because we believe the church expects us to avoid the master list of sins and to accept its implications without question. More specifically, we are discouraged from asking questions, from expressing anger toward God, and from struggling within our own Christian lives. Consequently, those of us who struggle are left holding the bag because we have nowhere to go with the resentment we don't understand and the inner conflict we feel.

Since the church has been emphasizing outward behaviors and not the inner states of being, we're actually unacquainted with our true "sinful" natures, and we're afraid of our true inner emotions and motives when they appear unexpectedly. *Those sinful feelings are only supposed to happen to those who don't know Christ, those unsaved persons who are on the road to hell. This can't be me. I've been living by all the rules.* These are some of the thoughts that surge through our minds.

Fear and Obligation

Perhaps the most difficult and far-reaching problem is the motivation behind many Christians' behavior. It seems that the Christian life is usually presented as a package with three parts: "Sin" that requires "Salvation" that results in "Service" out of gratitude for being saved from the despair of sin in the first place. Perhaps this follows Paul's outline in the book of Romans, which has the most systematic theological explanation of any book in the Bible. Paul, writing to persons whom he had not personally met, attempted to give a thorough explanation of Christianity and spent seven chapters discussing sin, one chapter outlining salvation, three chapters describing how the Jewish people fit into God's plan, and just over three chapters describing Christian conduct and service (the last chapter and a half being items of personal interest). Similarly, many sermons emphasize sin for twenty-five minutes and devote five minutes to salvation. When this type of sermon is delivered Sunday after Sunday, Christians are often left drifting with no clear direction for spiritual growth.

In the evangelical church, it seems that most of us never actually "experience" the despair of sin because it is defined in terms of a list to follow instead of an inner state of being. As we examine the danger points present in the church, it is obvious that to drive home the point of sin, we are told we are no good, which reinforces negative self-esteem. Then to motivate us toward salvation, the imminent fear of hell is graphically portrayed to scare us toward heaven. Consequently, instead of reaching out to salvation from a genuine understanding of our sinful state and God's grace, many of us have been catapulted into salvation through fear. At the same time, we are given the impression that expressing any negative emotion is sin, so we feel it's wrong to protest against what is happening to us.

Instead of being chosen as a positive option, God becomes the choice by default. Instead of saying "I love God because He loved me first," many of us find ourselves saying "I had better love Him because He'll get me if I don't." Usually, that's an accurate conclusion based on the manner in which the gospel was presented. When fear propels us into salvation, however, it's difficult for us to drop that fear with all its implications and serve God (the third stage) with a relaxed, confident, grateful attitude. The fear that prompted many of us into salvation often continues as the foundation for our lives. It's a persistent, gnawing obligation to "Christian duty" in order to keep the ever-present fear at bay.

This sets the same conditions in the spiritual realm that Rollo May has observed in the psychological area of emotions.[2] In the name of God, fear is used to take a young person's freedom away by not letting him "sin," experience himself, or even freely choose salvation. Instead the attitude is "Let's scare them into the Kingdom." And as May has pointed out, taking freedom away results in anger and resentment, which can lead to self-pity and low self-esteem. The church spiritualizes away this problem by calling such inner suffering self-denial, carrying one's cross, or even suffering as Christ suffered for us. This completes the trap for the sincere Christian who goes round and round without understanding what really hit him and who wonders why his spiritual life is not abundant living. If this has been your experience, you are not emotionally or spiritually free. You are not your own person psychologically, and the church doesn't encourage you to be yourself spiritually, either.

With lives crisscrossed by underlying conflicts and based on a foundation of fear that prohibits thinking for ourselves, many of us well-intentioned Christians are headed for trouble without even knowing it. In the next chapter we'll look at what frequently happens at some point in our lives.

The Shock
When Life Falls Apart

One fellow commented after hearing about some of my struggles, "I have never had a crisis type of experience such as you have, but I do have some struggles, especially with the feeling that anything that's fun is wrong to do." Many Christians struggle in varying degrees, silently, never baring their souls to anyone because they fear that what they're experiencing is terribly wrong because they've never heard it discussed in church.

The courageous ones often seek out a psychologist because they feel safer in a therapy session than they do in church. For other Christians who have been following the rules, keeping traditions, and even feeling rather secure in their self-righteousness, an unexpected crash of everything they believe can catch them on their blind side as their world is turned upside down. This sudden turn of events generally comes unexpectedly and causes a great deal of confusion. This chapter is directed primarily to those of you who have been caught up short—and by surprise.

Crisis Experiences

Dawn is a slender, attractive woman in her mid-twenties. She and her equally young husband were seated on the couch in my office, seeking help for a serious marital problem. The youngest child in her family, Dawn attended an evangelical church all her life. Her family life was without serious problems as she was growing up, although she didn't have a close relationship with her mother, who apparently had difficulty dealing with her own feelings.

In general, Dawn grew up within a sheltered environment, typical of other youngsters in her rural community, and she accepted what she was taught without question. In fact, she learned to agree with the prevailing winds so that she would be accepted by others, and she had few ideas of her own. Unfortunately, neither her church nor her parents encouraged her to examine her beliefs.

Her relationship with her husband began when she was fifteen and he was eighteen. When Evert wanted to date Dawn, her initial reaction was negative, but she felt some sympathy for him and didn't want to hurt his feelings. Continuing her established pattern of going with the flow, she continued to say yes whenever he asked her out. Weeks accumulated into months, and before she knew it, she had dated him all through high school. As graduation neared and many of her girlfriends were becoming engaged, Dawn caught the marriage fever as well. She laid aside her true feelings—"After all, how could you *not* get married after going together for three years?" she said—and began to push for marriage. Evert, eager to settle into the security of a marriage relationship, was quite agreeable.

Secure at last in his new marriage, he continued his life, enjoying his hunting and fishing activities with his friends. At this point, his version of what happened is somewhat different from Dawn's. She insisted that he often left her alone at home with their child and didn't communicate with her. She also maintained that he made no effort to change, even though she expressed her feelings about the matter. Evert maintained that he never was "that bad," and

177

if she did communicate dissatisfaction, it was not loud enough to catch his attention.

Dawn, being easily persuadable and not too wise in the ways of the world, was befriended by an older fellow employee who was separated from his wife. Without realizing it, Dawn began to enjoy her conversations with this fellow and the attention he gave her. Since he didn't have a strong church background and was more tolerant of ideas and behavior than members of her church and family, she didn't feel compelled to live up to any expectations to be accepted by him. As time passed, they began to spend more time together until she suddenly found herself in his arms and sexually involved, in total contradiction to her stated Christian values. Needless to say, a crisis was at hand.

Harry, in his late fifties, was a pleasant, friendly man who was dragged into my office by his angry, frustrated wife. A Christian couple, they were no longer living together because the tension between them had built to an unbearable level. Harry had grown up in an evangelical home with a father who was in full-time Christian work, and he had been taught along the lines discussed in this book—with an emphasis on the second movement of renunciation. This was compounded by the fact that he had a quick temper. To avoid angry flare-ups, he learned to circumvent conflict by going along, or giving in. This took its toll on his relationship with his wife, as well as with friends, because he often said yes when he wanted to say no.

In recent years, Harry felt his wife had become more demanding on his time as the children left home, and he gradually felt trapped with an overweight woman who kept hounding him. To avoid a hassle, he found reasons to stay away from home. By chance he gradually became acquainted with a thirty-year-old divorced woman who had three children. To his surprise, he learned that he could carry on a stimulating conversation with her (his wife talked on a more superficial level), and before he knew it he found himself sharing not only her coffee but her bed as well.

Eventually, his family and his wife learned about it and began to pressure him to drop the other woman, for whom he had now developed some affection, and return to his wife. Admittedly, he was in inner turmoil, somewhat confused by this sudden change in his life and puzzled by his own behavior. In spite of his initial reluctance about coming to see me, he was quite open about his dilemma. "I don't really understand it," he said. "I know I can't promise to go back, but I'm not sure I want a divorce. I wasn't even looking for somebody else. With all the pressure people are putting on me, my usual pattern would be to go back. But I'm not going to do it this time. My oldest daughter is taking it the hardest. She says, 'Dad, you're going against everything you taught us.' And she's right. I don't understand. I feel the worst about hurting my mother. I'd give all kinds of money if I could keep that from happening."

These examples illustrate how conscientious Christians often depart suddenly from their beliefs. Affairs are especially troublesome because they are so tangible and real. The erring Christians' actions undeniably contradict their stated beliefs; the discrepancy between how they actually live and what they say they believe is quite evident. Because they are unable to reconcile their struggles and behavior with their righteous self-image, intense anxiety and confusion develop.

Granted, not all Christians find themselves in affairs. For some of you, an unexpected illness or tragedy can force feelings into the open that had been hidden during the good times. But in each case there are similarities; you don't understand what's happening, and you feel all alone. Often you don't know where to look for support or solutions, especially if your life has taken a definite turn toward sin.

My Personal Call

To illustrate my point and lend support to those of you who have experienced an unexpected crisis, let me describe my own crisis experience. It has had a profound effect on my life. At the beginning of this book, I briefly described my experience at Cobo Hall, which was part of the culmination of my crisis, not the beginning.

In addition to the experiences I have already described about growing up at home and in the church, there were several other significant events that shaped the direction of my life. As a sophomore in college, I was seated in the right rear section of the Elkhart High School auditorium for a Saturday night YFC rally. During the rally, as I observed the director on the stage with his slicked-back, black hair glistening in the spotlight, I felt a sudden, deep, overwhelming conviction that God wanted me to enter YFC as my life's work. The exact moment and scene in the auditorium are still etched in my mind, and the sense of call was so strong that I decided to drop my language major and switch colleges in order to obtain an education that was more suited to YFC work.

This sense of call continued to guide me through the rest of my college years and served as a foundation for my entry into YFC, where I fully planned to spend the rest of my life. In spite of my definite sense of calling, however, I was unsure of my abilities and felt God directed me to a Scripture passage that I adopted as the basis for my budding ministry:

> Then said I:
> "Ah, Lord GOD!
> Behold, I cannot speak,
>   for I am a youth."
> But the LORD said to me:
> "Do not say, 'I am a youth,'

180

For you shall go to all to whom
    I send you,
And whatever I command you,
    you shall speak.
Do not be afraid of their faces,
For I am with you to deliver you,"
    says the LORD.
Then the LORD put forth His hand and touched my
  mouth, and the LORD said to me:
"Behold, I have put My words in your mouth" (Jer.
  1:6–9).

Beginning a YFC Career

Armed with this Scripture and my call from God, I left the Indiana farm to attend YFC's directors' school, and then I headed for Detroit to begin my career in YFC. Actually, my thinking was a bit immature and naive as I began my new venture. One of my first honest shocks took place when I arrived in Detroit at the city Campus Life director's house, where I lived until I found my own accommodations. To my utmost surprise and dismay, I saw that he drove a two-door Ford sedan, and an automatic, no less. My concept of an on-the-ball YFC guy was someone who drove nothing less than a convertible with a "four on the floor," which was popular at the time. And to blow my mind further, a fellow club director owned a Chevy *wagon*, while another had an equally "shoddy" sedan. One of the club fellows was losing his hair, and one had a minor speech defect. How could this be? I thought Detroit YFC was supposed to be the epitome of "Where it's at!" Apparently my concept of YFC was based on the image I had of my hometown director, who had a flashy style. Nonetheless, I survived that initial blow and found my niche within the program, but not without some trying moments.

My first year was a bit of a struggle because in spite of my great ideas and the concepts I learned at directors' school, I really didn't know what I was doing. A year or two before my arrival, Al Kuhnle had placed Detroit on the cutting edge within YFC by developing a discussion-based personal development group for Christian kids that was called Teenitiative. More than once I pulled a fellow club director aside and asked in quiet desperation, "How is this Teenitiative supposed to work?" not realizing at the time the extent of my own narrow view of Christianity. I also had frequent periods of discouragement and self-pity that I didn't understand. In retrospect, I can see that I was going through depression, but I didn't realize that at the time.

This sense of uncertainty about myself and my methods set the stage for the next major influence that entered my life. Through a chain of events, Bill Gothard met with our staff as he was developing his ideas, and his material became the guiding force in my life for the next several years. My uncertainty soaked up his tangible, definite principles like a dry sponge in water. It became a joke among my friends. "Look out! Here comes Sloat with his red notebook," they'd say with a laugh. "He has God's plan for your life." And I truly thought I did.

Gothard's strong teaching against sexual sin, including masturbation, intensified the guilt I was already feeling, and I attributed much of my depression to my guilt. Finally, after concerted effort, I was able to control my sexual feelings, but my periodic depression continued. I had to find another reason for my depression, and this opened the way for other influences that came through my reading.

Although I had discovered Eugenia Price, Rosalind Rinker, C. S. Lewis, and J. B. Phillips and found their ideas useful in my work with the YFC teens, they didn't really enhance my own introspection. Reading Keith Miller's honest account of his personal experiences in *The Taste of New Wine*,[1] however, opened my eyes to a new way of looking at myself, and I also began to emphasize the points of honesty and mixed personal motives in people when I spoke with my club kids. Combined with this was my contact with a dynamic evangelist who came to Detroit as a special speaker for our clubs. Vaguely sensing that I was needing some answers for questions that were not clear to me, I looked to him with a great deal of respect, not only because he was intelligent and articulate, but also because he had a master's degree in psychology. That impressed me and told me he had some insight. In my journal I noted, "He is probably the closest to the kind of man I want to be." He also told me to read *Escape from Freedom*[2] and *The Mature Mind*.[3]

During my first several years in Detroit, the director had been primarily responsible for raising the money for salaries. In early 1966, though, he decided to share some of this responsibility, which meant I was supposed to contact people personally to explain my work and ask for money. Being faced with this prospect, I was forced into a slow process of self-examination regarding my motives and why I was working with kids.

The World Collapses

Actually, my world began to fall apart in several stages beginning in the spring and continuing in varying degrees of disarray for the next several years. But the most severe shock occurred the first time that I suddenly and unexpectedly saw my life with a clear focus. As I struggled with the pressure of having to raise money, something I was very uncomfortable doing, I suddenly realized that I didn't want to win teens for Christ as much as I enjoyed the entertainment aspect of the rallies and feeling important as a Campus Life director. My motives were not pure. I was in shock.

The image that came to my mind was a picture of myself

on a stage, pedaling a stationary bicycle connected to a generator that produced electricity to light a small bulb. The faster I pedaled, the brighter the bulb became. This identical arrangement, the bicycle and bulb but not the stage, was one I had seen at the Museum of Science and Industry in Chicago. I felt as though I had been pedaling for my entire life, and the harder I worked, the more people cheered, but I was tired and wanted to quit. If I slowed down, however, I feared the people would stop applauding. I honestly wanted to stop pedaling, fall off on the floor, and pleadingly ask the crowd, "Won't you please just like me for myself even if I don't pedal?" I didn't want to have to prove anything.

A day or so later, I happened to begin reading Fromm's book in which he describes the fear that is attached to the responsibility of personal freedom, and the fear of feeling alone and insignificant in oneself. Statements such as the following hit me with great force:

> The other side is the attempt to become a part of a bigger and more powerful whole outside of oneself, to submerge and participate in it. This power can be a person, an institution, God, the nation, conscience, or a psychic compulsion. By becoming part of a power which is felt as unshakably strong, eternal, and glamorous, one participates in its strength and glory. . . .
>
> In discussing the qualities required in a Nazi leader and the aims of education of leaders, he [Fromm is referring to a labor movement leader] writes: "We want to know whether these men have the will to lead, to be masters, in one word, to rule. . . . We want to rule and enjoy it. . . . We shall teach these men to ride horseback . . . in order to give them the feeling of absolute domination over a living being."[4]

Suddenly, as the result of having the experiences described above and reading Fromm's book, I began to look at my entire past as though I had put on a badly needed new pair of glasses. With overwhelming clarity, I saw my deep feelings of insignificance extending into my adolescence and my pattern of attaching myself to bigger and more powerful wholes outside myself to make myself feel more important. The statement about the horses especially struck me, because I had always prided myself on being the only person who could handle Ginger, my extremely high-spirited mare, when I lived on the farm. Was my sense of tough, cowboy pride only the result of my inner feelings of weakness and need to dominate a horse? I was stunned.

And I had lived and worked in a funeral home, which also gave me a special sense of importance in the eyes of other college students because it was such an unusual living situation. At my church college, seven other fellows and I lived in dorm number "IV," so one of the guys cleverly created the name Ivymen for us. Not only did this give us more status than the rest of the dorms, but we also functioned as the prestigious group on campus. Finally, I was working with YFC in Detroit, the largest rally in the country and considered to be on the cutting edge. I could hardly believe it. I was really nothing in myself; I had to have something special around me to feel important. I believed God had called me into a ministry to save kids, and suddenly it was all a joke. I didn't care about some kid's soul—I just needed to feel important. *What do I do now?* I worried in quiet desperation. The fact that I had never known what it was like to talk to someone on such a personal level gave me an intense sense of jeopardy.

I considered talking to my boss but decided it would be too risky. On a Tuesday evening, I met with my best friend from college; he had moved to Detroit. We drove to a restaurant near the office, and with hesitant fearfulness I carefully explained my new insights. To my chagrin, he agreed with me. *Oh, no. It really must be true,* I thought. I was completely miserable and frustrated.

In desperation, I called the YFC director under whom I

had worked in college and to whom I looked up as my role model. Fortunately, he was pastoring a church in the Detroit area, and we arranged a meeting. As I talked to him, I again bared my frightened heart. Of all the people I spoke with during my crisis, he understood me the most. He said he had gone through a similar experience, and the answer he had found was to "get off the stage." I was unable to comprehend the total meaning of his point, but his understanding support was helpful.

Still trying to make sense out of my dilemma, I decided to call the young evangelist with the master's degree. After many calls to various people, I finally located him somewhere in New Jersey. "Jimmy, you've got to help me. I don't understand what's going on. I've been reading this book you recommended, and I'm seeing all kinds of stuff in myself I don't understand. What do I do?" He gave me two pieces of advice. The first one did no good, and I couldn't understand how it applied to my situation. He told me to "spend time alone in the Word, especially the first part of Acts." Second, he suggested that I contact a well-known psychologist in Flint who could help me "find" myself. I rejected that notion outright. *I'm no nut*, I thought to myself. *Can't anyone tell me what's going on?* I hung up the phone and felt even more alone.

The following months were characterized by ups and downs in my moods. I gained some new insight through reading, and then my depression returned. But I kept most of my feelings to myself since I had no one I could really trust with my frightful feelings. At times I felt as if I must be going crazy, so I tried to draw support from Keith Miller's account of his confused, crazy feelings. The predominant thought that came to my mind was, *I wish I had never been born! I don't want to be alive! I don't want to live forever. That's too long. I feel trapped. God put me here, and I'm forced to make a choice between two places I don't want—heaven or hell. I don't want either one. I didn't ask for all this. Who cares about what I want?* I pictured life as being on an escalator. I had been placed on it by no choice of my own, and the slowly moving escalator would eventually dump me off at the top into one of two bins—heaven or hell. My only decision was between the lesser of the two evils.

Then came the Teen Fair I described in Chapter 1. I didn't want to be there. I couldn't care about the lost kids, yet I had to act as though I did. I became very depressed and tired—tired of living and tired of God. *Why not stop the world and let me off?* I thought. There could be no doubt that Christianity was true, yet I had difficulty with the basics of it. I didn't like it. It was at this point that crashing my speeding Mustang into the sunbathed concrete pillars along I-94 began to have some appeal, but what would that accomplish? It would only speed my arrival at the top of the escalator.

Following my unsettling experience at the Teen Fair, I knew I had to make a decision about continuing with YFC. I resigned a few weeks later.

Common Themes

In my own experience and in the lives of those who have consulted me regarding personal crises, several common themes are apparent. Usually there is shock and surprise at the emotions and thoughts that have suddenly appeared, because they are so contradictory to past experiences and values. This causes anxiety and fear in addition to the sudden increase in tension caused by the release of pent-up emotions. Also, a feeling of "going crazy" often occurs. Generally, this is not a fact that is going to happen, however. As our habits of keeping unwanted thoughts and feelings under control are being pushed under by the escaping feelings, there's a sense of having less control, but most of us survive it even though we have strong doubts at the time.

When life falls apart, there is usually shock
and surprise at the emotions and thoughts
that appear suddenly, because they are so
contradictory to past experiences and values.

People often feel alone because they are embarrassed about their sexual sin, their apparent lack of faith, or their inner confusion that may lead others to think they are unusual or weird. A difficult but important task is finding someone who can lend support and understand the intense inner turmoil that is felt when such a crisis hits. The next chapter should also help you to better understand why things tend to fall apart eventually.

C H A P T E R   1 2

Understanding Why
Things Fall Apart

I sat in the conference room surrounded by psychiatric nurses, nursing students, occupational therapists, activity therapists, several social workers, a psychologist, and a psychiatrist. We were in the main building at Pine Rest Christian Hospital, a large private psychiatric hospital, and I was a member of the psychiatric team, completing the internship requirements for my master's degree at Michigan State. We met weekly in the "Bamboo Room," as we called it, to discuss the progress of and treatment strategy for the patients who were under the team's care. Many times the psychiatrist, who was the team leader, invited new patients into the meeting to become acquainted with the staff who would be working with them. This struck me as a rather formidable task for the new patients, who I suspected were already overwhelmed with personal anxiety without meeting a large group of strangers.

On this particular day, a new patient in his late thirties was led into the room to meet his team. The psychiatrist, who had already met the fellow, asked him to briefly describe his personal situation. He was a sincere, evangelical Christian who had begun to experience some personal anxiety and mounting confusion over the preceding months, but he was unclear about the cause of his difficulty. As he described his confusion, he made a point of saying that a few weeks before he was admitted to the hospital, a team of young people from a Christian college had visited his church, and he had made an earnest recommitment to Christ at one of the services in an attempt to resolve his distress. Even as he described this experience, he seemed bewildered by the fact that in spite of his sincere commitment to Christ, here he was, sitting in a psychiatric hospital. Apparently sharing my observations, the psychiatrist made what I perceived to be an accurate but insensitive remark. Somewhat curtly, he retorted, "It looks like your rededication to Christ didn't do you any good!"

No Quick Cures

This fellow's sincere effort to handle his personal emotional crisis through a renewed spiritual commitment is a common approach for evangelical Christians who "suddenly" find themselves in trouble, whether it is an affair, intense guilt, vague anxiety, unknown fears, or the appearance of painful childhood memories that had been forgotten for years. This sets a trap for them, as we saw in Chapter 10, where they not only have this problem but also find that their Christian faith is unable to overcome it. With no real relief forthcoming, the vicious cycle continues.

To move out of this confusion, the Christian who is suddenly in crisis needs to see the situation as it really is. Even though it often may seem at the time that the feelings suddenly came out of nowhere, an examination of one's life usually reveals that there was an accumulation of experiences, emotions, and situations that gradually led to the crisis. It is a culmination of emotional and lifestyle patterns that began developing in childhood and finally burst into the open. This is especially true for a Christian who was taught from childhood to push normal feelings aside and practice premature renunciation (remember the character Julie described in Chapter 9). And just as it took many years to reach this point, it also will take time to move past it.

"A great crisis experience of Jesus Christ,
as important and eternally valuable as it is,
is not a shortcut to emotional health.
It is not a quickie cure for personality problems."

Even in my struggles, I was looking for some type of spiritual cure for my doubt and turmoil, suspecting my level of commitment was the culprit. I finally learned through my experience the truth of Seamands's statement:

> We preachers have often given people the mistaken idea that the new birth and being "filled with the Spirit" are going to automatically take care of these emotional hangups. But this just isn't true. A great crisis experience of Jesus Christ, as important and eternally valuable as this is, is not a shortcut to emotional health. It is not a quickie cure for personality problems. . . . What I am saying is that certain areas of our lives need special healing by the Holy Spirit. Because they are not subject to ordinary prayer, discipline, and willpower, they need a special kind of understanding, an unlearning of past wrong programming, and a relearning and reprogramming transformation by the renewal of our minds. *And this is not done overnight by a crisis experience* (emphasis added).[1]

Seeing Clearly

In my work with people, I try to give them what no one gave me when I was going through my turmoil through the years: an understandable explanation of what they're experiencing so they can stop pressuring themselves to find a quick solution in order to avoid being a spiritual disaster. Even though I know they won't be able to understand all that I tell them, at least I'll have given them a framework they can use to make sense out of what's happening to them. I often say something similar to the following when a person is experiencing this fearful confusion:

"I hear what you're saying, and I know that now much of what you're experiencing doesn't make sense to you, but I have found through the years that once we're able to understand things more clearly, they're easier to handle—they don't scare us as much because we know what's going on. Because I've been through something similar to your experience and have listened to many people's struggles, I can see the entire picture more clearly than you can.

"First of all, what you're experiencing is a normal reaction for someone in your situation, and it doesn't mean you're a bad Christian, even though you may feel like it at times. What you're experiencing is an emotional problem because of the way you grew up, not a spiritual problem. And it's going to take some time for you to get through it, but that's okay. It took you twenty-six years to get here, and you won't get over it in three weeks. So, plan on the fact that it will take time.

"It does feel scary to say out loud what you're feeling, and that can be expected because you've had very little practice putting what you feel into words. God will not get angry with you for saying what you feel. I used to be afraid of saying things out loud, but I finally realized that God knows what I'm thinking anyway, so why not say it?

God will not get angry with you
for saying what you feel.
He already knows.

"Also, I don't want you racking your brain trying to find a quick, spiritual answer to this, because it just won't happen. Growing up as you did, you were taught to put yourself last and hide your feelings in order to gain approval. In effect, your parents and your church taught you to lie about your true feelings so that you could get approval from them. As a result, you developed a closet filled with feelings that you felt were wrong, and you weren't allowed to examine them or talk about them so you could understand them. You followed all the rules and thought you were a really good Christian, and now it blows you away because what you're feeling doesn't fit the picture you had of yourself. That's why it seems so confusing. You keep fighting it and saying, 'But these aren't my feelings. I don't feel this way!' You probably have felt this way for many years but didn't know it because you had trained yourself to think and feel what you were supposed to feel. Now you feel what you really feel, and it no longer works to pretend it isn't there. It shocks you because it seems so different from the picture you had of yourself. That's okay, too.

"You also appear to be a sensitive person. Your feelings are easily stirred, and this makes life more complicated because sensitive people have a harder time in life. Because you feel so much, you have more to handle than less-sensitive people do. As we go through the next several months, there will be times when you'll feel as if you're going to die, or else you'll wish you would, because the tension and anxiety will be so great. You'll live through it, even though you don't believe you will. And that's the secret. By living through it, you realize those feelings won't kill you, and you no longer need to be afraid of them.

"What you really want is the same thing we all want. It's simple, yet it's difficult. You just want to be loved and accepted for who you are without having to prove anything to anybody. You really want people to accept you as you are.

"For a while, you'll find that as you come here and talk, you'll leave feeling worse, which is normal. We usually think that after talking, *I should feel better,* but a part of feeling better is first feeling worse as we remember and feel all the painful memories we had forgotten. So when that happens to you, it's a *good* sign. It means you're making progress, even though it may be hard to believe.

"Let me give you a couple of suggestions as you go through this. First, there's a lot going on inside you, so now is not the time to make any major decisions. The world will go on without your trying to change it right now, and God will take care of things. What you'll be doing over the next few years is developing balance. You've had too much practice putting yourself last and everybody else first, so you need to learn how to put yourself first in a proper way so you can eventually do both. Then, when you do put others first, it will be because you want to, not because you 'have to.'

Once you understand your family,
you'll be ready to look more clearly
at the spiritual part of your life.

"And don't be surprised at what you may feel. You'll probably go from being afraid to being angry to perhaps feeling really nasty and rotten. But those are feelings that everyone else has, too, so don't put yourself down when it happens. What you're doing is becoming friends with your feelings instead of being afraid of them. The fear of God is probably connected to some things in your life that you don't understand now, but as we talk about it, it will become clearer and will make more sense. I'm sure that a lot of what you're feeling is connected to experiences you've had in your family, and we'll be looking at them eventually, too. I'll be giving you some things to read that will help you make sense out of what you're experiencing. Once you understand more about your family, you'll be ready to look more clearly at the spiritual part of your life."

People have often asked me, "How long is it going to take me to get all this figured out?" My answer is usually the same, "I can't say. It's hard to put a time limit on something like this. I do know that the more you try to avoid what you really feel, the longer it will take. But it usually takes longer than we think it will." As I have observed people through the years, I can say that a major upset in a person's life can take as little as one year to straighten out, or more than five. It's hard to predict because the emotional healing process can't be speeded up through voluntary effort. If you're looking for some direction, the next chapter has a number of suggestions you can consider.

PART FOUR

Finding Personal Peace and Freedom

CHAPTER 13

Sifting through the Past:
A New Beginning

Beth was a pretty woman in her early twenties who was having trouble with her husband. Actually, the problems were within herself, but they were showing up in the marriage. As we examined the patterns of her life, it became apparent that she had grown up in an evangelical home and had a mother who was a very active, dominant, "D" type of person. She kept her children under close control and held the reins on Beth quite closely. Her father was more submissive, or an inactive, weak type of personality who adapted to his wife's domination. In an attempt to counsel his daughter, who was contemplating divorce, he admitted that he, too, had considered leaving his strong-willed, dominant wife, but he had decided to stick it out because it was "the right thing to do."

Complications

Beth was well behaved during high school because she had little choice, and her personality was not strong enough to buck her mother. After high school, she attended a state university several hundred miles away from her home, and for the first time in her life she tasted freedom. However, having lived under her mother's iron hand, she had no experience in using freedom wisely. In the permissive environment of the university, she went wild, at least in comparison to how she had grown up. From her point of view, it was great fun. Psychologically, she was in delayed revolt because her mother had discouraged any rebellion while she was living at home. Not understanding that revolt was helping Beth to grow up, her panicked mother forced a sudden halt to her activities by making her quit school and move back home. She also scheduled a number of meetings with the minister, and together they pointed out the error of her ways. This combined outpouring of disapproval from a high "D" mother and the pastor was overwhelming to Beth; she gave up her fight and resubmitted to her mother's rules.

Two Methods

When we encounter problems, we must find a method that brings realistic relief, clearer personal understanding, and appropriate long-term benefit. Although this book is not intended to provide a detailed, step-by-step approach to emotional healing, there are useful, general principles that I'll describe to you.

In Beth's case, her mother and the minister used a method that worked for the moment—that is, Beth stopped her wild behavior—and it appeared that she had settled down. But the story didn't end as they had planned. Actually, their method of dealing with Beth's struggles was inappropriate and harmful to her. As mentioned earlier, a spiritual crisis experience is not the answer to the confusion that befalls people, and it was not the solution for Beth.

Working our way out of confusion requires effort, a serious commitment to honest soul-searching, and a willingness to try new ways of believing and acting.

Working our way out of confusion requires effort, a serious commitment to honest soul-searching, and a willingness to try new ways of believing and acting. There are basically two methods we can use to accomplish this effort. One is to try to figure things out on our own through reading, thinking, self-analysis, and discussions with friends. Friends, however, may discourage such open honesty because they don't understand. This approach has its problems, because when we're experiencing confusion, we often are unsure of the direction to take, and by following our noses we can meander down paths that lead nowhere.

This was the approach that I took, partly by choice, but also out of necessity because I was unable to find anyone who could explain to me what was happening. Also, when my inner feelings overwhelmed me in the sixties, self-help books and counseling services in the community were nonexistent compared to what is available today.

The second method is to seek out the assistance of someone who can provide wise counsel, preferably a Christian psychologist, social worker, psychiatrist, or pastor who understands the particular struggles that face the second-, third-, and following-generation Christians. Author Scott Peck's statement that "genuine psychotherapy is a legitimate shortcut to personal growth which is often ignored"[1] is certainly true, because it can save people from needless meandering on their own and speed the development of proper personal growth.

Unfortunately, there are instances when counseling doesn't help for various reasons. In Beth's case, her mother (not Beth) had sought the counseling for her, and the pastor may not have understood what was actually taking place in her emotional development. Either of these points could have reduced the counseling's effectiveness.

Purpose of Searching

Regardless of the method used to search out personal patterns, the goal is the same: to gain a clearer understanding of our lives and determine what can be done to improve them. At this point we begin to pick up the threads from earlier chapters, because searching for patterns means looking at the three primary areas in which the danger points occur to see how they fit together to form a complete picture—the type of personality one has, the nature of one's family, and the particular emphasis of church training.

These patterns can have several forms. Some people have experienced danger points in all three areas by having sensitive personalities and parents who used fear and guilt to control them while they attended a legalistic church that also emphasized fear of God to motivate people. Persons who have been on the receiving end of all three areas simultaneously will definitely have deeper struggles than others who have experienced only one or two of the danger point areas. Even sensitive children who grow up in homes in which the family attends a hellfire type of church have fewer difficulties if the parents are warm, accepting, and encouraging people who don't use the same fear tactics as the church.

As mentioned earlier, some of you may have difficulty understanding any of this because you have had positive experiences both at home and at church. If so, be thankful and continue with your life. When I mentioned the title of this book to my minister friend's wife, she reacted by physically shrinking away from me. The notion that growing up in a Christian home could be dangerous was totally unexpected and foreign to her. Her family and early church experiences were so totally positive that it was extremely difficult for her to understand the struggles that many Christians have.

An Environment for Searching

If we want our searching to be successful, we must do it in a proper environment. Searching for patterns and expressing emotions are not armchair exercises; we can't simply read, think, and analyze by ourselves. Thinking about our feelings without expressing them only makes the tension worse. We must express what we feel out loud to another person to find relief, whether the issue is a minor one or a major one. The basic ingredient in this proper environment is a relationship in which we feel safe and free to express verbally all the emotions we've been keeping to ourselves, a relationship in which we won't be judged or criticized. What we need is the security of knowing that someone cares and won't reject us for what we think or feel. Sometimes this can be a spouse, and in the security of a marriage two people can support and encourage each other in exploring their inner feelings as they search for patterns in their lives. This may also be a close friend or even a parent. The important point is the quality and security of the relationship.

My wife has been this special person in my life. With her, I really have *felt* loved. She had been trained as a psychiatric nurse and had conducted psychotherapy, so she understood emotions and people's struggles. For many years she was my chief listener as over and over again I talked, cried, got angry, and was sometimes silent as I struggled with my inner frustrations and depressions. It was because of her persistent and often demanding support that I learned to take the risk of saying what I really felt. She continued to love me, and the sky didn't fall in on me.

There are times when we are unable to find the type of relationship we need in our circle of family or friends because they are too close to us and can't see our situation objectively. Friends and family often have a hard time listening because they want to give their opinions about our feelings rather than just listen. For this reason, we may need to find a professional person who has been trained to listen and give direction, especially if we are dealing with heavy, confusing emotions.

We also need someone who can help us gain a clearer perspective of ourselves and what's happening. *Am I the only one who feels this way? Why is this happening to me? Am I going crazy? Am I really a bad person? Am I seeing things correctly, or are things not as bad as they seem to be? Is there life for me on the other side of this mountain of anxiety and emotion I see before me?* These are some of the questions that go through our minds, crying out for answers.

In this safe relationship, we can begin to examine what we feel and the ideas we have about ourselves, correct wrong conclusions we have drawn, and so on. We also need to experience the acceptance of another person after we have dared say all those terrible things we've been hiding. This is especially true when we have grown up believing that we have to behave and feel only the "right things" in order to be loved. This is a very important point, and we can only experience this acceptance once we take the risk of sharing our inner secrets. Incidentally, we don't have to share our secrets with lots of people. Sharing with just one other person is enough.

Obstacles in the Search

One of the first obstacles we encounter as evangelical Christians in the process of examining personal feelings and patterns is the fear of personal honesty. For years Terri had learned to push her true feelings aside and never voice her anger or any other negative thoughts about God and parents. Never defending herself, she was continually being pushed around, first by her father when she was a child and later by others even though she was an adult. This treatment further lowered her self-esteem. As she continued her sessions with me, she gradually became more comfortable exposing her feelings. One day she uttered a critical remark that seemed to simply fly out of her mouth. With a suddenness that startled me, she instantly clapped her open-palmed hand over her mouth in an apparent attempt to stuff the unwelcomed remark back into her subconscious and block any other honest remarks that might have been lurking there.

For the person who has been taught to be the passive, model child, hiding all his negative feelings to gain love and approval, it seems quite dangerous to think, let alone say out loud, thoughts that seem contrary to what is expected. When my world began crashing down around me in Detroit, this was one of the first difficulties I experienced. But because my inner feelings were so strong, I finally had to acknowledge them in spite of my reluctance. Such reluctance is also common. We generally try to avoid things that are uncomfortable until we realize we have no further choice but to face the truth.

Two thoughts finally helped me with this. First, I realized that God knows what I'm thinking even though I somehow had felt that as long as I didn't say my thoughts out loud, He wouldn't know them or hold me responsible. Actually, this insight brought some relief, because it removed the burden of trying to hide my unacceptable thoughts from Him. It also is consistent with the Scripture, "If we say that we have no sin, we are only fooling ourselves, and refusing to accept the truth. But if we confess our sins to him, he can be depended on to forgive us and to cleanse us from every wrong. [And it is perfectly proper for God to do this for us because Christ died to wash away our sins.]" (1 John 1:8–9 TLB).

A second insight helped me with my honest feelings of anger toward and rebellion against God. I had been taught that I had to believe in Christ to be saved from my sins, yet I didn't feel that I had committed any sins to be saved from. But I didn't want to believe and didn't want God, either. I was in a circle of trying to keep God off my back by doing things for Him and punishing myself. Like the suddenness of turning on a light in a darkened room, the truth of Romans 3:11 struck me: "There is none who understands; / There is none who seeks after God." God *expected* me to not like Him. God had known it all along. He just wanted me to realize it. I had been fooling myself. What a relief! There was no longer a reason to keep doubts away from Him. He knew all about them anyway. Now I handle such feelings by openly admitting them to God, saying, "I have this feeling, and I know You probably don't like it. But it is there, and I ask You to forgive me for it. I don't understand it and don't quite know what to do about it. I am willing to have You help me."

The second obstacle is similar to the first, but it has a different implication. As we explore our maps, or personal patterns,[2] we inevitably begin to look at our childhood experiences that have influenced us. For sensitive people, this almost invariably includes hurts that we have suffered at the hands of our parents, even though they had no intentions of hurting us. Hurt is usually accompanied by anger toward the person who has done the hurting, and here lies the problem. Christians first of all hit the obstacle of "I am not supposed to have angry feelings." And then once we admit our anger, we feel guilty for being angry with our parents because we have been taught to "honor thy father and thy mother." Many persons have sat in my office, struggling with the pain of their childhoods, and it is obvious that their parents have hurt them, some in quite unfair, insensitive ways. Observing their reluctance to genuinely spit out their anger, I comment about their hesitation. "But I really shouldn't feel this way!" they cry out. "It just isn't respectful, you know. We're supposed to honor our parents. And what I'm feeling isn't very honoring!"

The guilt produces yet another problem to be tackled in addition to the original hurt. The struggle is a familiar one to me because I experienced it myself as I began to feel and express the hurt and anger I had regarding my parents. I actually felt as though I were sinning. I finally decided that pretending I didn't feel the anger was useless for the reasons cited above and, further, that getting my feelings out of my system was not sinful or "dishonoring" because I was doing it for my own mental health with a person I trusted, as opposed to engaging in vicious, careless gossip with intentions of harming my parents.

I asked a colleague of mine who has training in both psychology and theology if the commandment about honoring parents applied to the point under discussion. His opinion was that it did not prohibit such therapeutic expression and was not a point to be used as a child-rearing principle to "keep children in line." Instead, he viewed it as a concept to aid in establishing social order, maintaining respect and care for the parental generation by being supportive as they advance in years.

Christians who keep their inner hurts and anger
to themselves for fear of disobeying the
fifth commandment
are doing themselves a tremendous disservice and
are furthermore preventing themselves
from gaining a true appreciation of their parents.

I have concluded that Christians who keep their inner hurts and anger to themselves for fear of disobeying the fifth commandment are doing themselves a tremendous disservice and are furthermore preventing themselves from gaining a true appreciation of their parents. Before some one misunderstands me, let me say that I am not advocating that you go to your parents and dump your stored-up childhood anger on them. That's not going to help the situation for you or your parents. A proper method to handle these feelings with parents will be discussed in Chapter 15. My point here concerns the need to appropriately vent these feelings in order to put them to rest and move on to a more mature level of personal functioning. I believe God understands this.

Common Patterns
of Struggling Christians

Let's return to our story about Beth who had resubmitted to her mother's control. Although she didn't understand it at the time, she had been deprived of the opportunity to become her own person, and under pressure she returned to being "Mom's person," which was her pattern during childhood and adolescence. As Mom's person living at home again, she decided that since she was unable to go to college, she might as well marry. She met a handsome, young Christian fellow, and he seemed to fit all the criteria that Mom wanted for her daughter's husband. Although Beth had honest moments of doubt, even as she walked down the aisle on her wedding day, she tried to dismiss them. Everything looked okay in principle, at least, and doing what Mom wanted instead of what she wanted was normal for her. Bucking the system by showing independence only caused more trouble, as her previous experiences at school had clearly demonstrated. So she married, believing that somehow it would eventually work out.

Stifled Rebellion Reappears

As the years passed, her interest in her husband slowly diminished, and as other stresses developed she became involved with another man. Although this second relationship upset her because it was contradictory to her Christian values, she also found it more satisfying than her marital relationship. As we discussed her current frustrations, it became apparent that her trouble had begun in her parents' home. Her mother had interfered with her development by insisting on having control over Beth and making decisions for her instead of allowing her to think for herself or develop her own viewpoint. She continued to do this through Beth's teen years, when Beth should have been developing her ability to make appropriate decisions. As a result, Beth's adolescence was extended beyond the adolescent years, and this pattern set her up for the big crash in her marriage.

As we worked together in therapy, I did not tell her she had to break off her relationship with the other man. Usually when people come to see me, they have many people telling them what to do: "Break off that affair!" "Get your heart right with God and everything will fall into place!" They don't need me to preach platitudes at them. If simple answers were effective, the struggling Christian would have accomplished the needed changes without me. My training as a psychologist tells me to help people realize what's taking place in their lives, not make their decisions for them. Besides, I don't know when they will be able to let go of the affair, but I do know that if it were so easy to discontinue, they would do so. I have confidence that God is able to work, and He can bring the eventual change in their hearts. It is the Holy Spirit's job to convict others of sin, not mine. My responsibility is to be caring and supportive. I also realize that people who are forced out of an affair before they are ready to do so are pushed into premature renunciation, the source of another problem.

Beth, similar to others who have consulted with me, was struggling with her conscience because she knew God's teaching about marital fidelity, but she also knew the intense emotional storm in her inner being that she could not extinguish upon command. So I listened and helped her understand what was happening in her life.

As her therapy progressed, Beth realized that she had married her husband not because she actually loved him but because she was caught up in the pattern of following Mom. In essence, it wasn't her choice at all because she was still living in the second stage of premature renunciation, having been deprived of the first stage of self-assertion and learning to make her own decisions. She had grown up living in the second movement, being trained in the same manner as Julie in the child's booklet described earlier.

Perhaps you're wondering how things worked out for Beth. For reasons she didn't fully explain, she discontinued her therapy with me, although I suspected that her family didn't like what she was learning about herself. I subsequently took a position in another town and eventually lost contact with her, so I never learned the final outcome of her situation.

Extended Adolescence

Instead of acknowledging young people's need to rebel in order to reach maturity, the church community generally sets up a system that attempts to extend adolescence past the "dangerous" stage in hopes that the teens will settle down and never get into trouble. This system generally becomes more apparent as children enter high school, and it is a spin-off from danger points listed earlier.

Instead of acknowledging young people's need to rebel in order to reach maturity, the church community generally sets up a system that attempts to extend adolescence past the "dangerous" stage.

Most of us know that adolescence is a difficult period as young people make the transition from childhood to adulthood. Rebellion is often part of adolescence, as teenagers throw aside the notions and values of their parents in order to sort them out and eventually emerge with solid values that are their own. This process is usually a difficult one for parents, especially Christian ones who fear any signs of revolt in their children.

To handle their concerns, parents (and frequently the church) often have a set of rules for their kids to follow (including the master list of sins), and they carefully supervise to ensure that the rules are followed. Youngsters are discouraged from questioning or challenging what they are taught, dating is monitored closely, and any tendency toward questionable activity or adolescent experimentation resembling rebellion is quickly squashed.

Having an apartment is often discouraged for young people who don't go to college. Most Christian parents prefer to keep their children at home until they are "safely married" and beyond the rebellion stage. Somehow parents believe that marriage places their children in a more secure position. Other parents send their teenagers to their favorite Christian colleges that have the same sorts of rules and regulations as the parents. They're basically asking the schools to continue as substitute parents who keep the kids in line. With this type of supervision and training, adolescence can easily continue to age twenty-two, when young people graduate from college. Consequently, since they have never rebelled or matured, they are actually functioning at an emotional level of fifteen or sixteen years of age.

This situation is further complicated by the fact that many Christian young people marry during this extended adolescence. When they finally begin to grow up and understand themselves, many find themselves in trouble, wondering why they married their spouse, angry because they have missed out on many singles' activities, and so on.

Suddenly, the Christian parents who so carefully extended their child's adolescence experience a divorce in the family and are stunned by it. Many times I have counseled women in their late twenties who married as teenagers, and now with several children they have suddenly realized that they have never had a job, lived in an apartment with other young women, or gone to college. The dilemma is intense as they realize how difficult it is to be single and eighteen when they actually are twenty-eight with a husband and two children. In my experience, this pattern of extended adolescence is almost always present in the life of a person who suddenly ends up in turmoil as an adult.

Before you misunderstand, let me underscore that I am not suggesting revolt for revolt's sake. The rebel who lives in a perpetual state of rebellion becomes a nuisance or danger to others while his own life revolves in an empty cycle. The purpose of rebellion, and I am using the term in a loose sense, is to develop a clearer sense of oneself as a separate individual, to try out different ways of doing things to learn which ones fit and are most effective, to learn to think one's own thoughts, and to make one's own decisions and learn from the consequences, whether good or bad. Part of this process involves questioning the values and beliefs that parents have taught.

It's obvious that well-intentioned parents can give poor advice. Remember Stan, whose father taught him to distrust women? Too often evangelical parents attempt to "protect" their children by making all the decisions, as Beth's mother did. Although this is necessary when children are very young, children should gradually be allowed and even encouraged to assume responsibility for personal decisions and opinions. Too often parents not only maintain the decision-making power for themselves, but also make their children feel so guilty about questioning their judgment that the children are afraid to challenge their parents' viewpoints. This parental stance prevents young people from maturing as separate individuals, and it makes it likely that the kids will have hollow beliefs that can collapse under pressure.

Following my multimedia presentation on this subject to a support group for divorced people, a woman in her late twenties approached me and asked a question that reflected definite insight. "How can I help my two children who are eight and ten become their own persons so they don't go through what I did?" she asked. We briefly discussed the steps she was taking to help her children develop their own points of view, and then she explained the background to her question. "I grew up in a rather strict home and got married when I was eighteen."

"Did you get married to get away from home?" I queried.

"Yes, I believe I did," she replied. "In fact, I never became my own person while I was living at home, and I married and simply became someone's wife. I lived that way for almost ten years. Now that I'm divorced I can see all this, and I'm finally working at becoming who I am. That's why I don't want my children to go through what I did."

Marriage is not a magical filter
that screens out the dangerous potential
in a person's life.

I knew nothing about this young woman's family, but her brief story highlights the disastrous consequences that can take place when young people don't become their own persons. Further, getting married doesn't mean that a person has passed the danger zone. The dangers quite obviously follow a person straight into marriage; marriage is not a magical filter that screens out the dangerous potential in a person's life. I'm sure you have experienced the truth of this in your own life or have seen it in the lives of others.

Another young fellow described how he had adopted his

father's views without examining them. He said, "My dad always emphasized how important it was to make money and support your family. I worked two jobs in order to do well, and I believed I was taking care of my wife and children. At the time my wife said money was not that important. She said I should spend more time with the kids, but I wouldn't listen to her." I nodded as I listened, but he was rolling and would have continued anyway.

"I thought what I learned from my dad was right, you know. Well, I didn't see it soon enough. Now I'm divorced, and I realize how much the family meant to me. I had to quit my jobs because I was so upset by the divorce. Now I'm working again, but not making as much as before. I am able to provide for my children, but in a different way. I don't see them as often. I wish I had seen this sooner." His voice seemed to trail off into the distance, along with his gaze, as his words obviously brought his hurt and loneliness to the surface. He wasn't looking for an answer; he just wanted to share his hurt. He knew that the answer, questioning—even challenging—what his dad had taught him, had come too late. Now he had to live with the hurt of what was and the unfulfilled agony of what might have been. My heart went out to this young man, a living casualty of extended adolescence.

Even though I didn't know it at the time, my crisis in Detroit was the culmination of my extended adolescence. Emotionally, I was living as a teenager until my late twenties. My parents' methods have already been described, and my adolescence after high school continued because I lived at home during my first year at a Christian college. I lived in a funeral home near campus the second year and needed to keep up the wholesome image of the business, and my last two years were spent on the campus of a Christian college more conservative than the first one! And besides, I felt God had called me to YFC, which meant I needed to live a Christian example. I apparently had some slight inkling of what was happening because during my senior year at college, I often said to my roommate, "I had better have my fun now because next year, when I start full-time in YFC, I'll have to behave." My senior year was one of my best years because I did as much "acting out" as my conscience would allow: coming back to campus late, messing up the resident adviser's room, taking pictures of a professor making out with his girlfriend who was a student, playing pinball machines at a local hangout, and so on.

YFC in Detroit continued my adolescence because there were staff rules against such things as smoking, drinking, and going to movies of any kind. Being caught breaking any of these would result in immediate dismissal from the staff. One part-time junior-high man was observed smoking in the grocery store by the director's wife, and he was gone the next day. In fact, I earnestly jumped all over a college volunteer who mentioned he was going to see *The Sound of Music*, giving him all sorts of dire warnings about such sinful activity. I was quite rule-bound and duty-conscious and never seriously considered doing anything on the list. I was not challenging what I had been taught any more than the young divorced fellow challenged his father's ideas about making money. I was going through empty motions without realizing it.

As important as this rebellion is for the healthy development of young people, the church has not addressed this point or helped Christian parents and teenagers through it. Paul Tournier has written, "God understands revolt, and allows it. He loves those who express it better than those who tepidly hide it (Rev. 3:15). For in respect of our heavenly Father, as with an earthly father, the way to adulthood lies necessarily through revolt."[1] In my opinion, the evangelical church and evangelical parents have ignored this concept to the detriment of growing young people.

Personality Style

The prominent personality trait that I have observed in struggling Christians and those who have experienced an extended adolescence is the tendency to withdraw into themselves when they encounter difficulties. Consequently, when their parents or other adults do something that hurts their feelings, they don't confront the person causing the pain, because that might only cause more trouble and pain. As we discussed earlier, this is typical of the weak, who give in to their fears and find conflict so uncomfortable that they prefer to avoid it, in contrast to the strong, who clear the path if it is cluttered and speak up if they are wronged.

Parents are powerful figures to children, and it is a heavy assignment for sensitive children to accept responsibility for fulfilling one's own destiny while living with parents who use God or guilt to keep children under control. Sensitive children, who are by nature unassertive, will not speak up and take a stand unless their parents encourage them to do so. The "i" personalities, though generally in the strong category, need approval, the "S's" need security, and the "C" people don't want to be criticized. Therefore, they are cautious with parents who aren't openly supportive, because taking a stand may anger the parents, and they may feel as though they are challenging God Himself. This is particularly true of the sensitive personalities who need all the support and love they can get and don't want to be rejected by the strong parental figures on whom they must depend.

This means they inhibit many of their normal emotional reactions, such as yelling back in anger at a parent or a friend who has hurt them. They try to please other people more than they please themselves, since they feel little self-worth. They may even believe that being apologetic is spiritual. They keep their feelings to themselves, remembering and collecting the hurts they have endured. If they're not careful, the hurts can build into resentments and even bitterness that eventually poison their entire attitude. Essentially, struggling Christians, and particularly ones with an extended adolescence, either have never begun to question their parents and the church or have attempted to strike their own course and eventually dropped their efforts out of fear, guilt, or being forced back into submission.

The strong children, the ones with "D" personalities, are naturally self-confident and are often more comfortable taking a stand with their parents. One high "D" woman recalled her teenage experiences with her father: "When I was out with my friends on a date, I knew what time I was supposed to be home and what my dad would do if I wasn't. So I made a choice. If I thought the fun I could have was worth the price I would have to pay when I got home, then I did what I wanted, and simply endured the punishment." Accepting responsibility for fulfilling one's own destiny was no problem for her. Her struggles will be different from those of the people with weak reactions.

Essentially, struggling Christians,
and particularly ones with an extended adolescence,
either have never begun to question their parents
and the church or have tried to strike
their own course and eventually dropped
their efforts out of fear, guilt,
or being forced back into submission.

Personal Patterns[2]

As I have listened to many struggling Christians who have sat in my office and poured out their hearts, several patterns appear repeatedly. I offer them to you here in an effort to help your search for patterns in your life.

1. Personal wishes, feelings, and activities were almost always subordinate to the parents' wishes (and then God's).
2. Approval was generally dependent on proper behavior.
3. There was a pervasive fear of disagreeing with or speaking up to the parents.

In response to the early influences in our lives, we all make decisions as we try to adjust and cope with the issues we face. Sometimes these are conscious, deliberate decisions, and other times we don't realize what we've done until years later. Beth was not completely aware of her decision until after her personal life was in trouble. The woman who came to my multimedia presentation began to make sense of things after her divorce. I made most of my decisions without realizing what I was doing, but there was one critical teenage decision that was quite deliberate, and I paid for it later.

When my dad made me quit the basketball team in high school, *I consciously gave up fighting to make room for my personal goals, decided that my life was not very happy, and emotionally withdrew into myself.* This decision was the culmination of a cycle that had been building up. Many times when I asserted myself for something that I wanted just for myself, I was turned down, or what was important to me was criticized. Being a sensitive person, I was deeply hurt, and I was afraid to yell back, get angry, refuse to milk the cows, or even calmly give my opinion. I became quiet and withdrew into myself with self-pity as I felt helpless to change what was happening in my life. My hurt turned to resentment as I sullenly obeyed, feeling unloved and misunderstood.

My sophomore year in high school was the turning point; so many things went against me that I gave up in despair. I had pimples, my girlfriend dumped me, my dad forced me to quit basketball, which was my one hope of gaining some social status, my mom forced me to go to

YFC and join the quiz team at the same time I had to quit basketball, and I felt guilty about masturbating, the one source of good feelings I had left. It seemed I spent my life doing what I *had* to do, not what I wanted to do.

The message at church was, "Do not want anything for yourself, for that is sin, and if you sin, you're going straight into the flames of hell!" My favorite high-school teacher asked me to smile, and I said, "I have nothing to smile about," and made a deliberate attempt to be somber.

By not fighting back, I allowed myself to remain in a subservient position, which fueled my resentment and feelings of helplessness and added to my distrust that anyone could really care about my feelings. I had surrendered control to my parents and was angry with them. I blamed them for years until I realized my part in it. I had made my own decision in responding to what they had done.

My decision was critical, because I eventually took the pattern I used to cope with my parents into adulthood and used the same method with other people, putting myself into the same emotional situation. Without realizing it, I had chosen a road that led me away from becoming my own person. By not speaking up, I allowed others to have control or influence over me, making me "their person." Being sensitive by nature anyway, I continued to be affected by things people said and did to me. But as I did at home, I increasingly kept my feelings to myself, which resulted in more inner tension. I was continually caught in the trap of feeling that I had to go along with what was expected and act as though I liked it, even though I hated it, or else withdraw in helpless frustration and hope it would go away and I could escape it.

My true feelings were never to be trusted or believed in; they were suspect, always subject to approval. They had to be ratified, and the ratification was always external. I had no control over it, and I therefore had no control over how I felt or how much worth or value I had. It became imperative to feel, think, and do only acceptable things in order to gain love and a personal sense of value. A lonely, fearful, empty feeling came over me whenever I was in a situation in which my feelings were not considered, and I felt like an object that was subservient to some external person or control. I felt powerless to get from my environment what I wanted, which was to be loved just for myself. To gain approval from God and people, I had to do what they wanted, not what I wanted.

Perhaps as you have faced your own difficulties, you have felt as I did. Encountering people or situations squarely not only seemed very dangerous to do, but even impossible. My insides turned to jelly, fear instantaneously gripped my heart, my knees felt weak, and my voice became shaky whenever I was in a position of having to defend myself. And the more I avoided and pulled away from situations, the less confidence I had that I could change. I didn't give myself the chance to experience the possibility of success and develop a sense of personal power. "What a way to live—always at the mercy of the other guy!" I noted in my journal.

Those of us who have not become our own separate persons have usually made a decision at some point to give in rather than resist or assert ourselves on our own behalf. Often we have good and necessary reasons for doing so— sometimes no other way would have worked for us in our relationships with our parents. Regardless of whether it was necessary when we were growing up, the essence of the pattern continues in our lives even after we've left home and are on our own.[3]

Dynamics

Fromm helps us understand the dynamics involved when we withdraw and assume a suffering role in an attempt to gain security from an outside power rather than assume personal responsibility:

> The masochistic person, whether his master is an authority outside of himself or whether he has internalized the master as conscience or a psychic compulsion, is saved from making decisions, saved from the final responsibility for the fate of his self, and thereby saved from the doubt of what decision to make. He also is saved from the doubt of what the meaning of his life is or who "he" is. These questions are answered by the relationship to the power to which he has attached himself.[4]

He further describes the reason for continued struggle and feelings of personal helplessness:

> Basically he remains a powerless atom who suffers under the submergence of his self. He and the power to which he clings never become one, a basic antagonism remains and with it an impulse, even if it is not conscious at all, to overcome the masochistic dependence and to become free.[5]

This means that to find security and love, we let others make our decisions and we don't learn to stand on our own. Although this approach may make us feel more secure, we never are completely comfortable with it because we have a deep, inner urge to break away.

If we continue to live under the thumb of our parents or the church, we do so at the risk of developing additional problems, as Rollo May describes: "Indeed it is not possible for a human being to give up his freedom without something coming in to restore the inner balance—something arising from inner freedom when his outer freedom is denied—and this something is hatred for his conqueror."[6] Let me add while we are on the subject that this idea is important to remember as we deal with our own children as well.

May also maintains that hatred in our society is generally suppressed and is not shown as hatred; instead it is experienced as resentment. In my opinion, this is especially true in the evangelical community, and I believe this tendency causes even more problems than we realize:

> Furthermore, if we do not confront our hatred and resentment openly, they will tend sooner or later to turn into the one affect which never does anyone any good, namely self-pity. Self-pity is the "preserved" form of hatred and resentment. One can then "nurse" his hatred, and retain his psychological balance by means of feeling sorry for himself, comforting himself with the thought of what a tough lot has been his, how much he has had to suffer—and refrain from doing anything about it. . . . Hatred and resentment temporarily preserve the person's inner freedom, but sooner or later he must use the hatred to establish his freedom and dignity in reality, else his hatred will destroy himself.[7]

As we look at these ideas, it is no wonder that numerous Christians feel discouraged, even depressed. Many of us have had our inner freedom denied by either our parents or the church. We have been scared into the kingdom prematurely and then not allowed to express our thoughts or develop our viewpoints. Tournier's concept of premature renunciation also encompasses the same concept of freedom denied as a young person is systematically taught to give up what he has not really been allowed to possess.

"If we do not confront our hatred and
resentment openly,
they will tend sooner or later to turn into
the one affect
which never does anyone any good,
namely self-pity."

My point to you is this: if you withdraw from the hurts you receive instead of speaking up for yourself, your hurt will remain inside you and turn to resentment toward the person who hurt you, and you will live with unhappy feelings about yourself. Once you understand this cycle, you can realize the reason for your discomfort and begin to do something about it. We will discuss what you can do in Chapter 15.

Whose Definition?

There is one more related point I want to mention before we close this chapter. A persistent problem I have seen in people who have grown up in the fashion described here is a gnawing sense that "I'm a bad person," and this becomes the basis for how they live. This truth is also evident in the lives of persons mentioned in earlier chapters.

Lacy, a caring, bright, sensitive woman with salt-and-pepper hair, began to struggle more openly with the issue of being her own person when she was in her late fifties. Gradually, as we explored her past, the patterns began to emerge from her childhood.

Her father was a bright but unhappy person who had been dominated by his mother. He apparently had mixed feelings toward women. He both feared and hated them, but he also needed them. To deal with his own discomfort regarding sex, he consistently spoke disparagingly about typical feminine qualities in Lacy's presence. Because he wanted his child to be a son instead of a daughter, he refused even to hold Lacy in his arms when she was a child. Lacy, being quite sensitive and intuitive, sensed Dad's attitude at an early age and realized that to obtain her father's love she would have to put aside her feminine qualities. This was a difficult assignment, since she also clearly knew she was a female like her mother, whom her father constantly belittled.

Consequently, Lacy developed a deep feeling that her feminine qualities and feelings were bad and had to be hidden. If someone were to see her as a truly feminine person with sexual feelings, she feared this would confirm her "badness" and result in definite rejection. To keep the bad feelings hidden, she worked consistently and determinedly to act unfeminine around her father and to keep him happy by anticipating his needs. Furthermore, any sign of displeasure on his part threatened to bring the bad part in her out into the open, which only prompted her to work all the more desperately to keep everything smooth and acceptable.

As she struggled with the intense feelings of being a bad person, it gradually became clearer to her that the definition of who she was had come from her dad, and she had believed it as though it were true. To gain his love, or at least so it seemed, she gave up her own notion of who she was (her own freedom was denied), did not fight for what she actually felt (she withdrew as described above), and lived under his shadow and influence. Life had become a vicious, unending cycle of having to live in the second movement of putting other people first to fend off the underlying fear of actually being that bad person. Gradually, she began to realize that her positive self-worth had been covered up by Dad's definition of her as a bad person. She wasn't really bad—that was simply her dad's opinion, and it came out of his own problems. She was free to discard it, she finally realized, much to her relief.

Many of us have had experiences similar to Lacy's. The feelings that we are bad started with our parents who were most likely expressing their opinions, not accurate assessments, of us. But as young children, we were unable to understand the entire situation, and we accepted those opinions as facts. Thus, we find it easy to live without becoming our own persons because we believe our attempts to please others will be more successful than trying to be "who I *really* am, which is bad!" And if the church and parents have repeatedly said that we are bad because we are sinners and God sends sinners to hell, the negative feelings are driven even deeper into our beings. Once we understand how these feelings actually developed, it's easier to break away from them and their control.

Many of us are not free, emotionally or spiritually. In fact, most of our freedom has been taken away in the name of God, and in the name of God we've been told not to be angry about it. It surely is a complete double-bind and an emotional box. But what do we do about it? How do we gain freedom? Mom and Dad and God are formidable forces to overcome in putting an end to extended adolescence and developing our own lives. Does God allow it? How is it done? We will look at these and other questions in the next chapter.

CHAPTER 15

Free to Be Your Own Person: Steps to Take

"Sometimes I'm not sure if what I think is what I really believe or what others want me to think." Dixie, a young woman in her thirties, was seated on the couch in my office, describing her struggles in becoming her own person. She had grown up in an evangelical home with very little personal freedom. I listened intently as she continued, "The other day my boss made some plans for me that I didn't like. But I didn't tell him that I disagreed with them—I don't want to get him mad and lose my job. I found myself going along with his plans, and later being mad at myself for doing it. This whole business of being who I am gets confused. He told me he was doing it for my own good, and if I just saw it that way, I would agree. After a while I'm not sure what I really believe!"

Toward Freedom

What Dixie says is true. When people have been raised in the second movement and the bottom suddenly drops out due to an affair, stress, or some other crisis, it isn't possible to straighten things out quickly and painlessly to become one's own person. There are difficult tasks to accomplish in achieving personal independence, and the way is not always clear.

Rollo May, in the same vein as Tournier, describes for us the process required of a person who has grown up in the second movement of renunciation and needs to gain balance by returning to the first movement of appropriate self-assertion:

> The basic step in achieving inward freedom is "choosing one's self." This strange-sounding phrase of Kierkegaard's means to affirm one's responsibility for one's self and one's existence. It is the attitude which is opposite to blind momentum or routine existence: it is an attitude of aliveness and decisiveness; it means that one recognizes that he exists in his particular spot in the universe, and he accepts the responsibility for this existence. This is what Nietzsche meant by the "will to live"—not simply the instinct for self-preservation, but the will to accept the fact that one is one's self, and to accept responsibility for fulfilling one's own destiny, which in turn implies accepting the fact that one must make his basic choices himself.[1]

Once we have spent time uncovering and analyzing our personal patterns, we usually will find a recurring theme: situations in which there is a fork in the road, with one branch symbolizing responsibility for fulfilling our own destiny by taking a stand for our personal viewpoint and the opposing branch representing putting ourselves silently aside in quiet submission.

In practical terms, this means that we must return to the emotional position we abandoned when we stopped fighting against our parents or the church as we were attempting to be our own persons. For example, Beth had to return emotionally to the point where she gave in to her mother and her pastor and then start fighting again for her own ideas. Lacy had to begin disbelieving the feeling that she was bad. I had to begin defending and asserting myself at the point where I gave up when I was in the tenth grade. I had to review what I had been taught and decide if I could believe it for myself. We must actively choose rather than simply go along with what our parents and the church have told us.

Dixie's account illustrates the problems and steps involved in becoming one's own person. She said, "My father worked for a Christian organization and was often gone for one to two weeks at a time raising money. I didn't see much of him." I nodded as she continued, "And when I did spend time with him, it usually was on his terms. He had a way of making me feel guilty if I disagreed with him [this took away her personal freedom], so I seldom came out with my true feelings [fear of accepting personal responsibility]. It's not that he ignored me. We did things together.

We must return to the emotional position
we abandoned when we stopped fighting
against our parents or the church as we were
attempting to be our own persons.

"I especially remember this one time when he had a business trip to Florida and took me along. It was supposed to be a special time for us together [good parental intention], but I knew he had the whole trip planned out in a way *he* thought would be fun for me [parent taking all responsibility, thus depriving her of personal freedom]. We were riding down the highway toward the ocean, but I kept seeing these signs along the road advertising other things to see [an awareness of true self and what she wanted], but I was afraid to say anything. I was afraid it would hurt Dad because he had the entire plan worked out in his own mind [giving responsibility for her own place in the universe and submitting reluctantly to an external power]. So we went to the ocean, and it must have been a good act. I laughed and splashed and had a great time, because I knew that was what Dad wanted [after putting her true self aside, she assumed a false identity and carried out the role of being "Dad's person" to gain his love]."

As Dixie talked, I observed a similarity between her statement about her boss and her anecdote about her father. In each instance she was faced with the identical inner dilemma. Actually, it was the fork in the road described earlier. Does she, as May says, take responsibility for her spot in the universe, choose for herself, and express her true opinion, or does she remain silent, giving superficial agreement? Does she choose to be her "own person" or her "boss's person"? Her "own person" or "Dad's person"?

It became clear as Dixie and I discussed her situation that the road to becoming her own person involved being aware of the fork in the road when it appeared and choosing to break the pattern she had started with her father by asserting her opinion, even when confronted by apparently insignificant situations. Each time she encounters this fork in the road, she must choose the direction her personal development will take, because the real nuts-and-bolts work of becoming her own person takes place in these seemingly small, everyday situations.

As time passes, we slowly shape ourselves in the direction of our choices— either toward the freedom of being who we really are or toward the frustrated, unfulfilled role of being under someone else's thumb.

Overall, however, these everyday experiences are accumulative. In other words, the more often we choose the branch toward being our own persons, the easier and more natural it becomes. On the opposite side, the more we take the branch toward being someone else's person, even in the small things, the harder it becomes to break away in our own direction. As time passes, we slowly shape ourselves in the direction of our choices—either toward the freedom of being who we really are or toward the frustrated, unfulfilled role of being under someone else's thumb.

Granted, there is risk involved. Parents and friends may not understand. The church may discourage questioning. Parents may become angry and threaten their challenging offspring. The road to being our own persons is fraught with difficulties, as Fromm points out in his book, and people often prefer to escape from the responsibility required to gain personal freedom.

Seeing Parents as People

At some point as we apply the "fork in the road" theory, we begin to run into the habits we learned from our parents, because they are usually the ones who have had the most influence on how we developed our style of reacting in the first place. We usually carry our childhood view of our parents as powerful persons with us into adulthood, and if we were afraid to question our parents' views while we were children, we continue to be afraid of questioning them when we are adults ourselves. This is because we don't see our parents as people with their own problems, struggles, hopes, and dreams. Mom and Dad are "Mom and Dad," not people. Usually, parents are the last persons that we see as people. It's easier to understand the neighbor as a person or Aunt Clara who has some unusual ideas of her own that we don't take seriously.

In order for us to move past the boundaries our parents have laid, we must feel comfortable laying aside their ideas.

My point is that in order for us to move past the boundaries our parents have laid, we must feel comfortable laying aside their ideas, and this is usually possible only when we are able to see that our parents' opinions are just that—their opinions as people and not God's truth for all time. For example, if Stan were to honestly view his dad as a person, he would realize that Dad's distrust of women was the result of Dad's reaction to his own experiences and that his viewpoint did not accurately portray all women. Then Stan would be able to make his own decision free of Dad's negative influence because he had seen Dad's belief for what it really was. But he can't move past Dad's belief until he sees his dad as a person.

Sometimes individuals begin to see their parents as people simply as the result of growing up and entering adulthood. There is an expression that "my folks really learned a lot in the years between my sixteenth and twenty-third birthdays." Growing older and facing life on their own often help people appreciate their parents and see them in a new light.

Becoming parents and dealing with growing children also can lead people to look more realistically at their own parents. As parents themselves, they realize they don't have all the answers, they make mistakes, and they often hurt their children without intending to do so. By realizing and understanding their own shortcomings as parents, they can begin to understand the "people" in their parents.

For others, it often requires special effort. The approach I have found useful for myself and for people who are working with me in psychotherapy has been to explore the parents' childhood experiences and the relationships they had with their parents. Doing this helps us understand the hurts and influences that have shaped our parents, and it also reveals the little boy or girl who resides in our parents.[2]

My parents said very little about their childhoods or their parents, and my dad said less than my mom did. Since I have an "S" personality with strong security needs directed toward the family, this left a large gap in my family picture. Grandpa Sloat was particularly intriguing because no one talked about him, and I couldn't form my own opinions because he died shortly before I was born. This only fired my curiosity to learn what had taken place, especially after I became an adult and wanted to explore the family tree to understand my roots. In my attempt to learn about him, I accidentally learned to understand my father as a person.

Grandma Sloat was my only source of reliable information, but she was reluctant to open up. Over a period of years and persistent questioning, I gradually began to piece together a picture of the family and some of the stresses my dad faced in his own growing years. I gained a new appreciation for my dad and his thinking. I also saw that he and I were very much alike. We both were born with sensitive natures.

Dad began to emerge as a person rather than the towering, parental figure I had pictured as a child. He was a human being, too, with his own share of hurts and frustrations. He had grown up, married, lived, and worked, trying to sort out his life and make things work for himself the best way he knew how. Even though I didn't like all his decisions regarding me as a youngster, he provided many positive experiences that helped me build a solid personal foundation. This gut-level realization of my dad as a person, not as Dad, paved the way for me to eventually put my anger to rest and truly forgive him. It also made me less afraid of him, because as a person he represented less power than as Dad.

Katie grew up in an evangelical home with a father who was a doctor and spent considerable amounts of time with his patients. Katie felt left out of his life because she didn't receive the attention she needed from him. She also had a hard time understanding his definite, unbending views on Christianity. As an adult, she became involved with other men in an attempt to find the security she had missed with her father. Fortunately, her father was still living within driving distance of her home. At first, with fear and trepidation, she began to have frequent discussions with her father in an attempt to learn more about him as a person. As she learned more about his lonely childhood, his social rejection at school, and so on, she began to see that he had channeled his energy into his studies and his profession because he could succeed and find acceptance there. Other avenues of life had been painful for him. They even went on a short trip to visit the spots where he had spent his youth so she could develop a more personal feel for him. As she continued this process, she became more and more understanding of her father and began to see him as a person. This process helped her clarify her childhood perceptions of him, and she began to understand that he really did love her when she was younger. It just didn't seem like it at the time because he was away from her so much. She also realized that her childhood perception of her father actually was her *mother's* perception; she had somehow learned to see Dad through Mom's eyes.

During your own personal search, I encourage you to seek out aunts, uncles, cousins, grandparents, or anyone else who might have information regarding your parents that would help you understand their inner feelings as people. If your parents are willing to talk about their childhood feelings and experiences, by all means talk to them as well.

Handling Anger

Another key step in becoming our own persons is facing and handling the anger that we feel toward the parent who has been discouraging or has not allowed us to have our own viewpoint. If you are struggling at this point of personal development, you know how intense this anger can be. Many people have told me during therapy, "I sometimes am a little afraid of my anger. It actually feels like rage. I could just go and tell my mom exactly what I think of her, and when I'd be finished, there wouldn't be anything left. Oh! I just hate her so much!"

Since I had stored up my adolescent anger toward my dad, there were times when it seemed to really build inside me. I was puzzled. I couldn't see how going to him and telling him how angry I was would do any good. At best it might make me feel better for the moment, but I didn't want my angry words ringing in his ears, especially after I had gotten over it. I wanted more for us than that.

The best solution for the anger is to find a good friend, an insightful counselor or pastor, or even a sibling, who will listen to the hurt. There is an advantage in talking to a brother or a sister because you can compare experiences and feelings. You may even find they had similar feelings. You'll know you weren't imagining your pain.

The anger definitely needs to be expressed, but to a third party, not to the parent involved. Notice I said *expressed*. Many times people mistakenly believe that simply telling another person about their anger or pain is sufficient. People have calmly said to me, "What my parents did made me angry, and now that I've told you about it, I don't have anything else to say." All they did was report that they were angry. They didn't experience the anger as they talked. Their emotion was not evident in their voices. They didn't strike the arm of the couch in frustration. Others bite their lips as tears begin to come. They are reluctant to experience their pain in full view of another person. But this is what they must do to empty the anger and pain from their inner beings. They need to work through this stage before they are ready to approach their parents.

Another technique some people have used is to write honest, uninhibited, scathing letters to the parent *but never mail or deliver them*. It may take a period of years to empty the anger completely. A time limit cannot be placed on it.

The best solution for the anger is to find
a good friend, an insightful counselor or pastor,
or even a sibling, who will listen to the hurt.

Gaining Closure

Graduate work for my Ph.D. at the University of Southern Mississippi began while I was in the final stages of understanding the concept of seeing my parents as people and dealing with anger toward them, but I didn't know how to put the entire issue to rest. My major professor, Dr. Gutsch, provided the final key that unlocked the puzzle by teaching me how the psychological concept of closure related to parents and the process of gaining autonomy in relationship to one's parents and the world. Gutsch's concept of autonomy is the same notion May called true freedom to be one's own person—the freedom to act in line with what one believes or feels without being unduly influenced by what others think, particularly parents.

Closure is similar to completing a transaction, or closing a deal with everything on the table. Let me explain. When I say to my daughter, "I really don't like what you're doing," my comments stir up emotions in her. If she states what these emotions are, she is completing the emotional transaction by returning to the situation the emotions that I stirred. She gets them off her chest. She has gained closure. If she doesn't state what she feels, however, she departs from that emotional transaction with feelings inside her that actually belonged to that particular situation. Thus, she doesn't achieve closure. When a person consistently keeps feelings inside, they begin to accumulate from all the emotional exchanges where the emotions were not returned to the situation.

Now let's apply this to relationships with parents. As we've seen, the "S" and "C" people—but especially the

"S's"—fear conflict and avoid a confrontation whenever possible. This means they typically have not reported to their parents how they feel about their parents' actions. For example, I never told my dad how I felt when he made me quit basketball or wouldn't allow me to do other things I wanted to do. Because I had never expressed myself to him or confronted the anger I had toward him, I remained under his influence as I described earlier. I was more "his person" than "my person." I was letting him dictate to me.

If people don't have closure with their parents in the small emotional interchanges that occur, they usually lack closure with them in their overall relationship as well. Consequently, all through the years the emotional flow in the relationship has been in one direction only—toward the children who are not taking responsibility for defining and defending their space in life or confronting their own hurt and anger. These submissive children are not doing what Rollo May says is necessary to have true personal freedom. Obviously, "D" youngsters are more likely to speak up and not find themselves in the emotional fix described here.

Gutsch agreed with my observation that dumping anger on parents is not productive, but he had an alternative that I had never heard before. He said people needed to talk with their parents not about their anger, but about the deeper, original feeling—the hurt. Hurt is always the first emotion, while anger comes second. In my case, to gain closure, I had to report to my dad how I had felt through the years in *my* half of our relationship, something I had never done before.

We need to talk with our parents
not about our anger, but
about the deeper, original feeling—the hurt.

Gutsch told me to summarize my hurt or my half of the relationship with my dad in one or two sentences to be used in reporting my feelings to him. Since I had been struggling with my feelings anyway, it was easy to summarize my pain: "Dad made decisions that affected me without taking my feelings into consideration." That one sentence described the essence of the painful portion of my years with him.

In preparation for actually talking to parents, Gutsch taught me several more important points. We must have a proper goal and expectations for our meeting, or it won't accomplish what needs to be done. We also have to realize clearly that the purpose of talking to our parents is to say what *we* have to say—to put back into the relationship *our* half of the emotion. With this as our objective, we can definitely reach our goal, because it depends only on our ability and courage. We can't enter the discussion expecting our parents to understand us, to apologize, or to sit down for a heart-to-heart talk. If they did, that would simply be a bonus. We have no control over what they might say or do, and having an expectation that depends on their response is asking for trouble, because we could be let down.

Talking to Parents

Armed with all this wisdom, I faced the most difficult task of my life—actually talking to my dad—and it was as awesome at the age of thirty-two as it was when I was fifteen and feared approaching him about basketball as he washed out the milkers in the milkhouse. I also knew that I had to grow up and accept responsibility for my feelings. I had examined my feelings through many discussions with my wife, and I realized I couldn't continue to avoid them.

I knew that in several months my wife and I would drive to Indiana from Mississippi for the Christmas holidays, and I had to talk to him then. I simply had arrived at the emotional point where I could not progress without doing so.

With fearful dread in the pit of my stomach, I anticipated the approaching Christmas season. My inner tension and anxiety were so great that large, painful boils began to appear on my back more than a month before we were scheduled to leave.

Knowing what I had to do made it difficult for me to enjoy the family Christmas celebration, because we were spending only a few days with my folks, and I had to either find or make an opportunity before the time was gone. Fortunately, on the second evening, Dad inquired about my graduate experience and asked me how a person's personality is formed. He and I sat on the living room couch, and I began to explain a theoretical view I had learned from Dr. Gutsch. *It's now or never*, I thought to myself, and with inner trembling I turned the conversation in the direction of my heavy heart. Without repeating our conversation here, suffice it to say I stated some of my feelings to him for the first time, and he listened. I assumed responsibility for my feelings by talking about some of my painful experiences. He also responded with his thoughts, and although he didn't quite say what I had expected, he did state his own position. Our talk helped me clarify things in my mind, because our ideas were out in the open. I was able to truly put the hurt behind me as I ventured further toward becoming my own person. A tremendous load was lifted from me, and my past pain ceased being a burden to me. I had finally freed myself from being stuck in the hurtful portion of our relationship, and this helped me develop a more positive view of him and what he had done for me.

I have seen this approach work for other people as well. Pat was a woman in her thirties when she finally realized the psychological work that needed to be done with her mother. In therapy I took her through the steps described above and helped her prepare for a discussion with her mother. With a broad smile on her face, she returned to my office and reported, "My mother not only understood what

I said, she apologized, too. And we had the best talk together that we have ever had!" She received the bonus.

Another woman came back and reported, "Well, I finally did it. I talked to my dad for the first time. But he said he would do the same thing over again. He didn't even understand that it hurt me. At least I know that his lack of caring for my feelings as a kid wasn't imagined. If he can't hear me now as an adult, I know he couldn't have when I was at home, either." This woman learned a valuable piece of information even though her father didn't understand her feelings. She also knew she would never have the close relationship with her father that she had always wanted.

A similar process needs to be followed in gaining closure with our mothers, but the words will be different because we don't have the same relationship with each parent. Since our parents' personalities are dissimilar, they will have reacted and treated us in differing ways.

Through the years I didn't feel angry with my mother because I couldn't point to anything specific she had done to hurt me. What she did always seemed to be for my own good. Who can criticize a mother for wanting her son to attend YFC at school or the services at church or to behave and be a nice boy? After a number of years, I finally began to understand her as a person, and I realized why I didn't feel angry with her.

Apparently in growing up, she had learned to assert her ideas without putting herself on the line. So, when she presented her ideas to me, she did it through the notion of either a third person or an appeal to some external duty or obligation that would inspire guilt if I didn't go along with her suggestion. For example, even after I became an adult and she was inviting the family for Sunday dinner, she never said, "I'd like you to come." Instead she told me, "Your uncle is going to be there and he has been asking about you. He's hoping you'll come." Refusing, at least on the surface, was not saying no to my mom, but disappointing my uncle. This usually caught my guilt button because I didn't want to disappoint my uncle. I finally realized that my uncle had nothing to do with it. My mother was using my positive feelings for him to get me to show up for dinner.

On other occasions she would ask me something like, "Would you like your brother to come over to the lake, too?" It really didn't matter to me, so I would mutter, "I don't care. It's okay with me." Then later I would hear her go to my brother and enthusiastically entreat, "Don says he wants you to come over to the lake, too!" I said that?

Once I began to see this, I realized why I wasn't feeling angry with her. Her comments made someone or something else responsible for my disapproval, whether it was God, my uncle, my dad (for example, she told me, "Your dad will not like your beard"), the family image ("Your beard does not look like a Sloat"), or whatever. She never made direct statements expressing her own opinion. Since everything she did was for my own good, I felt like a fool if I protested, or else my self-worth was questionable if I didn't go along. Her approach is similar to that of many mothers. People who have had similar experiences with their mothers have told me, "She killed me with kindness!"

Over the next few years, I began to dislike her approach, but I continued to be afraid to disagree or turn her down if she requested something. I felt I had no right to really express my feelings, and I was afraid that saying no would hurt her or upset her. Consequently, I continued being "her person" as long as I didn't speak up.

Settling things with my mother required several definite attempts on my part, since my first try took place before I had developed a gut-level sense of what was happening between us. During our first conversation, I pointed out that I felt she loved me only when I did what she wanted. She denied that such was the case because she had always loved me. We also discussed several other subjects, and I felt relieved at having had an honest talk with her. But I had more work to do in settling things for myself, and this gradually became clearer over the next few years.

During this period, I continued to struggle with my inner conflicts and depressed feelings. I had learned my lesson so well that I had a very difficult time taking a stand on things. In several business relationships, I let other people either make decisions for me or take advantage of my fear of speaking up on my own behalf. I gradually realized I was approaching an impasse in my life; I had to stand on my own or I was going to continue having trouble. I also realized that my fear of expressing myself stemmed from my feeling that I didn't deserve to. I knew, too, that I had to return to the source of my difficulty to take a stand. If I could speak up to my mother, the source of my fear, then I knew I could begin to handle other situations as well.

With all this building up inside me, a situation arose that I knew I had to handle. Just before Mother's Day weekend a few years ago, my mother called my wife on the phone. She already had a plan devised for a family function on Mother's Day and expected that we would go along with it. When my wife told her we already had plans with her parents for the day, my mother didn't take kindly to being turned down and attempted to push guilt on my wife. This really got to me.

Keeping our original plans, I decided that I had had enough. I knew that the time had come when I had to have another gut-level talk with her to declare my independence and be honest about my feelings. Although I had sensed this moment was coming, I was reluctant to state my feelings very strongly because of a persistent fear that she might fall apart if I took a stand with her (for some reason I sensed she was emotionally fragile). This time, however, I figured it was something I had to do. Although I knew I needed to speak up to her, I also didn't want to cause her personal difficulty in the process. However, the time seemed to be right. It was my best opportunity, and I didn't dare let it pass.

With tightness in my stomach, I mentally prepared my remarks as I sped through the waning sunshine of Mother's Day in my orange Fiat convertible to see her. With palpitating heart, I nervously walked to the door, but no one was home. "Of all the rotten luck!" I shouted to myself. "Here I've just gotten myself all psyched up for this, and now she's not here!" I was tempted to lose my nerve, but I knew if I returned home without talking to her, it would worsen matters. I knew I had come too far emotionally to back out. I had to do it. I had to take responsibility for myself and share my honest feelings with Mom.

So I nervously sat in my car, continuing to rehearse the points I wanted to make as I watched the clock slowly marking time. Finally, I saw her coming.

With my heart beating hard and with a sense of foreboding, I sat with her on the couch. After a few minutes of polite conversation, I began my speech, and as I spoke, a lightheaded feeling slowly came over me; I practically lost conscious control of the words as they poured out in rapid succession.

I basically told her I didn't like the way she communicated her wishes to me, and I described some of my painful reactions to other experiences when I was a youngster. She listened and replied with her own thoughts. She didn't fall apart, and she said that she wanted me to be honest with her even if I disagreed with her opinions and that I should not hide my feelings. As we were talking, I realized how different our conversation was compared to conversations of previous years; I had developed a definite habit of not being open about my true feelings, which of course made it impossible for her to adequately respond to me. I realized I had finally accepted responsibility for my own true self, something I should have done years earlier. Apparently, I had misjudged my mom—she was more willing to hear my honest opinions than I had expected. We continued our discussion and concluded that each of us needed to be more open about our thoughts in order to avoid misconceptions and communication problems.

I left with a definite sense of relief and felt that I had turned a corner. Since that time I have felt more comfortable expressing my true thoughts about her actions, and she has responded with her opinions as well. Now when she does something I don't like, I'm more comfortable saying so, and I feel we have had a better relationship—although she still pushes to have her own way. I realized that I was more afraid of disagreeing with my mom than I had to be.

Katie, mentioned earlier in this chapter with regard to her relationship with her father, also began to realize her mother had used guilt and manipulation in raising her. She decided she needed to declare her independence as the thirteen colonies had from England. When she talked to her mother, she began by saying, "I'm sick and tired of having a relationship based on guilt. If it continues that way, I'm going to come around a lot less often." After she had said a few more things, her mother responded, "Everyone else likes me the way I am!" Katie reported being flabbergasted to me. "Even though I said it directly, she still didn't really understand my feelings, and basically said she had done nothing wrong. I think she wanted to end the conversation and smooth things over, but I wouldn't let her until I had finished. I knew that if I stopped I would be falling into the old pattern of backing off from my honest feelings."

Perhaps you're thinking that Katie was overly harsh in her conversation with her mom. This was not the first time she had talked to her mom, however. In their earlier conversation, her mom denied any personal responsibility and also had continued an obvious pattern of manipulation in

Katie's direction. Also, Katie had never taken responsibility to speak up to her about it. She knew her mother had a way of seeing things the way her mother wanted them to be, and she knew she had to be quite direct to break through to her mother's awareness.

Subtle hints simply don't work with some people, especially those who like to control others. There are times when we have to teach other people (our parents as well) how to treat us. We may have to say to a parent, "I don't want you stopping over without calling first," or "This is my child, and I don't want you giving him chocolate candy. It's not good for him." Some relationships require more forcefulness than others, and to do less than is necessary is to be unfair to ourselves as well as to the other person.

I have also discovered through talking to people that Christian mothers in our society often use guilt to control their children, while fathers tend to use intimidation. I believe it is frequently more difficult to break away from a guilt relationship than from one with more open conflict, because the guilt-based one involves our self-worth. Also, as I have mentioned earlier, there is something basic about mothers. We depend on our mothers more than on our fathers in many ways, and perhaps this creates a more complicated bond that must be broken in our efforts to become autonomous.

I am reminded of Jesus' pointed response to His mother's guilt-inducing approach after she and Joseph had searched three days for Him. "His parents didn't know what to think. 'Son!' his mother said to him. 'Why have you done this to us? Your father and I have been frantic, searching for you everywhere.' 'But why did you need to search?' he asked. 'Didn't you realize that I would be here at the Temple, in my Father's House?' " (Luke 2:48–49 TLB). His statement is consistent with Rollo May's notion that we need to accept responsibility for fulfilling our own destiny and making our own choices. I find it significant that even Jesus had to take a stand with His mother—and that He was wise and mature enough to do it even as a boy.

For those of you who want to talk to your parents, I trust that the examples here have been helpful. If you are unsure about how forceful you need to be even after analyzing your relationship with your parents, I suggest that you start easy. You will have other chances, and you can always be more forceful later if necessary. Once you take the first step, it becomes easier to express yourself the next time.

Defining Success

Let's return briefly to Dixie on her trip to Florida with her father. "Your analysis sounds good," you say. "But what if Dixie had spoken up to her father, and he had gone to the ocean anyway? Or what if she did hurt his feelings? What good would that have done?" On the surface, it could appear that her efforts would have been futile in such a case, but a closer analysis of the situation reveals otherwise. Keep in mind that the primary issue here is Dixie's responsibility of choosing for herself and being her own person. By stating her true preferences and asserting her opinion, Dixie would have accomplished the psychological act of accepting responsibility for her existence. She would have taken a stand as a separate person with her own viewpoint, and this has value for her no matter what her dad says or does, or whether she is ten or twenty-five years old. He doesn't have to accept her opinion in order for it to have value in helping her become her own person. It certainly would help her if he did accept her opinion, and by doing so he would have encouraged her to think for herself, but it is not essential. If she had spoken up as a child and accepted responsibility, she wouldn't be struggling with who she is now.

The Process

Keep in mind that becoming one's own person is a more complicated process for individuals who have grown up living in the second movement of premature renunciation, because from an early age they have not been allowed to explore and express themselves. The remarks in this chapter do not adequately explain all the points that are involved, but this process has helped me, and I have seen it help others.

The basic steps are (1) identifying personal patterns, (2) seeing Mom and Dad as people instead of parents, (3) expressing the anger to a person other than the parent (talking to a sibling is often helpful, not only in emptying out the hurt and anger, but also in clarifying memories and viewpoints), (4) summarizing clearly the nature of the relationship in one or two sentences, (5) expressing this summarized hurt to Mom and Dad individually with the specific goal of saying what one has to say—not expecting or planning on a positive response—and (6) using the parent's response to either confirm one's original feelings or add new light to the situation.

Often, we have to continue defending our territory with a dominating parent, and this process helps sharpen our sense of identity, or "the person I am." Also, the pattern we have learned at home is often transferred to other relationships away from home and becomes an automatic way of reacting. The "fork in the road" concept is useful in changing this pattern as we face the challenge of taking the branch toward being our own person or the one toward being someone else's person. Simply talking to my parents was not an instant cure for me. It was the starting point in a process, and I have had to deliberately take deep breaths and face other people and situations as well. The other persons mentioned have had similar experiences. Of course, once we have become comfortable choosing the branch that involves self-assertion, we are in the position to choose the opposing branch because we want to and not out of obligation, fear, or guilt. Then we are making a choice from a position of strength, and a choice based on strength contains genuine virtue.

Rollo May offers a perspective that is helpful here:

> Obviously, the moral . . . is not that everyone get a gun and kill his mother. What has to be killed, as we have already implied, is the infantile tie of dependency which binds the person to the parents, and thereby keeps him from loving outwardly and creating independently.
>
> This is no simple job to be initiated by a sudden resolution and performed in one great burst of freedom, nor is it accomplished by one big "blow-up" against one's parents. . . . Actually in real life it is a matter of long, uphill growth to new levels of integration—growth meaning not automatic process but re-education, finding new insights, making self-conscious decisions, and throughout being willing to face occasional or frequent bitter struggles. A person in psychotherapy often must work through his patterns for months to discover how much he has been tied without knowing it, and to see time and again that this enchainment underlies his inability to love, to work, or to marry. He then finds that the struggle to become a person in his own right often brings considerable anxiety and occasionally some actual terror . . . .but the crucial psychological battle we must wage is that against our own dependent needs, and our anxiety and guilt feelings which will arise as we move toward freedom.[3]

Also, it is important to realize that the tension we feel will be reduced, but it may not automatically disappear completely and never return. Through the years I have observed a pattern in myself, and I have observed the same pattern with my patients. During the early stages of personal discovery, after we have struggled through a tough, depressing time, we usually discover a new angle on our struggles that helps us feel better. But the good feeling does not always last. Later, we often wrestle with the same issue. I have come to the conclusion that my earlier expectations were incorrect. I was expecting—hoping really—that I would someday have a brilliant insight or experience that would release me into freedom and joy that would never change. Life would reach a pleasant plateau and be relatively hassle-free. Perhaps that will happen eventually, but I have decided that the sensitive person, especially, will continue to have occasional experiences and insights that can be unsettling as new areas of thinking or personal faults are uncovered.

Hurts and frustrations are a part of life; the key is the attitude we choose as we face them. If we are to appreciate the positive things our parents have done for us, we need to put the hurts in perspective and learn from them what we can. This opens the way for a true appreciation of our parents.

Growing people are continually examining and revising their values, ways of thinking, and even notions about God. Growth is not always in a straight line pointing up, but it usually has ups and downs, with the overall upward slant only evident if one stands back and examines the entire picture. An excellent biblical example of this growth pattern is Abraham, who lived in an "S" style, needing family security and being reluctant to make drastic changes. His own faith grew very gradually with ups and downs, culminating in the extreme test of being willing to sacrifice his son Isaac upon God's command.

Once we begin to clear up our notions about our parents, we can also begin to look at God realistically, a subject we'll take up in the next chapter.

Seeing God through Clear Glasses

Jamie was a pretty sixteen-year-old girl with beautiful brown hair that barely touched her shoulders. After a YFC Campus Life meeting, she came to me with an obviously heavy heart. She was from a broken home, and she was caught in the intense conflict between her divorced parents. There were some bizarre events occurring where she was living, and with huge tears pouring from her eyes and the hurt evident in her sobbing voice, she cried, "I don't want to go back to my dad's house. I don't know if I can take it any more! He wants me to, but I can't! Do you think I should?" It sounded like an extremely unhealthy, complicated situation, and she was looking for support as well as direction.

At the time, everything, including emotional and spiritual issues, was black and white to me. I cockily thought I had all the answers, especially since I had Gothard's notebook under my arm. As I listened to her story, I totally failed to respond to her on an emotional level, and with complete confidence that I was right, I insisted, "You have to go back to your dad's. You have no choice. It doesn't really matter what you feel!" After all, Gothard had a chart about such matters involving parents. With pain in her voice, she pleaded with me, but I confidently brushed her hurt aside.

I ache and cry inside as I remember such instances from

my past when I was so uncaring and insensitive to the young people who looked to me for direction in Detroit. I have often wondered how much damage I did to them in my ignorance, and I wish I could see them again to correct my mistakes. Through the years I have learned that there are no easy answers, that life is complicated, and that struggle is inevitable because even though some things are black and white, there is a large area of gray in the middle. This is true of spiritual issues as well as emotional ones. And most critical of all, you and I have to find our own answers—and yours may very well be different from mine. There are several points you need to keep in mind as we explore the spiritual area of our lives.

Gaining Perspective

I am convinced that the emotional and psychological areas of our lives form the foundation for our spiritual lives, a point made well by David Seamands:

> If we have the idea that there is no connection between the *natural* (our temperament and personality structure) and the *supernatural* (our spiritual lives), we are seriously mistaken. Both our feelings and our faith operate through the same personality equipment. God does not come to us in special ways which bypass or short-circuit or sidetrack our personality equipment. He doesn't drill a hole in the tops of our skulls and with some magical, mystical funnel pour His grace into us. The mechanisms of our personalities which we use in faith are the same instruments through which our feelings operate.[1]

Since both our feelings and our faith operate through the same personality equipment, we are going to have trouble seeing God clearly if that equipment is malfunctioning or contains emotional distortions. Let me use an extreme example to illustrate my point. Some unfortunate individuals have such profound insecurities and problems in their personalities that they actually begin to believe they are historical figures, such as Napoleon or even Jesus Christ. Believing they are powerful historical persons helps them feel secure in an unusual psychological way. I'm sure you would readily agree that these people have faulty personality equipment and that their concept of themselves and of God is quite inaccurate. Their inaccuracies color everything they do, however, and if you talk to them, they will answer as though they really were people of the past. Before they can understand God or even other people realistically, they have to straighten out their confused thinking.

Since both our feelings and our faith operate
through the same personality equipment,
we're going
to have trouble seeing God clearly if that equipment
is malfunctioning or contains emotional distortions.

Since we are living in a sinful world and no one is perfect, each of us has distortions in his personality equipment, but not to the same degree as the fellow who believes he is Napoleon. The misconception of the misguided Napoleon is obvious, but our distortions are often so subtle that we don't even realize their presence or how they affect us. The woman who told me "I don't think anyone can love me without me giving them a reason to" is operating with an emotional distortion that will color her entire life just as surely as if she thought she were Cleopatra. Perhaps by now you can understand more clearly my point that our spiritual lives have a foundation in our psychological selves.

Therefore, clearing up our emotional distortions, becoming our own persons by assuming responsibility for ourselves, understanding the influence of our parents on us, and living out the first movement prepare the way for developing a more realistic spiritual relationship with God and clear out many of the subtle barriers that get in the way spiritually.

Dad and God

One day as I was struggling with my fear of and reluctance toward God, the similarity of my feelings toward God and my dad struck me. I had felt that my dad did not consider many of my feelings to be important, and it seemed to me that God had a similar attitude. Since I now knew that my experience with my dad could color my feelings toward God, my eyes were opened to a new possibility—maybe God does care, except I couldn't see it or had not allowed myself to feel it. As I began to understand my dad, I realized that he also had cared about me but had shown it in a way I hadn't recognized. This gave me a new avenue to pursue and a new sense of hope. Perhaps God also loved me, but I wasn't seeing it clearly.

Becoming a father myself has also affected me and my feelings about God. Since all through my life I have not *felt* God's love, and since my personality operates on my feelings, it has always been difficult, if not impossible, to picture God in heaven having warm feelings toward me. Many times as I have stood at the edge of my daughters' beds and quietly watched them sleep in the dim shadows cast by their nightlight, however, I have noticed my own indescribable feeling of caring and emotion for them and wondered silently to myself, *Does God—can God really look at me with the same kind of feeling that I have for Amanda and Molly? Does He really love me, and I don't know it? Are my feelings of not being loved incorrect?* I found my concept of God being challenged, and now that I have clarified my relationship with my dad, I can begin to work more directly with

God because I can see more clearly how some of my spiritual trouble has come from the emotional segment of my youth.

Remember Terri, whose father put her in the basement with the rats? Her concept of God has been definitely and adversely affected by her relationship with her father, and I realize that I can't encourage her to look to God the Father for comfort and assurance in her struggles until she has overcome her feelings about her father.

J. B. Phillips discusses the various concepts people have of God, including seeing Him as the "Resident Policeman," the "Grand Old Man," and the "Parental Hangover." His ideas have been very helpful to me, but there is insufficient space to describe his ideas here. You will find his book quite helpful in examining your own view of God.[2]

Mom and Grace

I also began to perceive the parallels between my relationships with my mom and God. I felt she loved me more when I did what she wanted, and what she wanted was not necessarily what I wanted. The same was true with God—at least that was the impression I received at church. As I began to understand my relationship with my mother, I was able to ask myself, *Is God really that way, or am I reacting to childhood feelings and what I learned about God at church?* As we deal with our emotional issues, more light is cast on the nature of our spiritual struggles. Seamands is right when he says:

> Many years ago I was driven to the conclusion that the two major causes of most emotional problems among evangelical Christians are these: the failure to understand, receive, and live out God's unconditional grace and forgiveness; and the failure to give out that unconditional

love, forgiveness, and grace to other people. . . . We read, we hear, we believe a good theology of grace. But that's not the way we live. We believe grace in our heads but not in our gut level feelings or in our relationships. . . . But it's all on a head level. The good news of the Gospel of grace has not penetrated the level of our emotions.[3]

Seamands correctly identifies one of the most difficult tasks the second-generation Christian faces—how to let the gospel of grace penetrate the level of our emotions. A person's self-image and sense of self-worth are closely related to being able to receive this unconditional acceptance and love. I have seen this difficulty many times in persons who have come to see me at my office. When I try to encourage them by being supportive and complimentary, they often will not accept it by protesting, "You say that to everybody! You're just saying that because it's your job!" It's hard for them to believe they deserve or are worth a compliment. If they can't take a compliment from me, how much harder will it be for them to believe God loves them?

I totally agree with Seamands's statement that "if this kind of low self-esteem has been programmed into a person, it is difficult, and in some cases almost impossible, for that person to feel beloved of God, accepted by Him, and of worth to Him in His kingdom and service."[4] For this reason, the mother's relationship with her child has definite pervasive, long-range effects that generally are in place by the child's age of two.

Checking Out Our Beliefs

As we grow up, we often develop childhood perceptions of people, events, theology, and so on that are inaccurate. Unless we adjust our ideas when we become adults, we will continue to live according to incorrect childhood ideas.

Most of us have had a common experience that helps illustrate this point. Do you remember thinking as a child how big the gym was at your school? Or maybe it was a room at your grandparents' house or a famous building you visited on a trip. Do you also remember returning to that particular location as an adult and saying to yourself, *This sure doesn't seem as big as I remembered. When I was a kid, this place looked huge!*

This happens in many areas of our lives, and the spiritual is no exception. Those of us who have grown up in church hearing sermon after sermon have begun at an early age to develop a concept of God, Christ, and the Christian life. Some of our perceptions are accurate, and others are colored by the dangers mentioned in this book, even though we don't realize it at the time. Other times we misinterpret what we hear. Regardless of how we arrived at our conclusions, they often contain various errors.

In the spiritual area, it is helpful to check the accuracy of our beliefs to uncover and correct distortions, just as we do with our emotions. A woman who had grown up in the church and struggled with many of the issues described here told me how she handled her situation. She came in contact with a trained, insightful theologian who also understood people and their struggles. To her, he appeared to have a proper grasp of spiritual issues, so she trusted his judgment. She spent time with him, openly describing all the spiritual truths she had been taught as a child, and asking him to examine their accuracy. As they discussed what she believed, he helped her see her misunderstandings, the points she had taken too seriously or misapplied to her life. Did she really have to be afraid? Was every little good deed she might have done but didn't really sin? Did she have to be perfect before God could love her? This was a liberating experience for her as she slowly began correcting the errors in the spiritual perceptions she had learned as a child.

Facts Vs. Feelings

There is insufficient space to thoroughly discuss this next topic, but at the risk of making a complex issue sound simple, I want to touch upon it briefly. Through my adult years, one of my greatest frustrations has been the conflict between what I feel to be true—what my experience seems to indicate—and what the Bible says is true. I have seen many other Christians struggle with this as well. For example, even though the Bible says God loves me, I have never felt it the way other spiritual people do. Others have struggled with the certainty of their salvation or whether their sins have been forgiven because they do not "feel" saved or forgiven. For me, since emotion plays a major role in my personality, this discrepancy creates a dilemma.

I often go by my feelings when I buy a car, look at a piece of furniture, or decide how much I want to trust a person. A situation or function has to "feel right" or else I become uncomfortable and don't want any part of it. I'm easily affected by what happens around me. You may have similar feelings.

When it comes to God and spiritual things, I use the same psychological equipment as when I buy furniture—I rely on how I'm feeling. I know all the right answers I learned years ago to the effect that fact and faith have to supersede feelings and that we can't base salvation on emotion. On the other hand, what do I do with emotions such as fear that are so strong they feel as though they have always been inside me? Not only are they strong, but they feel correct, yet they fly in the face of Scripture. What do I do with them? I have prayed, talked to people, and at times feared having them change, because there is a certain amount of security in their familiarity.

In 1963, I purchased a book that made a lasting impression on me, and one paragraph in particular because it dealt with this issue. I have often wondered if the writer, Watchman Nee, was correct or if he was one of those "easy answer" types with unrealistic spiritual solutions to difficult problems:

> All temptation is primarily to look within; to take our eyes off the Lord and to take account of appearances. Faith is always meeting a mountain, a mountain of evidence that seems to contradict God's Word, a mountain of apparent contradiction in the realm of tangible fact—of failures in deed, as well as in the realm of feeling and suggestion—and either faith or the mountain has to go. They cannot both stand. But the trouble is that many a time the mountain stays and faith goes. That must not be. If we resort to our senses to discover the truth, we shall find Satan's lies are often enough true to our experience; but if we refuse to accept as binding anything that contradicts God's Word and maintain an attitude of faith in Him alone, we shall find instead that Satan's lies begin to dissolve and that *our experience is coming progressively to tally with that Word*.[5]

The part that intrigued me was the statement that if I persistently believed what the Bible said, my feelings would gradually change. This sounded good to me, but I had trouble believing it enough to put it into practice at the time. Somehow the strength of my feelings had a ring of validity to them, and I felt I had to do something about them. As I look back to the sixties, I ponder what my life would have been like if I had determinedly taken Mr. Nee's statement in hand and treated my depression and anger toward God and my parents as the "mountain of apparent contradiction" that had "to go" in the face of faith. I genuinely think it would not have worked. I would have buried extremely strong emotions by not honestly facing my anger and going through the maturing struggle of becoming my own person. I would have become a superficial, not-in-touch-with-myself, pious Christian with shallow experiences.

Emotionally, I wasn't ready to do what Nee was advocating, to "reckon" myself on the cross with Christ. Back then I didn't know who "myself" was, which certainly would have made it difficult to "reckon myself"! I have had to go through the painful experience of discovering my true inner feelings as a prerequisite to applying spiritual concepts appropriately, and even after all I have been through, it still is not easy.

A young Christian woman who has been struggling unsuccessfully to extricate herself from an affair reported to me, "I'm sure learning more about myself, but I don't like what I'm finding!" She has tried with intense determination to break off the relationship, but her emotions keep pulling her back. This causes strong spiritual conflict for her, because what she feels is contradictory to the biblical standard of fidelity. I believe she needs to find out what is happening with herself emotionally, and once she is fully aware of herself and possesses her feelings, she will be in a position to apply Nee's ideas and work at reprogramming.

Reprogramming

Once we begin to understand who we are and realize the distortions in our emotional and spiritual lives, we should not expect that they will magically melt away. We still must deal with the concept we have of ourselves (self-image) that developed as we were growing up at home and in the church. For many of us, this is a difficult task that requires persistent effort and prayer.

Quite frankly, my professional experience and my own struggles have led me to believe that improving self-worth or self-image is extremely hard because it is a complex issue, and ideas that have been drilled into our heads since we were infants are hard to overcome. To change self-image, I'm gradually beginning to accept the concept of reprogramming that people such as Seamands[6] and Denis Waitley[7] advocate.

In essence, this reprogramming is similar to the concept described by Watchman Nee. You determine firmly and clearly the factual truth in your mind, and then you consistently believe it and act on it. You feed it into your inner "subconscious computer" in spite of the "emotional truth" you feel, and you constantly repeat the truth to yourself. Over time, your emotions begin to fall in line with the "factual truth" as your inner computer gradually starts to accept the new information as true. Waitley believes this approach works because your inner computer only records what is fed into it. It doesn't have the capacity to judge whether information is accurate or not. That is how inaccurate ideas often take root in your thinking and remain as powerful influences in spite of the truth.

You must determine firmly and clearly
the factual truth in your mind and
consistently believe
and act on it. You feed it into your
"subconscious computer"
in spite of the "emotional truth" you feel,
and you constantly repeat the truth to yourself.

Although C. S. Lewis was not writing about this specific subject, his thinking certainly parallels this point: "Do not waste time bothering whether you 'love' your neighbor: act as if you did. As soon as we do this we find one of the great secrets. When you are behaving as if you loved some one, you will presently come to love him."[8]

I often liken the process to my experience of living in Hattiesburg, Mississippi, when I was in graduate school. From the very first day when I drove into town, my sense of direction was off by one-quarter. In other words, what was actually east *felt* like north, and so on. Try as I might to change, this error persisted during the entire two years I lived there, and whenever I had to regain my bearings, I had to deliberately and consciously think out my directions. During reprogramming, a person has to consciously and deliberately orient himself to the factual truth despite his feelings.

Seamands describes three steps in the process.[9] The first is to correct faulty theology that says "a self-belittling attitude is pleasing to God." Then we need to develop a picture of self-worth based on God's love and promises, not on past hurts and distortions. This involves coming to grips with our hurts and distortions and putting them in perspective so we can see God's promises more clearly. He also asserts that Satan often uses our past painful experiences to keep us down, and if we have properly dealt with them, we have gained a spiritual victory as well. Finally, we must become partners with God and the Holy Spirit in this reprogramming, which is not a crisis experience but a process that takes place over time.

We need to develop a picture of self-worth
based on God's love and promises,
not on past hurts and distortions.

Seamands is correct in his process, but I believe it is easy for some people to apply this remedy too soon. More specifically, they take a spiritual approach to emotional issues before they have adequately emptied themselves of their hurt, anger, and other damaged emotions from the past. Trying to bypass pain by jumping into reprogramming prematurely, however, can have disastrous results, because the influence of the damaged emotions usually does not disappear immediately.

To simply repress past hurts in the name of spiritual reprogramming keeps us at risk. Because I have seen many spiritual people caught by surprise by too-long-ignored feelings (see Chapter 11), I believe strongly in the idea of facing all that we feel, knowing what our distortions are, taking them to God for forgiveness, and *then* applying the principle of living according to the truth in spite of what we feel and believing that our self-worth is based on God's love, not on what our past hurts tell us.

Another note of caution is needed here. It is also easy at times to simply wallow in our past hurt (remember how Rollo May said unexpressed resentment can lead to self-pity) and use our agony as an excuse to avoid the more painful steps of growth and letting go of our hurt. I am not advocating that. I believe that as we honestly express our hurt, there comes a time when we have plumbed our inner depths, explored all our inner secret closets, and emptied our wounds. If we have done our job properly, the eventual letting go of the hurt comes in a gradual, natural manner and prepares the way for reprogramming. If we continue to be angry or let a past hurt have an active influence in our lives, we have dealt improperly with our pain.

Also related to this is the fact that some of us usually have to experience the futility of our own efforts to solve our problems before we are willing or able to accept God's help, or anyone else's for that matter. This often takes place as we see all the overwhelming emotional trash in our lives and realize that we have made a mess out of things through our own efforts. Again, we are faced with another truth about ourselves, and we realize we need to turn to God and others for support. For these reasons, we must not turn our backs on emotions too quickly and attempt to force them into line with "the facts," or else more trouble will develop.

Fear of God

There's a complication that can interfere with the process outlined by Seamands. Recall again Terri, the woman whose father put her in the basement with the rats. She is unable to turn to God the Father because so much emotional anguish and distortion gets in the way. It will be difficult for her to base her self-worth on her concept of God and draw comfort from His love as she tries to modify her past distortions. The people who have such a negative concept of God based on experiences with an earthly father, or who are afraid of Him because of the fearful sermons they have heard at church, must first reprogram these fears before God can become a total resource on their behalf in the process of healing.

A number of years ago Robert Schuller sent me an E. Stanley Jones book because I had mailed a contribution to his "Hour of Power" program. I had never read Jones before, and I found his book very uplifting and practical. One paragraph opened my eyes to a point I had not realized before as he quoted a church member who had told him he "lived by fears rather than by faith."[10] This struck me deeply as I realized that I, too, was living more by fear than faith. With fear so prominent in evangelical teaching, I suspect this is true of many Christians.

As I examined my situation, I gradually realized that my fear was not limited to God; I had grown up afraid to speak up to my dad, I felt guilty if I asserted myself toward my mom, I was afraid of being hurt by others, and I often made decisions based on what would be "safe" instead of simply launching out in pure faith. A psychological test I had taken also revealed I was cautious in trusting people, being somewhat suspicious of their motives. As my wife calmly stated during one of our many discussions, "It's no wonder you feel afraid of God. You're cautious and suspicious about other people, too." Indeed I was. *Perhaps*, I thought to myself, *my fear of God was an extension of the other fears I had in my personality.* And I am an "S" type of person; "S" people are naturally fearful, anyway. I have a definite need to feel safe, and I mean *feel* safe.

One day as I was reading The Living Bible version of 1 John 4:18, the words of the verse jumped out at me: "We need have no fear of someone who loves us perfectly; his perfect love for us eliminates all dread of what he might do to us. If we are afraid, it is for fear of what he might do to us, and shows that we are not fully convinced that he really loves us." The truth of the verse hit me like a ton of bricks! It was true. I was afraid of what God might do to *me*. I had heard all the hellfire sermons as a youngster, fear had been used to scare me into salvation, God's will sounded like a life of suffering, and even heaven and eternity seemed like an endless nightmare with no escape—which it would be, I thought, to "spend eternity" with a God of whom I was afraid. John was talking about safety in being loved, and I realized that I hadn't reached the point where I could honestly feel loved enough to have no fear. But at least I understood it a little more. Still, I wondered if I could ever *feel* it. How was I supposed to make the switch? If you have had similar feelings, you are not alone.

Overcoming distortions that we have about God and His love often requires a positive, accepting relationship with another person who loves us just as we are. It is going to be difficult for us to get a handle on God's love if we haven't experienced love from another person we can see and touch. Unless another person actually loves us, we don't know what it even feels like to be loved. This point also highlights the need for a healthy, positive relationship with someone we can trust as we express our emotions, examine our distortions, and experience another person's love while we do so. God often shows His love to us through other people. Feeling loved by another person, we can begin to transfer what we have learned to our relationship with God.

Raw Faith

Many times the most we can do is honestly say to God, "This is where I am at and how I feel. Now, I know You may not like it, and please forgive me, but I don't know what else to do. Please either change it or show me how to deal with it." This is where our own raw faith has to come in—faith in the love of Christ that somehow it will eventually be okay even though there is so much we don't understand. In fact, I am convinced that this is the only true solution for unanswered questions regardless of personality style.

Many times we have to operate on raw faith—
faith in the love of Christ
that somehow it will eventually be okay
even though there is so much
we don't understand.

Often my fear related to God comes in the quietness of the night, just before I go to sleep, as the truth of 1 John 4:18 surfaces. It's hard for me to feel secure around God and truly believe that He has my best interests at heart, but as I see events happen in my life that I know I didn't bring about, I find myself slowly changing. When I heard a workshop leader state that "God is committed to making us feel secure," I was inwardly jolted because it seemed so different from the God I learned about in my youth.

Even though our experiences are not exactly parallel, I

have taken some comfort from Jay Kesler's comments about his own questionings in the night. Perhaps you will, too. He writes,

> I feel closest to God when I wake up in the middle of the night. It's dark and quiet, and I'm all alone. I listen, trying to focus my groggy brain back into consciousness, and wonder, "What's it all about, really? This Gospel I go around preaching—is it such Good News? Am I different from anyone else? Is life anything but a crazy, meaningless spin?" It's then that I cry out, "God! God!" and I am flooded with a sense of his presence. God never condemns me for falling down. That's the pain of growth. But goodness means not staying down.[11]

Many Christians have had that flood of closeness to God in the night, but others have had the flood of struggle. I believe there are no easy answers but a continual process over which God keeps a careful watch as we continue to make our way toward maturity. Once we have clearly defined the emotional areas and the spiritual ones, we must continue to move toward living by faith instead of fear, and we must remain open to experiences and answers that God brings our way. Let me close with a statement by C. S. Lewis that speaks to this issue:

> On the whole, God's love for us is a much safer subject to think about than our love for Him. Nobody can always have devout feelings: and even if we could, feelings are not what God principally cares about. Christian Love, either towards God or towards man, is an affair of the will. . . . He will give us feelings of love if He pleases. We cannot create them for ourselves, and we must not demand them as a right. But the great thing to remember is that, though our feelings come and go, His love for us does not.[12]

PART FIVE

Building a Healthy
Environment for Faith

CHAPTER 17

Making the Church a Safe Place to Be

Paul Tournier warns, "Theologians, and even psychologists, seem sometimes to be too sure of what line we ought to follow."[1] At the risk of committing the very error he describes, I have some observations about how the church could diminish the danger points described earlier. Perhaps one of the most important lessons I have learned is that there's a diversity of personalities, opinions, and ways of doing things. There is no *one way* that is always right for all of us. However, there are some general principles that apply to many cases. Some of the points discussed in this chapter apply to both church and parents; others relate more specifically to practices of the church.

Broader Perspective

The church needs to broaden its view of human behavior and development, particularly concerning the rhythm and flow between self-assertion and renunciation as described by Tournier. In my personal experience and in the lives of struggling Christians who have come to me for counseling, I have noticed a common thread: self-denial, premature renunciation, or whatever name you give it was taught exclusively, with no explanation or even appreciation for the fact that people cannot give up something they do not possess.

269

In response to this teaching, some of those people who have been unable to put self-assertion and self-denial in proper perspective ultimately reject Christianity,[2] and the ones who don't reject it remain in the church as frustrated, reluctant Christians. In my estimation, the type of Christian training advocated by the little booklet in which Julie was the exemplary model is all too common. There is an ebb and flow in the way people function and grow, and this concept needs to be incorporated into the overall picture of spiritual growth.

This truth is readily evident in dealing with small children. If my daughter is struggling with a puzzle that is too complicated for her, I'm doing her a disservice if I step in too quickly to help her. Once she has exhausted her attempts to solve the puzzle herself, *then* she's ready to ask for help and genuinely accept it. Her willingness at that point is based on her experience of not being able to solve it on her own. Incidentally, having the opportunity to accomplish as much as she can in the process also helps build her self-esteem.

I see this same principle in my life and the lives of other adults. Most of us need to do our best, play out our options, and eventually come to the place where we say, "I just can't do it! It's not working! I've made a mess of things!" At this point, we are usually willing to turn to God and accept a spiritual truth that has previously been resisted. But the very reason we can accept it is that we have had the prior experience of struggling and coming to the conclusion that we couldn't handle it alone.

For example, I recently counseled a young woman who had been deeply hurt by her father, who essentially abandoned her as a child. She tried to avoid the pain this brought into her life, and in order to escape more rejection and abandonment as a young adult, she developed a pattern of avoiding closeness with men. When boyfriends treated her kindly, she dropped them and dated fellows who used her, with their misuse being her reason for keeping emotional distance. She gained weight and blamed her appearance for her unmarried state, and she remained unhappy.

In therapy, we gradually uncovered many of the twists and turns in her life, and this caused her finally to face the true, original problem—her fear of being hurt. But she could accept the truth only after she had tried every other possible method to avoid the pain.

Too often church leaders or ministers, like protective parents, step into people's lives and try to stop them from going down the "wrong road." However, it seems that when people are rescued prematurely from their problems, they are not emotionally prepared for a true solution. They need to experience the futility of their own efforts first, and then they will willingly turn to God or to a person, not because they have to, but because they genuinely want to do it.

People need to live in the first movement of self-development, which is a preparation for the second, and God is over both. As Tournier says:

> The second movement, in fact, is also an affirmation of self, but on a much higher plane—a bolder and more adult assertion than revolt can ever be. In light of it the first movement can be seen to be a necessary but provisional stage, the point of which is that it prepares the ground for the second movement. One must have a place before one can give it up. One must receive before giving, exist before abandoning oneself in faith. We receive a place only so as eventually to leave it, treasure only so as to cast it away, a personal existence only so as to be able to offer it up. Thus, to deprive a man of his place is not only to take that place from him, but also to take away from him the chance of the religious experience of giving it up himself.[3]

Parents as well as pastors need to realize the truth in Teilhard de Chardin's statement as quoted by Tournier:

Thus, in the general rhythm of the Christian life, development and renunciation, attachment and detachment are not mutually exclusive. On the contrary, they harmonize, like breathing in and out in the movement of our lungs.[4]

When the prodigal son left home with his father's money stuffed in his pocket and headed for the "far country," he was asserting himself in the first movement (see Luke 15:11–32). He wanted to get away and develop his own viewpoint. It seems significant that his father did not argue with him, threaten to disown him, or bribe him to stay home. It is even more amazing that he gave the fellow his inheritance and financed the entire escapade. The father, who surely could see where his son was headed, was willing to give him the opportunity to venture out on his own, even though it must have pained and saddened him to do so. Clearly, the father was involved with the first movement and understood it. By allowing the son to leave, he gave him the chance to return on his own and have a meaningful spiritual experience. If the father had forced him to stay home, he would have deprived his son of this rich opportunity.

Although the son didn't realize it at the time, his trip into the far country was a step that prepared him for the second movement. His decision to return home with a changed point of view and a repentant attitude was possible because he realized his own emptiness through the first movement. He was grateful to be the owner's son, and he no longer took it for granted. There was genuine joy in his heart.

The harmonizing of the two movements is clear. Since the father represents God in this story, it is also reassuring to see that he is involved in both movements—each has its place in the overall scheme of things. The joy in the story is the father's love as he welcomed his son back with open arms, reinstated him as a son, and threw a party to celebrate his return. Helmut Thielicke believes that the essential theme of the story is about not the son who left home but the father (God) who waited patiently for his son. "The ultimate theme of this story, therefore, is not the prodigal son, but the Father who finds us. The ultimate theme is not the faithlessness of men, but the faithfulness of God."[5] The father in the story allowed his son to live in the first movement, and he loved him when he returned in the second one. God does the same for us.

Too often we think God only approves of self-denial. We wrongly assume He disapproves of the necessary first step, self-assertion.

God's love for humanity is the point of this story, and if we want to be instruments of His love, can we do any less than follow His example in our relationships with those who are struggling to find their way as the prodigal was doing? Can't we stand ready to say, "You are loved. You may come back home"?

All of this is easier said than done, however. When we see people we love going down the wrong road, it's difficult for us to patiently stand by while they experience the futility of their own efforts in the first movement. "Do you mean there is nothing we can do to help besides wait while a child we love is on drugs?" a concerned parent asked me. (For those of you who share this concern, you will find specific suggestions for dealing with teenagers in Chapter 18.) What if someone we love is going through a divorce or some other action that we believe is wrong? We can learn from the father in the story, says Thielicke: "He does not force the son to stay at home. He must have his freedom. God forces nobody. He did not force Adam and Eve to refrain from snatching at the forbidden fruit."[6] Too often we think God works only in the second movement. We shut Him out of the first. If we can see the entire picture more clearly, we realize that He is involved in both movements. Then we can see the hope that our loved ones' lives will work out, and we can understand that God is at work in their lives even as they live out the first movement. Allowing others the freedom to struggle and giving support are discussed later in this chapter.

Definition of Sin

There seems to be an implicit assumption that if children or even adults are not controlled, they will make decisions that move them away from God, or more specifically, they will live life only in the first movement of self-assertion, which is systematically seen as sinful.

If the church is going to broaden its concept of human behavior, it must also change the way it defines sin. I am referring here to the working definition of sin as it is typically applied to practical living. As I said earlier, when sin is defined and emphasized *primarily* in terms of behavior to be avoided instead of an inner state of being, the stage is set for a variety of negative and unhealthy responses to take place. First, church leaders and parents often become watchdogs to prevent children and other adult Christians from venturing into the forbidden areas. Such ventures lead to a loss of control. In order to maintain control, the persons in charge cannot encourage independent thinking, because people might go in the "wrong direction" and live "unsuccessful" Christian lives by not following the master list.

Second, Christians who do follow the list can easily begin to believe it is possible to reduce the inner sinful state of being by reducing certain external behaviors. In other words, the focus is on the manifestations of sin (the list), and not on the inner state of being, which makes it easy to develop a false sense of self-righteousness.

To maintain their sense of self-righteousness, the sensitive, fearful Christians become cautious about how they live for fear they will unwittingly commit a sin. They live as though sin were a contagious disease external to themselves, believing if they live cautiously and conservatively they can avoid catching it, when in reality sin is already inside them as part of their nature.

We cannot avoid sin by living only in self-denial
as the Pharisees tried to do,
because our "sinfulness" stays with us
no matter how "good" we are.

If the church would emphasize that sin is actually a state of being that is present in every person, many of the danger points could be avoided in the lives of growing children and adults. It reduces the amount of tension that people feel because there is less pressure to "perform" in order to be a good Christian. We cannot avoid sin by living only in the second movement as the Pharisees tried to do, because our "sinfulness" stays with us no matter which movement we're in.

In this light, we can be less afraid of our feelings and more open to ourselves, which is a necessary part of becoming our own persons. When we close off certain feelings because they are "wrong," we are also shutting out God, which prevents us from experiencing His grace. "If we say that we have no sin, we are only fooling ourselves and refusing to accept the truth. But if we confess our sins to him, he can be depended on to forgive us and to cleanse us from every wrong"(1 John 1:8–9 TLB). If we as Christians can see that sin is a state of being rather than the action itself, we can more easily face our feelings head-on and honestly say, "Yes, I really am angry and the anger is mine," which places us in a position to take our true feelings to God for open discussion and forgiveness. In other words, trying to follow a list to be self-righteous and holy takes us away from an attitude of gratitude and from a more positive Christian life, because it leads us away from knowing our true nature.

> Trying to follow a list to be
> self-righteous and holy takes us
> away from an attitude of gratitude.

Being more open to our feelings and experiences also has implications for how we arrive at salvation. The more we are able to experience ourselves as we really are, the more we will see that we miss the mark. The more we are allowed to try things in our own strength, the quicker we will realize that we cannot do it alone. The more we actually *experience* our missing the mark at a gut level, or as some may put it, "experience the misery of sin," the more inclined we will be to look at salvation for what it really is— salvation from ourselves. Then our motivation is desire for salvation, not fear of going to hell. This quite naturally leads to an attitude of gratitude, because then we are grateful for what God has provided and we enter the area of service with a joyful heart.

This process seldom takes place in the church community, because growing children usually don't appreciate their nature of missing the mark or actually "experience" their individual sinful selves. Instead, the church scares them into salvation before they are ready for it and expects them to be joyful servants.

Jesus told an interesting story during His visit at Simon the Pharisee's house. While Jesus was eating, a prostitute entered the house and knelt behind Him. As she wept, her tears fell on His feet. Not only did she wipe His feet with her hair, but she also kissed His feet and poured expensive perfume on them. The incident upset Simon, who thought that if Jesus really were a prophet, He would have resisted the woman's contact (see Luke 7:36–50).

In response to Simon, Jesus told a story about a man who loaned a great deal of money to one person and a much smaller amount to another. Neither of the borrowers was able to repay his loan, and the lender forgave both debts. When Jesus asked, "Which do you suppose loved him [the lender] most after that?" Simon correctly answered, "I suppose the one who had owed him the most."

Jesus summed up His response by saying, "Therefore her sins—and they are many—are forgiven, for she loved me much; but one who is forgiven little, shows little love" (Luke 7:47 TLB). Jesus seemed to be saying that there is a correlation between the number of sins forgiven and the amount of love and gratitude that follows forgiveness. This fact is evident in the apostle Paul's life. He demonstrated unfailing commitment to Christ, but he also described himself as the "chief among sinners" (see 1 Tim. 1:15).

In my own experience, most of the deeply changed and fruitful Christians I have known were people who grew up outside the church in an environment that allowed them to experience their feelings and come to a deep realization that they *needed* salvation. Consequently, their salvation experience had deep meaning. Others I have observed were strong-willed, "D" type personalities who rebelled against their evangelical upbringing, left the church, plunged into life enough to experience their emotions and needs, and eventually returned to sincere, meaningful Christian lives.

My point is that by more clearly emphasizing and defining sin as a state of being that manifests itself in certain behaviors, and that as part of our sinful nature we are always looking out for ourselves, we can allow our children the freedom to experience and understand their natures, which will provide a more solid base for them to eventually choose salvation out of desire, not out of fear. Tournier comments:

> The first movement is—not the fact of sinning, since that is common to all, but the intense, humiliating, overwhelming emotion that accompanies the conviction of sin. Then, and only then, the message of grace takes on its full value. The conviction of sin is the place where we encounter God's grace.[7]

The essence of this statement is readily visible in the prodigal son's life. The overwhelming benefit of his far country experience was his *awareness* of his sin—*the same sin that existed in him even before he left home.* When he returned home, he understood and appreciated his father's love for the first time.

We need room to live the first movement of self-assertion so we can genuinely approach the second movement of renunciation, and then we can continue living in the knowledge that life consists of constant movement back and forth between these two points. We will be emotionally and spiritually healthier as a result.

It seems to me that God was saying the same thing to the generations following Joshua who hadn't witnessed God's work in leading the children of Israel into the Promised Land. God knew they needed firsthand experiences observing Him at work in their lives, just as second- and third-generation Christians today need to experience God as a reality in their own lives rather than trying to live off their parents' spiritual experiences. "The Lord left [nations] in the land to test the new generation of Israel who had not experienced the wars of Canaan. *For God wanted to give opportunity to the youth of Israel to exercise faith and obedience in conquering their enemies*" (Judg. 3:1–2 TLB, emphasis added). Second- and third-generation Christians today need the same opportunity to exercise faith and obedience in their lives.

Free to Struggle

Crucial to being more open to our feelings and experiences is the knowledge that it is okay for us as Christians to struggle. If we redefine success and failure in the Christian life, struggle assumes a different meaning, as Jay Kesler points out:

> This account [an experience reported to Kesler about a family's failures] had a profound effect on me and prompted me to reexamine my own relationships. I began to wonder who started the lie that Christians have to succeed all the time. Perhaps some of it stems from always putting people who have succeeded in front of congregations and youth groups. This technique may be good strategy for sales motivation meetings but it seems to have done great harm to the church. In a world where success models are spotlighted and failures are shunted into the shadows we have learned to mask our feelings and defeats.[8]

Placing "successful" people before congregations and youth groups conveys the subtle message, "Be like these people—this is the way you should be!" There is no place for the people who feel defeated in their personal Christian lives.

"Who started the lie that Christians
have to succeed all the time?"

As a YFC staff person, I recall preparing for our annual sponsors' dinner where we presented our program and asked for funds. The staff carefully reviewed the past year's activities to identify "successful" teens with whom we had worked so we could have them give their personal testimonies to the sponsors. We didn't have struggling teens present their struggles.

Somehow the notion that perfect is better seems to have found a place in our lives and in our churches, because there seems to be something about human nature that believes being perfect is going to result in love and acceptance, whereas open admission of weakness invites criticism and rejection. Thus, to many of us, the admonitions toward perfection are attractive because we want to gain love and avoid rejection.

This desire is readily evident in my counseling when a person who has low feelings of self-worth talks about trying very hard to be perfect and not show weakness in order to earn love and approval from someone else. In reality, this usually doesn't work, because the "perfect" person eventually appears unreachable and becomes a source of anxiety for others who feel "that person is too good for me." I know that perfection in others troubles me, whether it is a person whose house is so immaculate that I fear to move about freely or a person who always does the "right things." I feel more comfortable with a "perfect" person once I have spotted a few flaws.

I'm not suggesting that we cast aside all scriptural ideals or that ministers should not exhort people to improve, but plain statements from the pulpit and church leaders are needed to place these issues in perspective. Sermons need to point out the various growth levels that people experience, including the fact that people arrive at their own maturity in their own time and in their own unique way. Ministers should not try to make people feel guilty for not attaining spiritual perfection in two or even twenty years. If the ministers' sermons consistently sound as though everything should be great and wonderful in the Christian's life, without making allowances for human emotion and struggle, what conclusion can be drawn by the sensitive, struggling Christian other than "something is wrong with me"?

But in reality, does being a growing Christian mean always thinking, feeling, and doing the right things? Is so-called failure, or admitting to a sinful state of being, really worse than a superficial, false self-righteousness that is based on following a few rules? As Tournier observes:

> It is nevertheless true that the most wonderful thing in this world is not the good that we accomplish, but the fact that good can come out of the evil that we do. I have been struck, for example, by the numbers of people who have been brought back to God under the influence of a person to whom they had some improper attachment. . . . In this world, our task is not so much to avoid mistakes, as to be fruitful. To be more and more able to recognize our faults, so as the better to be able to understand the price of God's mercy, and to devote ourselves more completely to him, makes our lives more fertile. But to become obsessed with the effort to recognize our faults, and to refuse to act for fear of committing some sin, makes them sterile. Our vocation is, I believe, to build good out of evil. For if we try to build good out of good, we are in danger of running out of raw material.[9]

Tournier's statement places so-called defeats in a different light, as he views them leading to eventual fruitfulness, which is a more realistic goal than continual success. We can be fruitful regardless of our successes, and even in spite of them at times. Looking at the Christian life from this perspective leaves us free to move about, to struggle, to take chances as we try new things, and to feel less inhibited about life and making some mistake.

"In this world, our task is not so much
to avoid mistakes, as to be fruitful."

Pulpit Support

In my years of church attendance, I have come to the conclusion that it is the rare minister who has a real understanding of people—at least judging by sermon content. In my home church as a boy, I can remember only one positive, practical sermon delivered by a visiting evangelist that made an impact on me because it was so down-to-earth. My primary recollection of my minister's sermons as a teenager was counting how many times he said "As it were" (there were many) during his sermon. I heard nothing in church that related to the loneliness, frustration, or guilt I felt.

Since most Christians base their concept of the Christian life on the weekly sermons they hear at church, they need to be given official permission from the pulpit to struggle, to ask questions, and to think for themselves. In my life, when I became aware of my internal struggles, I experienced a great deal of anxiety because I didn't know what was happening to me. What I was feeling had never been discussed from the pulpit, and it wasn't a part of the Christian life that had been laid out to me. Feeling that I was the only person in the world who felt the way I did only added to my intense fear. If I had heard sermons or discussions on this subject, I am sure my past struggles would have been less difficult, because I at least would have known I wasn't alone.

Instead, I had the impression that if I followed the master list and was spiritual enough, I would have peace that passes understanding, and life would be smooth. If anything came along that interfered with my peace, my Christianity was threatened. Sermons need to take account of the fact that life itself consists of struggle and difficulties to overcome, and that Christianity does not take the struggles away. Rather, it helps us deal with them.

As much as many people in the pews may need to hear such sermons from the pulpit, whether or not they hear them will depend on ministers and their particular personality styles. As mentioned in Chapter 6, ministers' individual personalities precede their theology and influence their theological interpretations. If ministers are going to tell their parishioners that struggle is acceptable in the Christian life, they must believe it themselves and be secure enough to allow their listeners to work out their own salvation. The ministers who personally prefer things to be black and white will tend to approach spiritual issues in the same fashion.

If ministers are going to tell their parishioners
that struggle is acceptable in the Christian life,
they must first of all believe it themselves.

Getting more support from the pulpit may be difficult to achieve for these reasons. Therefore, as individual Christians, we need to take a more active role in building our personal faith rather than depending on ministers to direct our spiritual lives. This of course is consistent with the notion of assuming responsibility for one's own destiny, developing a truly meaningful personal faith, and becoming one's own person. Relying too much on our ministers can become a method of escaping from freedom—in other words, relinquishing personal responsibility to an outside source because it's frightening to stand on our own.

Personal Support

As individual Christians, we can help one another and our children live in an atmosphere of freedom that allows struggle and questions. In my opinion, the key to accomplishing this is quite simple in principle but difficult to practice. The more we accept that struggling and thinking are acceptable, the more we can encourage and accept others when they struggle. People usually have difficulty allowing others to do something they are not free to do. For example, a person who carefully follows all the rules and develops a superficial sense of self-righteousness will have little patience with or tolerance for a person who is struggling and asking difficult questions.

An experience that comes to mind almost immediately took place with an old college friend I visited on a trip to my hometown. He had entered the ministry and was married to a minister's daughter who generally presented herself in a pious manner. During the course of my visit that evening, I made the comment, "I am a sinner in the process of being saved." Upon hearing this, my friend's wife pulled her shoulders back, tilted her head to one side, and with disdain in her voice firmly stated, "Well, Don! I don't know about you, but I'm not a sinner!" Whereupon both she and her husband began quoting Scripture in an earnest attempt to support their view and discredit my opinion. Realizing this was obviously not a healthy climate for a struggling Christian, I ended the visit as quickly as I could.

To me, her conduct is an example of not providing support in a relationship. Since she obviously saw herself as being perfect and without sin, she could not see me as a "sinner," either. To accept my struggle would force her to look at herself—something she obviously was unwilling to do. She was unable to allow me any more freedom than she possessed herself.

Relate without Judgment

We must also relate to children and people without judgment. One of my psychology professors emphasized that people coming for therapy do not like being imposed upon or evaluated. Actually, no one likes it. Judgment destroys a climate for sharing and eliminates opportunities to help others. As soon as a sensitive person feels judged, as I did in the example above, he will stop talking and withdraw, perhaps feeling even more discouraged.

One of the best ways to become nonjudgmental in our relationships is to develop a clearer sense of our own sinfulness (missing the mark) and diminish our sense of self-righteousness. How can I condemn someone who is no guiltier than I? Or as Jesus told the Pharisees regarding the woman caught in adultery, "All right, hurl the stones at her until she dies. But only he who never sinned may throw the first!" (John 8:7 TLB).

Tournier's thoughts on this subject have been very helpful to me. He writes about a friend who was obtaining a divorce:

> I cannot approve of his course of action, because divorce is always disobedience of God. I should be betraying my belief if I were to hide it from him. I know that there is always a solution other than divorce to a marital conflict, if we are really prepared to seek it under God's guidance. But I know that this disobedience is no worse than the slander, the lie, the gesture of pride of which I am guilty every day. The circumstances of our lives are different, but the reality of our hearts is the same. If I were in his place, would I act any differently from him? I have no idea. At least I know that I should need friends who loved me unreservedly just as I am, with all my weaknesses, and who would trust me without judging me. If he gets his divorce, he will no doubt meet even greater difficulties than those he is in today. He will need my affection all the more, and this is the assurance I must give him.[10]

In discussing another person, Tournier notes that he "took the greatest care not to make any pronouncement about the struggle of conscience which was going on in our patient, for one does not know by what roads a soul must travel in order to achieve its full stature."[11] We are in process as people and as Christians. We are not what we once were or what we eventually will be. Our level of maturity varies and shifts as we have new experiences and become older.

We all learn in our unique way and have to mature at our own pace. And we don't know what types of experiences our neighbor needs to grow. So, what right do we have to criticize others before they have reached their destination? Besides, is there a final arrival point this side of the grave? So let's look at something positive we can do for others.

Need for Support

Some Christians who are "failing" and struggling are already experiencing inner turmoil and may be condemning themselves for their misbehavior or lack of faith. They do not need my condemnation as well. It seems to me that my job is to love and support a person as he struggles with his particular set of inner feelings. As someone has said, "The Christian army is the only one that shoots its own wounded!" And the wounded Christian certainly needs my love more than my condemnation. Is failing to support the struggling Christian in line with the biblical injunction to "bear one another's burdens" (see Gal. 6:2)?

Now, you may ask, "If I listen to and support someone who is doing something wrong, am I not condoning what that person is doing?" I don't think so. For one thing, your neighbor's spiritual life is between him and God, and it is the Holy Spirit's task to convict him of sin—not yours. You can listen and care, but judgment and forgiveness come from God, not you. You can love someone without loving what he is doing, and loving doesn't mean you sanction what he does. Besides, if you withdraw your love because you disagree with your neighbor's actions, your love is conditional and manipulative. In effect you say, "I will love you when you behave the way I think you should." This is not consistent with God's love, which remains steady and unconditional in spite of our behavior.

As the apostle Paul wrote, "They are God's servants, not

yours. They are responsible to him, not to you. Let him tell them whether they are right or wrong. And God is able to make them do as they should" (Rom. 14:4 TLB).

Tournier, in describing what people need when they come for therapy, clearly summarizes what our fellow Christians need in their struggles and what we as parents need to provide our children:

> The majority of those who consult us are not primarily seeking advice. They have already said to themselves, over and over again, all that can be said about their problem. They may even have an idea of how it can be solved, but they have not dared, or have not been able, to follow it out. The support they want is a support to counter their own weakness. They need to express themselves, not to have an arbitration award pronounced against them. They need a place where they can be completely sincere, and feel themselves completely free. That is so rare in this world! Freedom is a wonderful support to have. They need to be able to say what is holding them back, before they can manage to overcome their inner resistance. . . . The ideal support, then, is a presence, a vigilant, unshakeable, indefectible presence, but one that is discreet, gentle, silent, and respectful. We want help in our struggle, but do not want our personal responsibility to be taken from us. A look, a smile, an intense emotion—these are the things that can help us win our victories over ourselves.[12]

Danger of Gossip

Even though we can become more comfortable with our own struggles and in turn can accept the same in others as we provide the support of freedom, one other element must be present within the church fellowship or else our efforts will certainly fail. That element is confidentiality. The opposite of this, in scriptural terms, is gossip. If gossip exists within the personal relationships that develop, destruction of everything positive is inevitable. Gossip is so clearly prohibited in the New Testament because it destroys trust, which is the foundation of relationships. Indeed, without trust, true Christian fellowship is nonexistent. Gossip destroys Christians and church life. From this perspective, gossip is probably the most destructive manifestation of sin within the context of Christian fellowship. In fact, I have often wondered if the prayer chains at church become a form of permissible gossip, because the remarks about a faltering soul are couched in terms of how much the hurting person needs prayer support.

Fear as Motivation

The use of fear to motivate sensitive, vulnerable children toward the gospel is one of the most damaging methods used in the church, and in my estimation it has caused untold suffering among Christians, even causing many to flee the church and turn away from God. Just the other day, a fellow in his forties sat in my office. Somehow the subject of church and fear came up. He quickly stated, "When I was real small, about five or so, I used to go to church, but I went to one where I heard hellfire sermons. It really scared me! I don't go much now. It sticks with you!" It is unfortunate that fear is his prominent childhood memory of church, and it keeps him away from church as an adult. Helmut Thielicke observes, "Whenever the New Testament speaks of repentance, always the great joy is in the background. It does not say, 'Repent or hell will swallow you up,' but 'Repent, the *kingdom* of *heaven* is at hand.'"[13] In the name of good sense and for the sake of the potential Christian, why does the church preach repentance in a fearful fashion today?

In a conversation with an evangelical minister, I was amazed at his lack of understanding in this area. As we discussed the use of fear to motivate people toward salvation, he openly acknowledged that he did it and knew he was doing it. Even though his philosophy placed him in the company of the late evangelist D. L. Moody, I felt his attitude bordered on callous noncaring as he emphatically stated, "Well, I think the main point is to get them in [the kingdom] any way we can, and we can worry about their motivation later. Most of us got in that way, and we usually get it straightened out." Perhaps he thinks so, but I don't share his optimism. Besides, I have never heard anyone in church talk about how to change one's motivation from fear to gratitude, yet it is an issue that countless Christians must face. It appears to me it is an issue that the church has not begun to address. J. B. Phillips makes a useful observation related to the use of fearful guilt to motivate people toward salvation:

> It is interesting, though rather pathetic, to note here that the success of a certain type of Christianity depends almost wholly on this sense of guilt. For the "gospel" will be accepted only by those in whom the sense of guilt can be readily awakened or stimulated. Indeed, missioners of this type of Christianity (flying incidentally in the face of Christ's own example) will go all out to induce and foster "conviction of sin" in their hearers. The results of such efforts are usually small, a fact attributed by the missioner to the hardness of the hearts of his hearers. It is really due to the healthy reaction against artificial guilt-injection possessed by all but those few whose unhappy childhood has left them peculiarly open to this form of spiritual assault.[14]

Different Personality Styles

A related issue is the fact that different personality styles will express their Christianity differently, and some will experience problems that others will breeze through, yet each has his own place. Although we often mouth the words that "each part of the body is important," in practice we usually try to put Christians through the cookie cutter so they come out saying and doing all the "right" and same things. Being different is usually not acceptable and is often seen as possibly even dangerous.

As parents must recognize the differing personality styles of their children, so must the church accept and appreciate the differing personality styles of its members and the way in which these differences will influence learning as well as expression of one's Christian life. For example, "S" persons with fearful personalities in need of security do not need threatening sermons, but they are steady, dependable people. Since high "i" people are naturally optimistic, they can easily launch out on faith and inject enthusiasm into a project. "C" people prefer to have their questions answered in a concise fashion before they act, and they will pay attention to details. They will find it difficult to launch out on faith. "D's" will find it difficult to lean on God because they prefer to be self-reliant, but they can give leadership in the face of obstacles. A full discussion of these points is not possible here, but I trust the general point is clear. When the church begins to teach children and adults in a manner that is compatible with their personality bent or style, danger points that currently cause enormous trouble in the spiritual area will be avoided.[15]

CHAPTER 18

Homes without Dangers

God places a high priority on children and on parents' responsibility toward the children He has given them. In recognition of and in response to God, most Christian parents publicly vow to train their children in the ways of the Lord as part of an infant dedication or baptismal service. Recently, as I listened to some young parents making these vows as they stood before our congregation, I suddenly realized the solemnity and the depth of responsibility they were accepting. It also dawned on me that I had done the same when my daughters were small—and I felt a surge of guilt. *Did I promise to do all of that?* I thought. *How well am I doing? How can I teach my daughters the truth about God? Am I doing what I can to help my daughters avoid the dangers listed in this book?*

Often in the excitement of the public service, it's easy to forget the profundity and seriousness of these vows. In the years that follow, we as parents are often so caught up in daily living that before we know it the children are half or fully grown, and we wonder where the time has gone and whether we adequately trained our children as we promised we would.

Many volumes have been written about child-rearing principles, and I don't intend to cover the entire subject here, but there are several points I want to emphasize for those of you who are concerned about your own children.

291

As with most things in life, it is easier to list or describe these points than to actually carry them out. The first set of suggestions relates to parents themselves, and the second group of suggestions consists of guidelines for helping parents relate to their children.

Parents Helping Themselves

Parents first of all have to be aware of the dangers present in their homes and be willing to admit they are there. I frequently emphasize this basic principle to the people who consult with me about changing a pattern they have. Before people can change anything, they have to be aware of what they're doing.

In order to help your children,
you must first help yourself
to be the best person you can be.

The second point is a broad one with several related issues. The best way to help your children is to first of all help yourself become the best person you can be. Some Christians have trouble with this idea because they believe it's selfish, but a child's adjustment is usually tied to the parents' adjustment. This is especially evident when I work with a person who has been divorced and whose children are having a difficult time adjusting to their own pain. I tell the divorced parent (usually the mother) to work on her adjustment to the divorce first, not neglecting the children, but to work out her own pain. As she does so, the children become calmer, better behaved, and more open about their feelings. By taking care of themselves, Mom and Dad not only provide a better environment, but they also serve as examples of how to properly handle life's difficult situations.

Since the quality of children's adjustment usually depends on their parents, it is important that young adults do as much maturing as possible before having children. They need to identify, understand, and clear up their own distortions about God, life, feelings, anger, sin, and so on. If young adults don't come to terms with their own parents and their own beliefs—in other words, become their own persons free to think for themselves instead of simply doing what their parents did—they quite likely will pass their distortions to their children without realizing it.

In my work, I often see habits and patterns being handed from one generation to the next because no one ever stopped to examine the validity of the habit, just like the daughter who cut off the end of the ham before she placed it in the oven. This also was true of Stan in Chapter 2, who accepted his father's distortion that women could not be trusted. Since he has kept this distortion without questioning its accuracy, he will eventually pass it on to his son without realizing what he's doing.

Following one of my multimedia presentations on this subject to a divorce support group, a fellow in his forties described his father to me as a domineering man who demanded unquestioned obedience. "I raised my boys the same way my dad raised me, but I had all kinds of trouble. Now they hardly ever want to come and see me. They wanted communication, but I wouldn't let them. I thought the way my dad did it was right!"

"Have you ever gone to them and explained that you raised them the way your dad raised you, and you can see the problems it caused? And told them you're sorry?" I asked him.

"No, I haven't," he replied. "I didn't know what I had done wrong until tonight!" He had raised his children for over twenty years using a distorted notion of how he should relate to them.

A concerned mother sat in my office and expressed her

worried thoughts about her seventh-grade son. She said, "I found several notes in his jeans' pocket before I put them in the wash. The notes talked about being depressed and wanting to kill himself. Even though I'm a teacher and work with kids, this really scared me. I want you to talk to him. Is he feeling things that a normal boy his age would feel, or does he have some serious problems?"

After I talked with her son and tested him, I realized that he had a definite conflict with his father, who tended to be demanding but talked very little. He seldom shared his thoughts with anyone, even his wife. The son was emotionally hungry—or perhaps more accurately starving—for positive attention from his dad.

When the son and I met with Dad, we learned that Grandpa also was quiet and had spent no time with the father. I emphasized repeatedly to the father how important he was to his son, and I said that when he was quiet his son had a hard time knowing whether he was angry, thinking about something else, or just being silent. The son usually believed that Dad was angry with him, which burdened his sensitive heart. Dad subsequently made a few attempts to spend time with his son, but it was short-lived. Although he did express a genuine desire to talk more with his son, he seemed unable to appreciate what his son needed from him. He continued to live as he had learned to do from his father.

Of course, this is not an ideal world, and many young people marry and have children before they're aware of the issues discussed here. Realizing these facts can create a dilemma for those who become aware of their own struggles after becoming parents.

Parents' Dilemmas

Molly, my five-year-old daughter, and I were sitting on her bed talking just before her bedtime. Suddenly, she turned toward me and with deep strength of conviction stated, "We're supposed to read the Bible every night, you know! Why don't we?"

I was taken by surprise, and many thoughts flashed through my mind as I felt a surge of guilt. Stalling to think of a face-saving answer, I responded, "Who told you that?"

"My teacher in Sunday school!" came the instant reply.

What could I say? I believed that I should read the Bible every day, but I also knew that I didn't practice that belief. In an instant, my daughter's remark exposed my personal hypocrisy, inconsistency, or whatever it is. Not only did my poor example bother me, but it also made me feel guilty. *What kind of father am I, anyway?* I thought. *I have enough struggles of my own. How can I teach my daughter truths that are still unclear to me? And I am supposed to be the psychologist who tells other parents to help themselves first? How well am I doing?*

As a youngster, I was convinced that being a kid was a tough job because of my struggles, but when I became an adult and counseled parents, and finally became a parent myself, I saw the other side. Now I'm convinced that life is often difficult not just for the children, but equally so for the parents.

Although there are many parental dilemmas, from whether children should be forced to eat carrots to what time is appropriate for teenage curfews, the most distressing problems are those that force us to face ourselves and our own inconsistencies. In their innocence, children are able to cut through adult pretenses, bringing our own inner doubts and unresolved problems to the surface. Oh, we often know all along that they've been there, but it's much easier to ignore our inconsistencies when we're not responsible for presenting good examples for our children to follow. It's easy to take comfort in the fact that we know what we *should* be doing, even if we're not living up to our beliefs.

A young father told me, "When I was growing up, we

were allowed to play tag or hide-and-seek outdoors on Sunday because it was clean and we didn't get dirty. Now that my own son is twenty months old, I realize that I'm facing a decision in the next year or so. Am I going to let him play football and get dirty on Sunday, or do I do what my parents did?"

Another father described his experience: "You know, I never really thought that much about what I believed until my children began to grow older. When I started teaching them about God is when I definitely had to examine what I really believe."

Handling Parental Dilemmas

How do we maintain an air of authority when our children are asking questions and raising issues that make us look dead wrong and as hypocritical as the Pharisees? Perhaps the critical dilemma in this discussion is, How can we be positive, constructive parents when our children know that we don't have our own struggles straightened out? What can Christian parents do when the inconsistencies that were safely tucked away out of sight are suddenly thrust into plain view?

One thing we can do is ignore it, pretend it isn't there. However, that doesn't change the reality of the situation; the problem still exists. Our children, who observed the discrepancy in the first place, also know it remains. When we ignore it, they see us lacking courage and honesty. As a result, they lose respect for us. When nothing changes, all involved lose an opportunity to grow.

A second option is to fake it. We can pretend that we believe something when in reality we are unsure or don't care. Or we can act the way we think we should even though it may not seem to fit our nature. I doubt if there is any benefit in our "faking" values or behaviors that we don't genuinely believe, because children can spot phony behavior, and they reject it.

A third approach is to use admonitions to compensate for our inconsistencies. Although it is at least more honest than ignoring or faking, it still smacks of the old saying "Do as I say, not as I do." This approach fails to benefit our children, because we all know that "actions speak louder than words" and that our children "learn what we live." At most, this approach alleviates some parental guilt because we can say, "At least we *told* them the right things, even if we didn't live it."

The best approach, in my opinion, is also the most difficult. It is to face the problem openly and honestly. Although it is distressing, and even embarrassing, to admit that we don't have all the answers or that our behavior isn't always consistent with our stated beliefs, everyone can benefit if we handle it properly.

When we face the issues, some hard questions arise. If I believe daily Bible reading is important, why don't I do it? Do I believe it as much as I say I do? For the young father mentioned earlier, it is, "Do I continue to believe that getting dirty playing on Sunday is wrong, or do I change what my parents taught me?" Such questions triggered by our encounters with our growing children force us to examine ourselves and re-evaluate the issues. Although time consuming, this process is important not only for us but also for our children. We may need to make some definite changes so our lives will be honest examples of God's truth. As we help ourselves, we help those who look to us as role models.

Openly admitting our shortcomings to our children may not help us save face, but it certainly develops a more honest relationship and sets a good example. Our children know the truth about us anyway, and instead of losing respect, we will gain more of their respect when we admit we're wrong and don't have everything figured out. Every person who has had a parent who was "never wrong" and has come to me for therapy has expressed frustration and disgust at the rigid, unbending, "I'm always right" attitude that spoiled their relationship. "I can show my dad right to his face in black and white that he's wrong, and he still won't admit it! I can't get anywhere with him!" I have heard these words many times, and whenever they're spoken, I realize that the chance for a supportive, positive relationship between parent and child has been lost.

Admitting your shortcomings helps your children see that life isn't always perfect and free from struggle. This gives them the freedom to be comfortable with their own struggles and feelings.

Admitting our shortcomings helps our children see that life is not always perfect and free from struggle. This gives them the freedom to accept and be comfortable with their own struggles and feelings. It allows them to be themselves without the pressure that they must be perfect, and they will be comfortable admitting when they are wrong because Mom and Dad have set the example.

Depending on the particular issues that may arise with children, it is useful to invite them to participate in our self-examination and search for answers, particularly with junior-high-age and older youngsters. If, for example, the question relates to sex before marriage, parents and teenagers alike can read and discuss books and articles on the subject, study the Bible in detail, and search together for meaningful answers. This can also be done on other issues such as Sunday observances, the use of certain slang words, and attitudes toward people. Obviously, children must be old enough to participate, and a working relationship between parents and children must be in place for this to be effective. It requires extra effort and courage on the parents' part to pursue such a program, but it is worth the effort.

Not only will this approach improve communication between parents and children, but it also teaches a method for problem solving that children can use for themselves later in life. In addition, it will teach and encourage children to think for themselves and base their opinions on ideas that have been seriously evaluated.

Through your example, your children will see that God can use us in spite of, or perhaps because of, our failures.

This shared approach to finding solutions is also an opportunity for us as parents to share our feelings about life and teach our children what we have learned from our mistakes. Such sharing, when done with genuineness and sincerity on our part, can be a powerful example for children who are old enough to understand.

Finally, as parents, we need to face our dilemmas not only with our children but also with God. In the area of values, we often fail to live as we know we should. With the Holy Spirit's direction, we need to examine ourselves, ask forgiveness, and make changes where necessary. It is best to admit whatever we find to ourselves, to God, and to our children—they know it anyway. Through our example, our children will see God use us in spite of, or perhaps because of, our failures. If handled properly, what seemed to be a parental dilemma can become a blessing for parent and child alike.

Parents Helping Children

There are excellent books available that describe proper parenting principles, and I won't attempt to repeat their points here. Also, the danger points discussed in Chapters 4 and 5 essentially are examples of what not to do, so it follows that the correct way is to do the opposite of the listed danger points. Awareness plays a definite role here. Parents need to be constantly aware that their own ordinary, everyday actions have a powerful influence on their children as described earlier and that these actions will often have more impact than pious family practices. Having said that, however, I want to emphasize several particular topics.

Adolescent Masturbation

Let me make a few observations on the issue of masturbation and teenage development. As parents, we have a tremendous responsibility and opportunity in this area with our children. We can either push them into deep problems with guilt, or we can help them avoid the guilt.

Many people in the church have regarded masturbation as a sin, and of course this attitude has been conveyed to young people by well-intentioned Christian parents. I have known people (particularly fellows) who have grown up in very spiritual homes with parents who induced deep guilt in their sons over masturbation, and this guilt has caused tremendous emotional problems in their adult lives. During his therapy, one young fellow said his Christian mother repeatedly stood quietly outside his bedroom door and then suddenly opened it—hoping to catch him in the act of masturbating. She was convinced he was doing something wrong and wanted to correct him. The fellow had a sense of humor, and when asked if she had ever caught him, he slyly replied, "The hand is quicker than the eye!"

In his film series "Focus on the Family,"[1] Dr. James Dobson pointedly discusses this subject, and he emphasizes that he is giving his opinion and not trying to speak for

God. As he points out, research reveals that 95 percent of all boys and 60 percent of all girls will engage in masturbation. In other words, whether parents like it or not, masturbation is going to occur with teenagers. And as Dobson emphasizes, parents (regardless of whether they believe it is a sin or not) have a responsibility to help their children with the devastating guilt that masturbation brings. Dobson believes young people have left the church because of guilt over masturbation; they had to get away from a God who did not seem to understand their struggles and the pain that flowed from a habit they felt they couldn't control.

According to Dobson, his father concluded after extensive prayer and Bible study that normal teenage masturbation is not a sin that is going to affect a young person's spiritual relationship with God. Dr. Charlie Shedd takes a similar stance. He told his own children that "*masturbation is a gift of God.*"[2]

Dr. Dobson and Dr. Shedd are the first Christian authorities I know who have taken a positive public stand on this issue. I support their belief that teenagers should be told that masturbation is a normal adolescent activity that does not destroy their spiritual lives. Otherwise, the notion that it is sinful *will* drive the sensitive young people into guilt, and this will definitely affect their spiritual attitudes. It undoubtedly is one of those subjects that many of us have secretly struggled with in our hearts, but few have discussed it openly.

Also, with sexual energy at its peak in adolescence, some acceptable outlet is necessary, and masturbation can help divert sexual energy away from heterosexual relationships.

Dobson lists three areas in which masturbation is clearly harmful. First, when it is associated with unrelenting guilt. Second, when it occurs in a group. (This can swing a particularly vulnerable young person's sexual interest toward the same sex.) And third, when it is continued into marriage as a substitute for sex between husband and wife.

Shedd states that if masturbation becomes an all-consuming, "I've got to do it all the time" pattern, the habit is beginning to have too much control and can lead to problems. Space does not allow a detailed discussion here, so I encourage you to read the books by Dobson[3] and Shedd for more information, and see film number five in Dobson's series if you have not done so already.

As parents strive to reduce the dangers in their homes, they need to have open, direct discussions with their teenagers (usually such discussions need to take place before the actual teen years) on this as well as other sexual issues. Of course, this presupposes that a positive, mutually respectful relationship between parent and teen has been established.

For parents who are a bit shy in initiating a discussion, using a book such as the one by Charlie Shedd can be an excellent start. In fact it would be very helpful for the family to read a chapter together as part of family devotions, then use the book as a springboard for discussion. This allows the young person an opportunity to express personal views as well as a chance for parents to offer guidance. Dobson also has prepared an album of cassette tapes in which he speaks directly to pre-teens about adolescence.

God has created the world and all that is in it. Sex is an experience that is too good to be spoiled or misused. We as parents can help our sons and daughters develop healthy attitudes toward sex, as well as help them avoid the destructive, unnecessary guilt that can drive them away from God. Sex is a wholesome gift from God that can add immeasurably to our lives when it is practiced as He intended.

Appropriate Self-assertion

Parents should not teach their children systematic renunciation such as Julie, whom we met in Chapter 9, was taught. Instead, parents need to see the balance between self-assertion and renunciation for themselves and their children. (The explanation of this topic in Chapter 16 relative to the church also applies to parents and will not be repeated here.) Parents need to realize that children have to learn how to reach out, how to develop the confidence that they can make things happen and that they can put themselves first. In fact, they have to if they are ever going to be able to genuinely and truly put themselves last. As Tournier writes, "Finally, to assert oneself does not mean only to defend oneself and impress others, *but to assert oneself as a human being—a being who is able to think and to choose, and to formulate a view of what life is*" (emphasis added).[4]

Tournier remarks:

> Parents who put the brakes on their adolescent children confuse these two movements together. Self-assertion must come before self-denial. And one is the better able to deny oneself for having first asserted oneself. . . . A negative education of this kind destroys a child's self-confidence and pushes him into neurosis, because it blocks the spontaneous force of life within him.[5]

Parents as well as the church need to realize that "the first movement is not an end in itself; it is a beginning."[6] Perhaps many evangelicals are uncomfortable with self-assertion because they fear their children will live only in the first movement and overlook the second. Or they see the first as living in "sin," while the second is "spiritual," with the two movements being mutually exclusive, not interrelated.

Action in the first movement often frightens parents. When a teenage girl begins to pull away from her parents so that she can gain a more accurate viewpoint of her own, the parents try to quickly close the gap by chasing after the girl. Mother may secretly read her diary or check through her purse for clues to what the girl is doing. They peek down the hall to see what time she turns her light off to go to sleep. Her breath is checked when she comes home to see if she has been drinking. The list goes on and on. As the parents follow their natural impulse to close the widening gap between their daughter and themselves, they unwittingly deprive her of the distance she needs from them. They are denying her the possibility of going through the first movement.

So in order to develop herself, she has to move out even further from her parents, and her behavior becomes more severe. She may drink harder than she would have otherwise to prove a point. She may become sexually active because she knows they don't want her to. If the parents are unsuccessful, they may use a heavier approach consisting of the minister, Bible verses, and God. Remember Beth and her parents? Her mother yanked her out of college and set up a series of meetings with the minister. The frightened parents appeal to the church rules, the master list of sin, in hopes that they can generate enough guilt in their daughter that she will drop her efforts in the first movement. If they're successful, they breathe a sigh of relief: they headed off the rebel before the big trouble began. But they have also succeeded at creating a situation more subtle and dangerous than what their daughter had in mind.

By stopping her, they have taken away her chance to have the experience of coming home voluntarily as the prodigal did—with genuine joy. She has lost the opportunity to have a meaningful foundation for herself. Instead, she lives an inhibited, stunted life of duty, stuck in the second movement with the potential that her inner feelings will burst forth in later years with even more vengeance and pain. If the parents are unsuccessful in halting her and continue to pursue her relentlessly, this cycle builds, and eventually they unknowingly help push their daughter off the edge. They have failed to learn from the father of the prodigal.

Unfortunately, children who are trained to live in self-denial and guilt will become fearful adult Christians, not powerful personalities able to work in the kingdom.

Safe Rebellion

One of the ways we can help our growing children is to recognize the need for rebellion and allow "safe" rebellion to take place. If parents don't allow safe rebellion, they definitely run the risk of pushing their youngsters into unsafe rebellion, because the tighter the hold, the stronger is the push to break away. The exception to this is when the child is a sensitive fearful youngster who withdraws into silent, emotional conflict.

One of the ways we can help our growing children
is to recognize the need for rebellion
and allow "safe" rebellion to take place.

By safe rebellion, I mean activity in which there is no potential for physical or irreparable emotional injury. In the late sixties and early seventies, many adults were becoming quite nervous about high-school students' wearing long hair, and they took definite steps to keep their youngsters in line. Some schools even stipulated in their dress code that boys' hair could not cover their ears or extend over their collars more than a specified distance. There were schools that actually measured hair length with a ruler! Since I worked in an adolescent counseling center at the time, I could see the parents' worry about hair length causing more problems than their teenagers' behavior.

After leaving YFC, I enrolled at Michigan State University in 1967, which was during the hippie period. Being away from the confines of home and YFC, I decided to venture out in a few areas of life, so I began growing a mustache and goatee. This experiment lasted only three weeks, but it brought definite and unanticipated results. After I had about two weeks of growth on my chin, I unexpectedly had to visit my parents' home to pick up my photography equipment. Upon seeing my beard, my mother became very upset and, as usual, voiced her disapproval indirectly. "Your dad won't like that! You ought to shave it off. It's not nice. It doesn't look like a Sloat!" Ironically, my dad said nothing. Several days later I received a letter from my mom stating how the matter was weighing on her and Dad. She related how she had dreamed that I had returned home and was clean-shaven. She concluded by writing, "I see riots started by guys on TV with long hair and beards. We are praying that you don't lose your Christian witness."

I became quite discouraged and despondent. As I pondered what was happening, I realized that the situation with my mother was precisely what always had happened—there was no room for testing or trying different patterns of behavior. The whole situation was tangible evidence that there was no room to be myself. Mom was more concerned that I "act and look right" than that I "feel right." But what I wanted was to be understood, loved, and accepted for what I was—without having to prove anything or be somebody. "Is this the same pattern I have with God?" I noted in my journal at the time, wondering about the connection between my experience with my mother and my feelings toward God.

On one occasion while I was working in YFC, I visited a college friend and his wife who had been married for only a year or so. Both had grown up in my denomination, and her father was a minister. To my surprise, they quite boldly pulled out a pack of cigarettes during my visit and with nervous fanfare began to light up. I could hardly believe it!

What were they trying to prove? *Don't they know that smoking's wrong?* I wondered.

With puzzled disbelief, I listened to their explanation. "We both decided to rebel and thought that one way to do it was by smoking. We talked about it, and we both feel the same way. We may not do it very long, but at least we tried and it helps us prove our point!" In a way I admired their courage, and I left with mixed feelings, wondering if I should consider some revolt of my own.

While I was working in a drug program, I frequently fielded calls from panic-stricken mothers, and the mothers' concerns generally followed a similar pattern. A typical call was from a mother who was doing routine cleaning in her son's bedroom and found a small quantity of marijuana hidden under his underwear. "I just don't know what to do. I can't believe it really is marijuana! I didn't think David was that kind of boy. His dad is so angry he's ready to throw him out of the house. In fact, he yelled at David for twenty minutes last night! He said if he can't live by our rules, he can get out. I don't like it, either, but as his mother I can't go that far—it just wouldn't be right. I feel like I'm caught in the middle. My husband wants to call the police, and David says he was keeping it for a friend and that he's never used the stuff. I don't know what to believe. Besides, David thinks I was snooping and I had no business being in his room. But you should see his room! If I didn't clear it out, things would start to grow in there!"

Many times the parents' reactions in these situations pushed their sons away from them even further, which was the last thing the parents or the children wanted or needed. In their anger over their sons' behavior, the parents lost sight of the relationship and said hurtful things that made healing more difficult. I always tried to slow the mother down, help her see the situation more realistically, and gradually help her see the person in her son rather than focus only on the marijuana and his behavior. When I asked, "Did you ask him what he feels when he smokes it? How does it benefit him or help him? Why does he think he uses it?" the answer from the mother was always a no, which was accompanied by mild surprise at this approach that had never occurred to either her or the father. I'd tell them, "Even though you don't like what your son is doing, you can discuss it with him, learn what he's thinking, and use this as a topic of communication rather than let it tear the family apart. The important thing is that you keep talking with your son, because if you lose the relationship, you have nothing at all."

It's useless for parents to make rules they can't enforce, such as choice of friends. If a teenager wants to hang out with a forbidden youngster, there is nothing Mom and Dad can do to stop it. The result is intensified conflict, and the parents set themselves up to look foolish and helpless. It *is* appropriate, on the other hand, for parents to express their opinions. "I'd rather you didn't hang out at the fast-food restaurant, but I know I can't stop you," they might say. "I'm counting on you to use your good judgment."

At the same time, parents *can* set rules they're able to enforce. "I know I can't stop you from being friends with Jamie, but I don't want her in the house." "If you get a ticket, you'll have to pay for it yourself." "I don't want any smoking in the house."

Married women in their twenties have told me that the only reason they married their husbands was that their parents' attempts to break them up brought them closer together. "If they had left us alone, we would have broken up, I'm sure," I've heard a number of times.

For many average teen situations, we as parents need to set basic guidelines with positive and negative consequences according to the teenagers' behavior. For example, being home on time means being able to go out again, while coming home after curfew automatically forfeits the next time out. Within these guidelines, the teens need room to move about on their road to growing up and assuming responsibility. It is better to have our youngsters fall on their faces while they're living at home and we can support them and help them learn from their mistakes than it is to protect them so much that they are unprepared for the real world when they leave home.

The hardest task facing us as parents is standing by when our children make their mistakes.

The hardest task facing us as parents is standing by and restraining ourselves from stepping in to rescue our children when they make their mistakes. We all know that experience is the best teacher, but sometimes we have difficulty letting our youngsters have the experiences they need in order to learn. As I mentioned earlier, we often have to come to the end of our rope before we are willing to accept help, and our children are no different.

"Does that mean we just have to stand by while our kids get on drugs? Isn't there something we can do so another person doesn't have to go through so much agony in order to learn his lesson?" one concerned parent asked me. I'm not suggesting that parents should throw all caution to the wind and let children do whatever they want; that would be sheer irresponsibility. However, each of us has to make his own decisions and handle his own pain, and we often have to find answers the hard way. As youngsters advance into their teen years, they should be given more and more freedom and responsibility. Of course, this gradual assumption of responsibility should have been a process that began during their infancy. We can lend support, as mentioned in Chapter 17, while they are struggling with their difficulties. And there are times when we need to learn from the father in the parable of the prodigal son. Remember how he waited for his son and was ready to welcome him home after he had come to his senses. It also goes without saying that we need to pray for our children, but we must also work as hard as we can in our everyday relationships with them.

There are occasions when parents need to step into their children's lives. If a youngster's behavior is getting out of control—if there's evidence of consistent lying, stealing, running away, breaking and entering, heavy drug use, fighting, or similar sorts of serious problems—the parents should seek professional help and seriously consider residential programs that can work with the youngster in a controlled setting. Many youngsters with bad behavior habits are somewhat pliable in the middle teen years, and such extreme behavior can reflect deeper emotional problems that will not simply go away. I have told parents, "If you want to give it your best shot, you should consider placing your teenager in a program, because once he reaches legal age, there isn't a thing you can do."

Let me hasten to add, too, that a youngster's behavior doesn't have to reach such extremes before professional help is sought. Many conflicts between parents and adolescents can be ironed out when a professional helps the family look at their problems in a new light. Sometimes the parents are upsetting the teenager and don't even know it because the teen is afraid to speak up. In the safety of a counselor's office, a young person often is able to express his true feelings, and the family can work out a plan that helps the youngster develop positively.

Wise parents recognize that hair styles, clothing fads, loud mufflers, ragged jeans, and so on are not issues worth fussing about with teenagers because they represent healthy forms of self-assertion. Arguing about these things can interfere with the more important priority of maintaining a relationship with growing young persons. And if parents force a halt to such activities, the determined youngsters will simply find other (and often more serious) ways to rebel, and the sensitive ones will be pushed into developing emotional problems. No one gains as a result.

Fear of Rebelling

Revolt typically receives very little support in the church community, and when I was a youngster growing up, I often heard adults make frequent critical remarks concerning local young people who apparently were taking the wayward way. Often the so-called wild kids eventually took their place in the community, appearing no worse for their "wild" times, while I remained well-behaved, feeling unappreciated in a manner similar to the prodigal son's brother.

Even after I left YFC, revolt was something I pondered more than I actually carried out. At the time I saw revolt as primarily taking the form of using alcohol, smoking, or having sex, about which I knew very little. Intellectually, I knew that any of these routes would ultimately lead nowhere, so I didn't seriously pursue them—but perhaps that was an excuse for my fear. I have since realized that I was defining revolt too narrowly, and that alcohol use and the typical teenage rebellion activities are merely symbols that represent the underlying need to "be my own person by doing what I know you don't want me to do." I have gradually realized that for me, simply doing what I want because I want it feels like revolt (and probably is) against the backdrop of my upbringing. Even now I feel twinges of guilt if I pay over a hundred dollars for a sport coat, because I feel as though I'm being selfish and should be giving that money to missionaries instead of spending it on myself.

For the sensitive "S" and "C" personalities, rebelling even in small ways can be difficult within the church environment because it is often so closely linked with sin, which is, of course, to be avoided. Consequently, the cautious ones tend to edge toward revolt slowly and carefully, if they rebel at all. My friends who tried smoking were doing it within the privacy of their home where they could control who would observe them.

In high school, I didn't have my own car to fix up, but that sort of thing always appealed to me. When I finally bought my Mustang, I wanted to put dual Iollywood glasspack mufflers on it, but while I was working with YFC I felt it would have been wrong to use money from my paycheck—money that other hard-working people had earned to support teenage evangelism—to buy something as "selfish" as loud mufflers! Within about two months after leaving YFC, I returned to Detroit to visit my mechanic friend John with "my own money" in my pocket—money I had earned working in a mobile home factory. Now free from the previous guilt, I got John to help me install a dual exhaust system with the loudest mufflers I had ever heard. He jokingly said it was "loud enough to make your ears bleed." It was so loud that first day that I wondered if I could stand it. My mother said she could hear me coming a half mile away, but I enjoyed it. I felt I was finally doing something for myself.

My attempts at trying new things had their dangers, however. One time during my stay at Michigan State, two fellow students, a professor, and I had gone to the county jail to interview inmates for our practicum experience. On the way back to campus, the others wanted to stop at a bar. Feeling some social pressure as well as curiosity, I decided to order a beer. I could hardly stand the taste of it, but I didn't want to appear conspicuous by leaving the glass three-quarters full, either. Taking it a few sips at a time, I managed to down most of it before I began to feel the effects in my head. This frightened me a bit, not knowing quite what to expect, but I managed to hide my anxiety from the others.

Meanwhile, in another class I was studying the psychological aspects of physical disabilities, and one of the diseases was multiple sclerosis with its symptoms of lightheadedness and dizziness. Several days after drinking the beer, I noticed with sudden panic that I was feeling lightheaded and a bit dizzy on my feet. The first thought that shot through my mind was that I had damaged my brain and nervous system with the beer, and God was paying me back! After some reflection, my panic subsided when I realized that I had a cold combined with an inner ear infection, and these accounted for my symptoms.

As I grow older, I am slowly beginning to understand that God can work in our lives through many types of events, through other people, and as Lewis suggests,

> through experiences which seem (at the time) *anti-*Christian. When a young man who has been going to church in a routine way honestly realizes that he does not believe in Christianity and stops going—provided he does it for honesty's sake and not to just annoy his parents—the spirit of Christ is probably nearer to him than it ever was before.[7]

Bread and Fish

Fathers have a tremendous responsibility toward their children, because by their everyday treatment of their children they are building piece by piece the foundation for their children's concept of God. It is absolutely essential that fathers (and mothers as well) give their children "bread and fish," not "stones and snakes." Children's physical and emotional needs must be met if they are going to have any type of positive, solid foundation for adult life. Meeting a child's needs says, "I see you as a valuable, worthwhile person. You can count on me to come through and be here when you need me." This is communicated by spending time with growing children, reading to them, playing ball with them, going on walks, playing games, giving hugs, and even taking time to put aside the newspaper to listen to their latest knock-knock joke. Treating them as the important people they are develops inner security and a base from which they can approach God, believing that God is similar to their own fathers and will meet their needs as well. It also builds a healthy sense of self-esteem, which is so vital to every area of life.

Fathers must also examine their relationships with their wives. Does the relationship exemplify Christ's relationship to the church? Is it service-oriented and supportive, or autocratic and domineering? Is Mom treated as someone special and worthwhile or as the live-in cleaning lady? A young fellow at school was disciplined for striking another student, a girl. He protested the punishment by insisting, "That's what girls are for—to hit! Dad hits Mom all the time!" He was learning from his parents, but what he was learning was not preparing him for a positive life with other people—or God, either, for that matter.

Mothers also have the responsibility for giving acceptance and love as the foundation for the concept of grace. They have to be very careful, because it is so easy for evangelical mothers to misuse biblical principles as a device to control children's behavior. This is particularly true in the area of self-assertion, expression of anger, or any other tendency that is seen as selfish or sinful. Again, this relates to the way mothers hear sin defined at church, and if they hear sin defined primarily as a list of behaviors to avoid, in their attempts to be good Christian mothers they will do their best to keep their children from sinning by using *whatever* method works. The church seems to communicate its fear of emotion and self-assertion to parents, who in turn are afraid of it in their children. This sets up a vicious cycle in the name of God, and it often causes more trouble in the process, even though people's intentions are good.

It's easy for mothers to use the same methods on their children that they experienced at their mothers' hands. If their parents used fear and guilt to keep control and if the church uses the same approach, it is natural for mothers to employ fear and guilt unless they realize the dangers and make changes so they do not continue to pass the negative pattern to the next generation. Mothers who communicate genuine acceptance and love are giving the most precious gift they could possibly give to children, because it is a vital foundation for adult emotional and spiritual life. Mothers, as well as fathers, build this foundation through ordinary, everyday actions.

Children's Personality Styles

As a parent, you need to tailor your child-rearing methods according to the God-given personalities of your children. To do otherwise communicates not only a lack of respect, but even a message of rejection. You don't have to be a trained psychologist to understand your children's personality styles. You live with them every day, and after reading the brief description of personality styles in Chapter 3, you should have a good start toward understanding your children. For example, "D" youngsters will require consistency and dependability from you. Communication with them needs to be clear and direct, because they don't want someone to take advantage of them. Trying to pull the wool over their eyes will stir their anger. You also need to see the positive side of high "D," or strong-willed, children. Instead of trying to break their spirits and make them docile, appreciate their drive and desire to achieve. Help them, too, to channel their energy into constructive activities

The "i" children need social approval and will not handle confrontation well. Discipline should not be done in public, because this will strike the "i" children's fear button: loss of social approval. Harsh and insensitive discipline will damage the self-image. A mother told me she had a method that always worked when her high "i" child refused to behave in the grocery store. When all else failed, she warned her child, "If you don't behave, I'll spank you right here in front of everybody!" Even though this method worked, she was able to see the problems it could cause as she began to understand her child's personality style.

The "S" youngsters are sensitive to security issues, adjust slowly to change, and need to belong. They need a consistent routine and assurance that they will be a part of the group. They also are extravulnerable to guilt and are easily hurt if their feelings are not considered. Since they naturally withdraw under pressure, you should not automatically interpret their silence as acceptance. You need to repeatedly encourage your "S" children to express their opinions.

The "C" children need to have their questions answered. They also need to have situations explained to them ahead of time so they feel prepared and know how to act. For example, "When the waitress comes to take our order, she'll talk to Mom and Dad first, then she'll ask you what you want. When she does this, you speak right up and tell her what you've picked from the children's menu. She also will ask what you want to drink. If you're not sure, you may ask her what they have." These children need enough time to do tasks "right" according to their own standards. Criticism must be carefully worded and given in a supportive manner.

As you deal with children (and adults as well), keep in mind what each personality style needs or fears. Then give them what they need to feel safe, and you will be loving them by providing a safe environment in which they can grow. This approach personalizes the relationship between parent and child and ensures that your teachings sink into the youngster's heart. Teaching that is done contrary to a child's natural bent is met with resistance and not assimilated. A detailed discussion of this particular point is not possible here, but the suggested books in the Appendix will provide additional valuable information.

You must be especially careful with your tenderhearted children, those sensitive ones who can be hurt so easily. As long as they're living with you, you are helping them build a foundation for the rest of their lives.

The Price

Doing a proper job as parents is a difficult task for which few adults have been adequately prepared. And it's so easy to become caught up in the rush of today's society and the demands of maintaining the household that we forget the individualized attention our children need. As Jenny and I looked at her relationship with her father, this fact was quite evident. Her father worked for a Christian organization and apparently worked extra hard to prove himself. Said Jenny, "He would work extra hours and make double mortgage payments on the house. There was never money for extra things around the house. Even in the summer, when we returned to his boyhood neighborhood where he owned several acres of blueberries, we stayed at a nice camp that had a swimming pool, but we had to pick berries. Why didn't he just once say, 'Let's go swimming and have some fun together. We'll pick berries tomorrow morning when it isn't so hot!' But now he's gone. And what good did it do that he worked all the time?" Charles Swindoll writes with great insight:

As a parent, you cannot afford the luxury of simply housing, feeding, clothing, and educating your offspring. . . . We as parents have a homework assignment from God that will take years to complete. We are assigned the responsibility of coming to know our child. And what we observe and hear must not be ignored. We are to draw upon that information as we train him or her. . . . I warn you, however, that this personalized investment will require two exceedingly valuable ingredients: concentration and time. It is impossible to make correct observations without concentrating on your child at given moments each day—not all day, of course, but periodically each day. . . . And—as is always true of important projects—your schedule must allow the time for such a procedure.[8]

Since the foundation we provide for our children is the one they will use in every area of their adult lives, it is so important that we build it as solidly and strongly as we can, and in such a way that we don't erect emotional barriers that complicate their adult spiritual lives.[9]

Passing the Torch of Faith

Watching the mile relay in track and field events is always exciting. As the runners sprint into the first leg of the race, the tension begins to build. Even though one team is ahead after the first quarter mile, the lead often changes during the course of the race. Giving it all they have, the runners go all out for their quarter mile responsibility, then hand the baton to the next teammate. Passing the baton is the most critical, risky element of the race. Teams with superior speed have lost to slower opponents because of errors in passing the baton. Not only must the runners train for speed and endurance, their own part of the race, but they must also train to pass the baton smoothly without hesitation or error. If the baton is dropped, precious time is lost. A team may have the fastest runners alive, but if they cannot pass the baton successfully, they will never win the race.

I see similarities to Christians. We all have to train for our own lives. We must develop our own strength and endurance. No one else can do it for us. But in the Christian life, as in the relay, the critical, risky phase is passing the torch to the next generation. It is at this critical point that many things can go wrong. And because life is not as simple or obvious as a relay race, the baton can be dropped without our realizing it. Or we can easily do something early in the race that affects the transfer, but we fail to see the connection. Then we wonder why the next generation has trouble running enthusiastically with the torch of faith.

My goal in this book has been to show you some of the dangers that affect the critical overlap where generations touch and the baton is passed. I believe we can do a better job of passing the torch than we have, and I trust I have been able to give you a clearer understanding of the dangers that are often felt but unseen.

In spite of its dangers, the Christian home is a good place to be. Many people who have become Christians as adults have looked with envy at other Christians who have the richness of a Christian upbringing. People with a Christian upbringing often look with restrained envy at those who grew up outside the church. But that's often the way we are—we think the grass on the other side is greener, and we don't fully appreciate what we have until it's gone.

My hopes for you, as we end our time together, are that you have found some new insights in these pages and that you will feel encouraged to think, to struggle, and to ask questions as you become your own person. Remember above all that whatever you think or say or do, the sovereign God loves you.

Notes

Chapter 3

1. John G. Geier, *Personal Profile System Manual* (Minneapolis: Performax Systems International, Inc., 1979, Revised 1983).
2. Ibid., 3.
3. John G. Geier, *The Personal Profile System* (Minneapolis: Performax Systems International, Inc , 1978), 2 audiocassettes.
4. Paul Tournier, *The Strong and the Weak*, trans. Edwin Hudson (Philadelphia: Westminster, 1976, first published in English by SCM Press Ltd. in 1963), 20–23.

Chapter 4

1. J. B. Phillips, *Your God Is Too Small* (New York: Macmillan, 1961), 21–22.
2. John Stapert, editor of *The Church Herald* (official magazine of the Reformed Church in America), personal communication with author, 1985.
3. Merrill C. Tenney, general ed., *The Zondervan Pictorial Bible Dictionary* (Grand Rapids: Zondervan, 1963), 322.

Chapter 6

1. Jane C. Duckworth, *MMPI Interpretation Manual for Counselors and Clinicians*, 2nd ed. (Muncie Accelerated Development Inc., 1979), 113.
2. John G. Geier and Dorothy E. Downey, *The Inspirational Pattern*, vol. 6 of *Library of Classical Profile Patterns* (Minneapolis: Performax Systems International, Inc., 1979), 16–17, 19–20.
3. Bobb Biehl, president of Masterplanning Group International (Laguna Niguel, Calif.), personal communication with author, 1985.
4. Portions of this section were previously published in "Reluctant Christians," *The Church Herald*, September 3, 1982, 6–9.
5. Paul Tournier, *A Place for You*, trans Edwin Hudson (New York: Harper & Row, 1968), 128.

Chapter 7

1. Denis Waitley, *The Psychology of Winning* (Chicago: Nightingale-Conant Corp., 1978), audiocassettes, tape 2.

Chapter 9

1. Tournier, *Place*, 93.
2. Ruth McNaughton Hinds and Faith McNaughton Lowell, *Why* (Wheaton, Ill.: Scripture Press, 1966).
3. Ibid.
4. David A. Seamands, *Healing for Damaged Emotions* (Wheaton, Ill.: Victor Books, 1981), 70–71.
5. Tournier, *Place*, 107–8.
6. Seamands, *Healing*, 49.
7. Waitley, *Winning*, tape 3.
8. Ibid.
9. Tournier's book should be available in many church or public libraries. At the time of this writing, the book had gone out of print, unfortunately, and it may require persistence to locate it. It is the best book I have ever seen on the proper biblical perspective between self-assertion and renunciation.
10. Ibid., 93.
11. Ibid., 99.
12. Pierre Teilhard De Chardin, *Le milieu divin: An Essay on the Interior Life* (New York: Harper and Row Publishers, Inc.), 77f.
13. Tournier, *Place*, 99.
14. Ibid., 115–16, 128–29.
15. Ibid., 130–31.
16. *Grand Rapids Press*, July 28, 1985, sec. A.

Chapter 10

1. Portions of this section were previously published in "Reluctant Christians," *The Church Herald*, Sept. 3, 1982, 6–9.
2. Rollo May, *Man's Search for Himself* (New York: Norton, 1953),

149. This book offers excellent insights on the subject of becoming one's own person.

Chapter 11

1. Keith Miller, *The Taste of New Wine* (Waco, Tex.: Word, 1965). Even though this book was published over twenty years ago, its emphasis on personal honesty is still helpful.
2. Erich Fromm, *Escape from Freedom* (New York: Avon Books, published in arrangement with Holt, Rinehart & Winston, Inc., 1941, 1965).
3. H. A. Overstreet, *The Mature Mind* (New York: Norton, 1949, 1959).
4. Fromm, *Escape*, 177, 249.

Chapter 12

1. Seamands, *Healing*, 12, 13, 14.

Chapter 13

1. M. Scott Peck, *The Road Less Traveled* (New York: Simon and Schuster, Touchstone Books, 1978), 57. This book contains many beneficial ideas.
2. For an enlightening discussion about personal patterns, read Peck, *The Road*, 44–58.

Chapter 14

1. Tournier, *Place*, 119.
2. For an excellent description of the types of patterns people have with their parents, along with suggestions for gaining true independence, see Howard M. Halpern, *Cutting Loose* (New York: A Bantam Book, 1976). Insights into a person's inner child are clearly presented by W. Hugh Missildine, *Your Inner Child of the Past* (New York: Simon and Schuster, 1963). A helpful description of an individual's caution in relationships can be found in John Powell, *Why Am I Afraid to Tell You Who I Am?* (Niles, Ill.: Argus Communications, 1969).

3. For a broader discussion along this line, see Paul Tournier, *To Resist or Surrender?*, trans. John S. Gilmour (Richmond: John Knox Press, 1964).
4. Fromm, *Escape*, 177–78.
5. Ibid., 178.
6. May, *Man's Search*, 149.
7. Ibid., 153–54.

Chapter 15

1. May, *Man's Search*, 168–69.
2. Halpern, *Cutting Loose*. This book has useful material related to seeing our parents as people.
3. May, *Man's Search*, 136–38.

Chapter 16

1. Seamands, *Healing*, 117.
2. Phillips, *Your God Is Too Small*.
3. Seamands, *Healing*, 29–30.
4. Ibid., 64.
5. Watchman Nee, *The Normal Christian Life* (Fort Washington, Penn.: Christian Literature Crusade, 1961), 56.
6. Seamands, *Healing*, 58–75.
7. Waitley, *Winning*, tape 3.
8. C. S. Lewis, *Mere Christianity* (New York: Macmillan, 1960), 101.
9. Seamands, *Healing*, 70–75.
10. E. Stanley Jones, *Abundant Living* (Special Hour of Power abridged edition published by arrangement with Abingdon. Nashville: Abingdon Press, Copyright 1942 by Whitmore & Stone, Copyright renewal 1970 by E. Stanley Jones), 59.
11. Jay Kesler, *Growing Places* (Old Tappan, N.J.: Revell, 1978), 117.
12. Lewis, *Mere Christianity*, 102.

Chapter 17

1. Tournier, *Place*, 192.

2. Ibid., 96.
3. Ibid., 136.
4. Teilhard de Chardin, *Le milieu divin*, 77f.
5. Helmut Thielicke, *The Waiting Father*, 29.
6. Ibid., 21–22.
7. Tournier, *Place*, 130.
8. Jay Kesler, *The Strong Weak People* (Wheaton, Ill.: Victor Books, 1976), 18.
9. Paul Tournier, *The Person Reborn*, trans. Edwin Hudson (New York: Harper & Row, 1966), 80–81.
10. Ibid., 71.
11. Tournier, *Place*, 86.
12. Ibid., 192.
13. Thielicke, *The Waiting Father*, 26.
14. Phillips, *Your God Is Too Small*, 20.
15. Portions of this chapter were published previously in "Reluctant Christians," *The Church Herald*, Sept. 3, 1982, 6–9; and "Free to Struggle," *The Church Herald*, April 15, 1983, 6–8. Used with permission.

Chapter 18

1. James Dobson, *Focus on the Family; Preparing for Adolescence: Peer Pressure and Sexuality,* film five (Waco, Tex.: Educational Products Division of Word, Inc. A 16mm film series. 1979).
2. Charlie Shedd, *The Stork Is Dead* (Waco, Tex.: Word Books, rev. ed. 1968), 70.
3. James Dobson, *Preparing for Adolescence* (Ventura, Calif.: Vision House, 1978).
4. Tournier, *Place*, 136.
5. Ibid., 115.
6. Ibid., 143.
7. Lewis, *Mere Christianity,* 148.
8. Charles Swindoll, *You and Your Child* (Nashville: Thomas Nelson, 1977), 24.
9. Portions of this chapter were previously published in "Parents' Dilemmas", *The Church Herald*, January 20, 1984, 6–8. Used with permission.

Appendix

Suggested Books for Additional Study

Dobson, James C. *Dare to Discipline*. Wheaton, Ill.: Tyndale, 1970.

———*Hide or Seek*. Old Tappan, N.J.: Revell, 1974, 1979.

———*The Strong-Willed Child*. Wheaton, Ill.: Tyndale, 1978.

Dreikurs, Rudolf, and Vickie Soltz. *Children: The Challenge*. New York: Hawthorn Books, 1964.

Ginott, Haim G. *Between Parent & Child*. New York: Macmillan, 1965.

———*Between Parent & Teenager*. New York: Macmillan, 1969.

Leman, Kevin. *Making Children Mind Without Losing Yours*. Old Tappan, N.J.: Revell, 1983.

Swindoll, Charles. *You and Your Child*. Nashville: Thomas Nelson, 1977.

Ziglar, Zig. *Raising Positive Kids in a Negative World*. Nashville: Thomas Nelson, 1985.